"Life As A Waking Dr[...] simultaneously and powerfully, illustrating as it does how we can become conscious of the inner workings of our lives."

— *P.M.H. Atwater, Lh.D.,*
author of The Big Book of Near Death Experiences

"A powerful tool for those interested in gaining self-awareness, living more consciously, and finding greater meaning and purpose. A concrete strategy for transforming life experiences into mirrors which reveal the self in a new light."

— *Linda Reisser, Ed.D.,*
coauthor of Education and Identity

"Incisive, profound and inspiring."

— *Barbara Marx Hubbard,*
author of The Shift from Ego to Essence

"The old Hindu prayer has it right: 'Lead us from the unreal to the real.' This book does just that."

— *David DeBus, Ph.D.*

"As we balance our lives by using our daily experiences and relationships as our teachers, a whole new world of insight, adventure and amazing self-discovery is ours to enjoy. Bravo for this fine treasure!"

— *Betty Bethards,*
author of The Dream Book

"This is an important book. We must find the connections between our interior life and the external world, and this book shows us how."

— *Michael Murphy*
founder of Esalen Institute

Books by Diane Kennedy Pike

As Mariamne Paulus:

The House of Self

Awakening to Wisdom

Four Paths to Union

As Diane Kennedy Pike:

The Love Project Way (with Arleen Lorrance)

My Journey Into Self: Phase One

Life Is Victorious!
How to Grow Through Grief

Cosmic Unfoldment

Channeling Love Energy (with Arleen Lorrance)

The Wilderness Revolt (with R. Scott Kennedy)

Search

As Diane Kennedy:

The Other Side (with James A Pike)

Life As A Waking Dream

How to Explore Your Most Vivid Life Experiences and Find the Meaning Within Them

By Diane Kennedy Pike

Teleos Imprint ~ *Scottsdale, AZ*

Teleos Imprint
Wisdom Books
Published by LP Publications
7119 E Shea Blvd.
Suite 109 PMB 418
Scottsdale, AZ 85254-6107

The Teleos Institute World Wide Web site address is
http://www.teleosinstitute.com

Library of Congress Cataloging-in-Publication Data
Pike, Diane Kennedy.
   Life as a waking dream : how to explore your most vivid life
experiences and find the meaning within them / Diane Ken-
nedy Pike.
      p. cm.
   Includes bibliographical references.
   ISBN-13: 978-0-916192-50-1 (alk. paper)
   ISBN-10: 0-916192-50-4 (alk. paper)
1. Symbolism (Psychology) 2. Self-actualization (Psychology)
1. Title.
   BF458.P54 2007
   158—dc22

                                        2007051233

Printed in the United States of America

Cover Art by Rev. Rebecca Hanna Ph.D.
Life As A Waking Dream teacher and artist (see page 318)

To

ARLEEN LORRANCE

my partner in creativity and transformation

for believing in me

for supporting my creative process

for contributing her intuition and insight

and for being such a vivid part of my waking dream

Contents

One: The Great Unknown 3

Two: Life As A Waking Dream 21

Three: The Sense of Self 49

Four: The Creative Forces: Yin & Yang 81

Five: Communicating with Self 109

Six: Symbols and Meaning............................ 147

Seven: Realizing Our Potential 189

Eight: Life Themes 223

Epilogue 259

Appendix 269

Notes 297

Glossary 303

Bibliography 311

Illustrations

#1: Senses of Self... 61

#2: Expanding Senses of Self 65

#3: The Creative Forces................................. 93

#4: Primary Characteristics of
    The Creative Forces........................... 98-99

#5: Instinct & Sensation:
    Expressions of the Body 111

#6: Feeling & Thinking:
    Expressions of the Psyche 119

#7: Instinct & Wisdom:
    Expressions of the Spirit......................... 131

#8: The Flow of Self-Communication 139

#9: Knowing & Direct Perception:
    Expressions of the Integrated Self.............. 142

#10: Images & Symbols
    Used in Self-Communication.................... 177

A Note to the Reader:

If you find words in the text that are not familiar to you, or that are used in a way that seems unusual to you, you may want to look for them in the Glossary in the back of the book.

Life As A Waking Dream

The great enemy to spiritual progress is the belief you know already. Knowledge is unfolded. Pray to be willing at every stage to be ignorant so you can be really taught.

— *Thuksey Rinpoche*

Beyond the limited circle of light bounding our conscious mind is the vast darkness of our unconscious mind. Conscious knowing, what we know that we know and can explicitly spell out, is a small part of the mind. Most of our knowledge is unconscious — tacit, implicit, and difficult to verbalize. The very ground upon which consciousness stands is the unconscious mind.

— *Stephen LaBerge*

2 LIFE AS A WAKING DREAM

Chapter One

The Great Unknown

When I was 32 years old, I was confronted with a large unknown. My husband had died suddenly, and I wanted to know what I was meant to do with the rest of my life.

I asked a friend to guide me as I went into a deep state of relaxation so that I could focus on the inner knowing to which I did not have access in my ordinary consciousness. During that guided meditation, I had a profound experience in which I seemed to recall a past life. The experience was like a dream,[1] in that it occurred only in my mind, but I was totally awake and alert as I watched the scenario unfold.

I remembered being the Mother Superior of a cloistered order of nuns in Spain in the sixteenth century. I saw in vivid color and with great detail the convent and the other nuns with whom I lived. When the memory ended, I felt certain that I would be able to find the convent were I ever to go to Spain.

Through the years, that experience remained vivid in my consciousness though it did not clarify my life purpose at that time. It was like a dream whose meaning had not been fully revealed.

Fifteen years later I had an opportunity to explore that vivid recall more fully. My partner Arleen Lorrance and I took a four-month sabbatical leave from the work we had been doing for twelve years. We traveled in Europe and deliberately included Spain in our itinerary so that I could look for "my" convent.

I did not know the precise location of the convent, but I felt intuitively that it would be in the northern part of Spain. Just after crossing the border from France, we spread a map out before us. I breathed into my lower abdomen where the knowing about the convent seemed to be lodged. Then I put my index finger down on the map. I asked Arleen to look in our guidebook for towns in the vicinity of where my finger had landed. One of them was called Soria.

Arleen read the description of Soria. She said there was a Carmelite Convent there, founded by St. Teresa of Avila in the sixteenth century. Adrenaline rushed through my body and the two of us got goose bumps all over, as if we realized that this could be it. We were full of expectancy. What if we were actually to find my convent?

When we started south toward Soria, the road took us higher and higher into mountains. The land got rockier and drier. In the recall I had sensed that the convent was in high country, though flat, and I had seen dry, rocky soil. As we drew closer, the terrain was exactly as I had seen it. Soria sits in the center of a high, arid plateau.

I asked directions at the Tourist Information Office. A quick walk through the center of town took us to a building on which there was a plaque which read: CONVENT OF THE BAREFOOT CARMELITE MOTHERS, FOUNDED PERSONALLY BY SANTA TERESA DE JESUS ON JUNE 2, 1581.

During the drive toward Soria, my rational mind kept saying, "You know, this is really crazy. You can't have a so-called past-life recall and then expect to find the place.

You know nothing about the Carmelites or about Spain." But my strong feeling that I would find it won out. It did not surprise me to be standing in front of a building from the very period I had remembered in that experience fifteen years before. It was a meeting of inner and outer realities, of the known and the unknown.

We stepped inside. A small posted sign informed us that we were too late in the day to visit. I thought "visit" meant to see the ancient building that had once been used by the nuns. I surmised it had been preserved as a historical site. We made a note of the visiting hours and retired to our hotel.

The next morning we arrived at the convent shortly after 9:30 A.M., the beginning of morning visiting hours, which lasted until 11:30 A.M. I rang the bell. A tall man emerged. "We would like to visit the ancient convent," I told him eagerly.

"That's impossible," he replied. "They are cloistered."

"You mean the nuns are still using it?" I asked in surprise.

He nodded, adding, "And they are entirely cloistered."

I asked to speak with one of the sisters. The man rang a bell. We heard footsteps in the inner courtyard. Then a voice spoke from behind a dark window. The old čaretaker told her that some women wanted to speak to one of the sisters. He motioned me to the window, and then left Arleen and me alone in the reception area.

I stepped up to the small opening, grateful that I spoke Spanish fluently. "I have come from the United States," I began. "Several years ago I had a vision of a convent such as this — I believe it was Carmelite — and I have come looking for it."

From behind the dark window the nun answered, "Just a moment, I will get the Mother Superior."

Perhaps you can begin to sense how the "real world" and my inner experience began to merge. I was to be given an opportunity to meet the Mother Superior; in my recollection, I had *been* the Mother Superior.

The Mother Superior pushed a key through a small window. She directed us to a second-story parlor and told us she would meet us there. When we entered the parlor, we found two chairs set on either side of a round table, under which there was a small heater. The nuns, we learned, had no heat in the convent, but they provided that comfort for their guests.

The table sat in front of a large, grilled window without glass. Soon the shutters were opened on the other side of a matching grill. There was a foot of space between the two grills. A light went on, and the Mother Superior greeted us. She was dressed in a dark brown habit, just as I had worn in my recall, with a white cloth fitting close around her head and neck, and a black veil over her head. She wore glasses. Her round face and eyes peered eagerly at us. She said, "Now we can talk."

I had been hoping that the Mother Superior would allow us inside the convent, even though I fully understood the nature of their cloistered life. But the moment I saw her, I became totally absorbed in the vividness of the moment and all prior thoughts and desires fell away. At the same time, any sense of myself as an outsider dissolved and I felt like one of the nuns.

Before we had gone very far in our conversation, a second nun joined us. She was introduced as the assistant to the Mother Superior. In an intense hour and a half, the three of us had a lively exchange. Arleen was a silent witness, since she spoke no Spanish. I told them of my memories (which I called a vision out of deference to their heritage). They confirmed the majority of the details for me.

Most startling for me was the moment when I told them about my death. "I was quite old, lying on a large bed, not in my regular cell. All the members of the community were gathered around the room praying for me, and I experienced their prayers literally lift my soul up out of my body and toward heaven."

Their eyes opened wide in wonderment. "How could you know such details about a Carmelite's deathbed experience? No one but a Carmelite is allowed to witness such a death, because it is considered to be the most sacred event of a lifetime." They went on, "We do all gather around the room. Those who can, kneel and pray. The others stand. And we use our prayers to lift the soul of the dying one toward God."

My meeting with the nuns was thrilling and confirming, and certainly confounded my rational mind. There was no objective explanation for how I could have known so much about the lives of these cloistered nuns. Neither was there any way to "prove" that this was the same convent of my recall since I could not visit the interior. However, I was satisfied that there was truth to the memory and that was enough.

Still, it was clear to me that there was something more important for me to uncover about the visit. The Mother Superior had asked if Arleen and I were dedicated to the worship of the Holy Mother. Learning that we were a Jew and a Protestant, the two nuns lamented that we were missing a great deal by not having the Mother. "Not to take anything away from God the Father and from our Lord," they were quick to point out, "but as in any family, it is the Mother who is the soul. We need the Mother. We cannot live without the love of the Mother."

Near the end of the conversation, the assistant to the Mother Superior was overcome with excitement when it occurred to her to say, "Never mind that you are Jew and Protestant! We should all do what we want. Therefore, you must love the Mother in any case!" The Mother Superior joined her with enthusiasm. "Yes, you must love the Mother, and pray to her. She will answer your prayers. You must love the Mother."

As we left the convent, I knew the primary reason for my visit had been to hear the nuns' message about loving and praying to the Mother. But I did not know how to integrate that into my life. I had no past experience or religious training in prayer to the Mother. In my Protestant heritage, we always prayed to God the Father. Prayer used words and appealed to God as "other," outside of self, usually with the feeling of reaching up. I felt awkward just thinking of loving the Mother, and I had no idea how I would pray to Her.

As it turned out, the answer to my dilemma was contained in the experience that had just unfolded. It occurred to me to look at the visit to the convent as a *waking dream* to see if I could unveil its deeper meaning for me. This was the first time I had approached one of my life experiences as a waking dream.[2]

As I worked with this approach, trying to penetrate the inner meaning of my convent visit, I began to reach realms of understanding and perception previously unknown to me. The method of work I present in this book began to take form. It developed through my inner exploration of the unknown realm of "prayer to the Mother."

Here is how I worked with the experience as a waking dream. I received the cloistered convent as a symbol for a space in my own consciousness where the work of prayer goes on constantly. I had not consciously recognized this yin space of prayer before and I welcomed bringing it into my awareness.[3]

In my past-life recall, I had seen myself as a Mother Superior. In my waking dream, I had met the Mother Superior and her assistant. I understood the waking dream to indicate that I had made direct contact with the inner authority of my feminine polarity. In this way, I began to integrate a growing sense that I *already knew* how to pray to the Mother.

The waking dream was made up entirely of feminine symbols: the nuns who lived in the convent, the Holy Mother to whom they insisted I pray, my partner and I, and even the woman who gave directions to the convent at the information center. The only masculine symbol was the caretaker at the convent, whose specific function was to make contact with the outer world for the cloistered sisters. He was the perfect symbol for the energy that enables me to make my inner process of prayer known to others. I am activating that polarity now, as I write these words.

This is how I began to internalize the meaning of both my past-life memory and the waking dream of the convent in Spain. For me they symbolized the awakening of a highly developed facet of my consciousness that had long been in place, but which I had not brought into active awareness during the first forty years of this life. The waking dream seemed to say that buried in my unconsciousness was vast knowledge of the Mother-God and the ways of praying to her. This recognition enabled me to begin to consciously integrate the feminine polarity of wisdom, as represented by the "Mother," into my sense of self.

The Realm of the Great Unknown

For many years I have been a student of the Ancient Wisdom, a body of fundamental principles that is found at the heart of all great religions. The teachings are born of direct perception by awakened beings from ancient through modern times. These beings are in surprising agreement about the nature of the universe and the place human beings have in it. Seers from all times have perceived certain laws that govern our consciousness and our creative self-expression. They also offer certain truths that, when understood, free us from suffering.

In these teachings, the Great Mother is understood to be the energy that enables the invisible pattern of the Father Force to come into what we call manifested form. The Mother is everything that gives form and everything that has form. In one of her aspects She is Mother Nature. It is She that gives us birth and nurtures and sustains us as long as we have form.

About nine years into my study of the Wisdom, I began to explore the darkness, the whole realm of the unknown. I was motivated by a desire to know more of my emotional nature, my deepest feelings, and to reveal them to others. Not only did I explore feelings, but I became fascinated with all that was hidden and unknown within.

I found there were many urges, motivations, desires, needs, longings, etc., of which I was almost entirely ignorant. Eventually, I came to understand them as forms of inner communication: instinct, feeling, and intuition.

Soon I was probing beyond my personal psyche into the Great Unknown, the vast mystery that I came to call the Mother-God through my study of the Ancient Wisdom. My first trip to India in 1979 was a waking dream in which I felt I was walking in the body of God, that is, in the Mother. Love was palpable everywhere, even in circumstances that I would have ordinarily termed unpleasant or horrible.

I acknowledged then that my aspiration to know God had been one-sided. I had sought only the light. Without also knowing the dark, the mystery, the embodied power, my understanding was incomplete and misleading. I was moved to let go of my spiritual aspirations to become *more* than human, realizing I needed to become *fully* human first.

In the years following that trip, I became more and more fluent in the language of the Mother-God: feelings, intuitions, symbolism, archetypes, myths, desires, instinctual urges, etc. I learned how to see in the dark, how to find what is not yet revealed by or in the light.

I gave myself fully to an inner process that was like groping in the dark. I had no road map to guide me in my exploration. I relied entirely on my feelings, intuitions and instincts, languages of the unconscious, of the feminine polarity, as I went from one area of darkness in my consciousness to another. By the time I arrived at the convent in Spain, I was ready to hear the message of the inner authority: "You must love the Mother and pray to Her. She will answer your prayers."

I interpreted that message to mean that it was time to

bring into conscious focus what I had been learning and to formulate it in a way that would serve my further development. The Life As A Waking Dream method presented in this book is that formulation.

After the experience of visiting the Spanish convent, I understood that *to pray to the Mother is to give reverent attention to what is, to what has manifested, to what has come into being. My prayers to the Mother are answered in the forms and shapes that life takes as me and around me. The Mother answers my prayers through the experiences of my life.*

Take some time, now, to record a meaningful experience from your own life as if it were a dream. See what meaning you can find in it. The questions that follow will guide you in your exploration. You may want to wait to respond to each of the questions about the experience until you have read the chapter of the book that elucidates the question.

QUESTIONS TO GUIDE YOUR EXPLORATION OF A VIVID LIFE EXPERIENCE (VLE)

Title of Your Vivid Life Experience:
Record this only after you have completed your work on these questions. Have fun choosing the title. Often you can capture the spirit of your inquiry in the title.

Step One: What Was the Event? [See examples in Chapter Two.]
Choose a specific event from your life that remains vivid for you because:
(a) It still has a lot of energy charge on it;
(b) It had a formative impact on you;
(c) You still can't understand it.

Then write a very simple, one-sentence statement of the event on which you wish to focus. All elaboration will come in the steps that follow, and will require you to re-enter the event consciously again and again. This sentence is like an anchor; it will hold your attention on the time-space you are examining. *[Examples: When I responded to the doorbell, I found two policemen on my doorstep and knew at once that my son was dead.* Or, *I met a man to whom I felt I was already married.]*

Step Two: Describe the Event [See Chapter Two.]

Write a description of the event *as if it had been a dream.* Speak in the present tense and use lots of descriptive words. Be sure to include your feelings, intuitions (knowings), and body sensations as well as words and actions. Do not include a lot of background. Get right to the core of the experience and describe it concisely. Generally speaking, *one page* should be sufficient to describe the event. Elaboration follows under the questions.

You may want to set this aside for a day or two after writing the description, so that you can return to it with more detachment.

Step Three: Revisit the Experience

Aware of yourself as the dreamer who has now awakened from the waking dream episode you have written about, ask yourself the following questions and write your responses.

As you stand back in yourself from the dream, identified with the Power-to-be-Conscious of the dream rather than with the sense of self in which you dreamed the dream, call into your awareness the larger context of your life in which this experience took place. That will help you to gain perspective on the given event.

1. What was your sense of self in this experience?
[See Chapter Three.]

When you touch how you felt during, or in the aftermath of, the waking dream, continue to breathe into that feeling while you ask yourself, "Who was I?" Sometimes your sense of self will be determined by how you felt in relationship to the other person or persons. Sometimes it will be the result of a self-image. Sometimes your sense of self will emerge as a result of something you said or an action you took or something you did not do or say that you wished you had.

You are looking for *a name or an image* that expresses the feeling you have found in your body and memory. When you find the words, you will sense a kind of agreement in your body. A sigh may come, or a feeling of relaxing or releasing tension.

Try to find a noun to name your sense of self, though you may want an adjective or two or three to go with it. Examples might be: rule maker, eager learner, ripe virgin, big bully, lost soul, etc.

2. How were you expressing yin energy in this experience? How were you expressing yang energy? [Chapter Four.]

Both polarities of energy are working in us and through us at all times. Here you will reflect on your participation in this event to see if you can identify both polarities within yourself.

3. What were your strongest feelings, sensations and intuitions in this experience? [See Chapter Five.]

The real Self attempts to awaken the sense of self through the arousal of emotion or intuition. Strong feelings or knowings (even when you don't know how you know) knock on the door of awareness and say, "Pay attention." The body reflects those feelings and intuitions as muscular tension, pain, discomfort, shivers of recognition, etc. Here you will record what feelings and intuitions were awakened and in relation to whom or what, and/or what reactions you noticed in your body.

4. What symbols stand out for you in this VLE?

[See Chapter Six.]

Look at the other persons, animals, key objects or places in the dream, especially those that seemed to evoke feelings, sensations or intuitions. Use plenty of descriptive words about what you were experiencing in the event about the symbol. (Do not include other information you have about the person, place, etc., that was not active in the incident you are exploring.)

Then see if you can identify what this person, object, or place symbolizes in you.

Do not include yourself as a symbol. You talk about yourself under the "sense of self" question. Here you look at those facets of yourself with which you were not identified in this experience. (Not being identified with them is not necessarily negative; it can also mean that you know those things in yourself but were simply not identified with them at the time.)

Summary retelling of the event: After you have identified what the symbols represent in you, tell the story again, briefly. This time translate the symbolism so that it reads like an inner event. See the example at the end of Chapter Six.

5. What don't you know about your VLE? [Chapter One.]

Usually we are so busy paying attention to what we *do* notice in an experience, that we fail to pay attention to all that we *do not know*. It may be precisely in that area that we can discover what we need to learn. Make a note of what you don't know.

6. What is the theme of this event? [See Chapter Eight.]

The theme is the central idea or issue in the event. Only you can know what the theme was. It reflects your feeling responses to the event, what you were dealing with, and what you were learning about. (Examples: Handling a Crisis, Being Abandoned, Hurting Someone I Love, The Seduction of an Innocent, Taking Charge of My Life, Collapsing Under Pressure, Hiding Feelings from Self and Others, Taking Risks.)   Themes are related to our life purpose. Although we usually live out these themes unconsciously, by identifying them we can begin to gather information directly related to our life purpose.

7. Of what other experiences in your life does this one remind you?

Make brief notes here, notes to yourself. Often the experiences you are reminded of will be other instances in which you were identified with the same sense of self and/or the same theme was in play. By bringing these other experiences into your consciousness, you will become conscious of Life Themes: that is, themes that have played out over and over again. When the themes keep repeating, it is because you have more to learn in that area and thus need to wake up to what your real Self wants you to see, know and do.

8. What is this experience telling you or asking of you?

This question is key to the awakening process and may be hard to come to by yourself, because it is so integral a part of your life dream. To the degree you remain identified with the "I" that had the experience, that is, with the sense of self within the waking dream, to that degree it will be difficult to see what the event was telling you. You might ask yourself, "What does this experience show me that I hadn't seen or acknowledged or known in quite that way before?" Or, simply, "What did I learn through this VLE?"

For clues to new information, look at what you did and did not do or say, what you felt, what aspects of yourself you let others play out rather than being/doing them yourself, what you don't know, what you were protecting or defending, what the theme is, etc. In effect, look back at all you have said about the experience and stay alert for things you haven't seen before, or haven't seen in quite that way.

Also, what questions do you ask yourself as a result of this exploration and what changes can you make in yourself as a result of it?

It is a well-known psychological fact that at moments of very intense experience, great joy or great suffering, everything happening around seems to a [hu]man unreal, a dream. This is the beginning of the awakening of the soul. When a [hu]man begins to be aware, in a dream, that he is asleep and that what he sees is a dream, he awakes. In the same way a soul, when it begins to realize that all visible life is but a dream, approaches awakening. And the stronger, the more vivid the experiences of a [hu]man, the quicker may come the moment of consciousness of the unreality of life.*

— *P. D. Ouspensky (1920)*

Too many mystics and enlightened beings have independently arrived at an understanding that our world is a dream for us to ignore what they say.

— *Malcolm Godwin (1994)*

*Bracketed material ("hu") inserted by D.K. Pike.

Chapter Two

Life As A Waking Dream

Sometimes our life experiences seem almost unreal, as if orchestrated by an unseen composer. We feel caught up in something not of our own choosing, much as we might feel during a dream at night. Those are the very experiences that have the potential to reveal deeper meaning in our lives. As the Russian philosopher P. D. Ouspensky says, "A soul, when it begins to realize that all visible life is but a dream, approaches awakening."[1]

Looking at life as a waking dream helps us to awaken and to learn to live with greater freedom, purpose, creativity, and power. If we are in some sense "dreaming" while we are awake, then what we experience says far more about us than it does about the world around us. We can discover the power of our own consciousness by giving up the illusion that our lives are happening *to* us, and learning instead how to change them by changing ourselves.

Here's an example that illustrates this approach:[2]

Lois, a 38-year-old single mother, social worker, and divorcee was looking for a way to get her life under control. When asked to tell the story of an event which evoked very strong sensations, feelings, or intuitions, Lois recounted a recent episode in her life which had puzzled and disturbed her. She told her story simply, without trying to explain it.

> One Friday afternoon about a month ago, I took a few hours off work to take my son to the downtown train station. I do this every four to six weeks, so my son can visit his father. On that day I planned to use my Visa card for the $25.00 train ticket. I was embarrassed and ashamed when my card was not accepted because I was at my credit limit. Distraught, because I needed to get my son on the train on time, I negotiated with the female ticket person. She agreed to give me the ticket and to keep my wallet in reserve while I went to get cash.
>
> I found a branch of my bank nearby and used the automatic teller to withdraw the money I needed. I felt a mixture of shame and gratitude as I exchanged the cash for my wallet. The ticket person seemed glad to have been able to help.

Lois's account gave strong indications that she had been caught up in a waking dream. She mentioned powerful feelings: embarrassment, distress, shame, and gratitude. Because her feelings lingered long after the event, they can be seen as caution lights that were flashing, "Pay attention, Lois! There is something for you to see that you are not seeing. what don't you know? Wake up!"

But Lois did not wake up. She described how the event evolved further:

> I then put gas in my car and headed back to work. When I overshot the approach to the freeway by a block, I was angry at myself and became preoccupied with the quickest way to backtrack. My mind did not adjust to where I was, and I turned the wrong way onto a busy, three-lane, one-way street. I went one-and-a-half blocks before I realized I was going the wrong way.
>
> Then I became very frightened and ashamed. I quickly tried to pull out of the lane I was in, seeing three lanes

of heavy traffic stopped at a light. They would soon be
coming at me. Then I saw a police car with its lights
flashing.

Not only did Lois's feelings continue to be strong,
but they began to interfere with her functioning. This is
another indication that she was in a waking dream. She
was angry and preoccupied, so did not grasp where she
was. When she saw that she was going the wrong way on
a one-way street, she became frightened and ashamed,
further diminishing her capacity to make sound decisions.
Still, Lois did not snap out of it. She was so totally immersed in the event that she felt it was happening *to* her.
She could not change it.

She continued:

A policewoman parked in the lane in front of me. She
got out of her car and came to my window. Angrily she
asked, "How could you drive on this one-way street
and not know it?" I answered honestly that I knew it
was dumb, but I was preoccupied. She took my license,
car registration, and proof of insurance, and wrote me
a ticket. I just sat there, my face hot and red. Traffic
rushed by. One man stuck his head out and yelled, "Ha!
Ha! Ha!" Another man shouted, "You are blocking traffic."
All I could think of was, "I have to get home and stay
there for a long time." I was terribly upset. But I had
errands to do before going back to work, so I carefully
went on, trying to breathe, cool off, and pay special attention to one-way signs.

In a waking dream we often feel trapped in our
experience, sometimes even the victim of it. We say to
ourselves, "How did I get into this?" We feel out of control,

much as we do when we are in a sleeping dream. Many people live a whole lifetime feeling this way.

To explore a vivid life experience we ask ourselves, *"What sensations and feelings was I aware of during the waking dream?"* According to Lois:

> I was totally shocked and ashamed to find myself in this situation. I felt like I had gone totally unconscious for a short time. I felt like I couldn't breathe. My chest felt constricted and painful. I felt young and stupid and very out of control.

Perhaps you can recall times when you have had feelings similar to those Lois describes. Strong feelings are signs that we are caught in a waking dream, as contrasted with those moments of lucidity when we are not totally immersed in our life circumstances and can stand back and look at the life we are living. During those lucid moments we can make choices about the quality and direction of both inner and outer experiences. To one degree or another we know we are the "dreamer," the one who brings the reality into being, even if we do not know exactly how we do it.

Discovering that
Life is a Waking Dream

Our whole life is a dream, but it is only gradually that we become aware of that fact. We begin to notice episodes within the life-dream, experiences that stand out from the rest of the day or the week because of their intensity. Emotions aroused may jar us to an awareness that something important is happening, or a strong intuition might say, "There is a message for me in this." Sometimes sensations in our bodies, such as restlessness, pain, or uneasiness, alert us to a need for heightened awareness. Sometimes we are not able to get the experience out of our minds. We wish we could rewrite the dialogue or relive the event differently. We tell the story over and over again to friends and colleagues. The repeated mental review may eventually make us realize that more is being asked of us than the mind has grasped. In any or all of these cases, we can begin to identify given events as waking dreams. Eventually the awareness that our whole life is a dream develops.

To call our experiences waking dreams implies that there is some way in which such experiences are not real, or are "all in the mind." Yet it is clear in Lois's account that her experience felt very real to her. Was the experience real? Or were her feelings pointing beyond the experience to a reality in Lois's consciousness that she needed to bring into her awareness? How do we know when an experience is real? According to Carl Jung:

> There are, and always have been, those who cannot
> help but see that the world and its experiences are in the
> nature of a symbol, and that it really reflects something
> that lies hidden in the subject himself, in his own tran-
> subjective reality.[3]

Is it possible, then, that the life events to which we give so much of our time and energy are waking dream episodes that offer messages about what is going on within us? I, and others, have explored this question repeatedly, and the answer to it is, I believe, one key to empowered living. As the physicist Ilya Prigogine says, "Whatever we call reality, it is revealed to us only through an active construction in which we participate."[4]

If the question "What is reality?" seems too abstract to be important in your life, you might want to think of this approach as a metaphor. It is *as if* life is a waking dream. It is *as if* we get up from a night's sleep and go through the day thinking we are awake but we continue to dream.

Our waking dreams hold information for us. They are a form of communication from the unconscious, from the Great Mother. When we learn to understand them, we come to know far more about ourselves. This understanding enables us to heal divisions in our sense of who we are, to integrate new qualities and skills into the way we know our personalities, and to expand the scope of the world in which we function. With practice, we are able to awaken, and to know ourselves as the observer and director of our lives.

Sometimes we can better appreciate the waking dream metaphor by reflecting on the experiences we have while we sleep. We lie in our beds and have no awareness of functioning in or through our bodies. Yet we have experiences, many of which are very powerful and seem very real. Many are interactions with others. Occasionally we travel to other places. Sometimes while we sleep we receive teaching, or clarify something with which we have struggled during the day. Upon awakening, we are aware that all these things took place in dreams. Nothing happened in the objective reality to which our bodies appear to belong, because sleeping dreams are totally subjective, or internal.

What is a dream, then? *A dream is an experience we have while our consciousness is not awake to the world around us.*

According to ancient wisdom, life itself is a dream. To call life a *waking* dream distinguishes experiences we have while in our ordinary state of awareness from the dreams we have when we are asleep, though they are actually the same phenomenon. As Ouspensky says, "both states of consciousness, sleep and the waking state, are equally subjective."[5]

The wisdom tradition tells us that life is a dream because we are asleep to the real Self, the Self that is our true nature. Just as dreamers at night are unaware of their physical bodies and the objective world around them, so we are unconscious of the real Self and the energy world in which we live. If we were to wake up, our life experiences would seem no more or less important to us than a dream, according to those who have awakened.

In order to wake up to our real Self, we call to our attention how we think and feel about ourselves. This helps us to know who we *believe* ourselves to be while we are asleep to our true nature. So we ask the question, *What was my sense of self in this waking dream?"* Lois commented:

> I felt like a child who had just done something stupid
> and dangerous, but with no idea how stupid and danger-
> ous until I had done it and had come back to conscious-
> ness.

It was only when Lois came back to consciousness of herself as she usually knows herself that she recognized just how unconscious she had been. This is very much like awakening from a disturbing dream from which we felt unable to escape. When we finally wake up, we feel relieved because we can say to ourselves: "That was horrible, but it was only a dream." We recognize that we are not the person who was caught in that dream. We are the person who has just awakened. In this case, Lois was not a child but rather a grown adult, yet it was *as if* the waking dream had been the experience of a child, for she felt like a child in the midst of it. The "adult" is not Lois's entire Self either, and one day she may awaken from the experience of her "usual adult self" and realize that that too was a dream.

Three Stages of Awakening

As we begin to pay attention to waking dream episodes, we discover that our sense of self shifts and changes throughout the day. It shrinks and expands. During the experience of being caught going the wrong way on a one-way street, Lois felt like a child. Later in the day, she returned to feeling like an adult. She felt almost as though she had been unconscious during the experience in the car. She had asked herself, "What on earth happened to the usual very competent and prepared me?"

The child who lived the waking dream is only one fragment of what Lois knows herself to be, a small constellation of feelings and characteristics that does not include being competent and prepared. Lois does not usually feel like a child. That is what was so disturbing to her. While she was functioning as an adult taking care of her son, she *felt* like a child. Then she "woke up."

There are three stages of awakening within a lifetime, and the sense of self is key to all three of them. Terry wrote about one of her experiences:

> I dreamed I was a student in a class in which I was ex-
> periencing performance anxiety, feelings of inadequacy,
> and judgement. I was fumbling for answers, feeling
> trapped in the literal. I felt like I just wasn't "getting it" I
> thought, "I can't even write the dream. Everything seems
> important. I live in details! It keeps me from seeing the
> symbolic message."

Terry was beginning to realize the extent of her identification with the content of her daily life. She recognized
that as long as she was focused only on the details, she
could not find any meaning in her experiences. Her feelings were very strong:

> I felt emotionally disconnected from my life and reluc-
> tant to take time to think about what I'd been through.
> I was simply dreading doing the assignment and pro-
> crastinating for all I was worth. I was not satisfied with
> what I wrote and was embarrassed. I was afraid of being
> judged, evaluated and criticized.
> My sense of self was the scared child looking for approv-
> al, security and a sense of worth from outside myself,
> from the teacher.
> I discovered I had given up my power.

This is a clear example of what I call *stage one: beginning to recognize that we are asleep most of the time.* Even
though we decide we want to gain insight into ourselves
and our lives, as Terry had done in joining a waking dream
class, we often continue in the dream. Terry was beginning
to know through her own experience just how unconscious
we usually are. To realize she had given up her power, as

we do when we live as though life just "happens," was to begin to take it back.

> Realizing this, my sense of self expanded. I no longer dreaded the class, but looked forward to it, knowing I would learn and grow no matter what. I now felt like a co-creator of my experience *as I was experiencing it*, not just looking back at it. I felt empowered, relieved and at peace.

In this first stage of awakening, we begin to have moments when we perceive clearly that what we are caught in is not real. Terry, for example, saw that she was not being judged by the class or the teacher. She wrote:

> I realized I was the one doing the judging. "I am doing it to myself!"

That realization empowered her, because it meant her experience was not being determined by some external reality. She could *change* her experience. When we begin to see our personal experiences as dreams, highly subjective and ever-changing, then we can begin to experiment with new possibilities.

Terry changed her sense of self:

> In this experience, I felt separate from the teachers, saw them as authorities who could validate me, my existence, and my worth. I now feel I have a new sense of self. I feel as a student I am also the teacher. That it is an equal partnership to help guide and empower each other to find answers within.

When Terry changed her sense of self, she found great meaning in the dream:

Not only was there the message telling me to own my
role as co-creator of my life, but there was the **feeling** of
the "aha" of awakening, and the joy and inner peace of
being there consciously. "I got it."

Even this first phase of awaking makes a big difference in the way we see ourselves and understand our lives.
The philosopher A. R. Orage put it this way:

> The truth is that just as in night-dreams the first symp-
> tom of waking is to suspect that one is dreaming, the
> first symptom of waking from the waking state — the
> second awaking of religion — is the suspicion that our
> present waking state is dreaming likewise. To be aware
> that we are only partially awake is the first condition of
> becoming and making ourselves more fully awake.[6]

Seers from ancient times through the present have said
that when a lifetime ends and the body and personality die,
our real Self awakens. Our real Self may remember the
life-dream in fragments, just as we often remember only
fragments of our sleeping dreams. If our real Self recalls
only vague images, much of what was experienced during
our lifetime will be lost.

Most of our sleeping dreams are forgotten when we
wake up in the morning. But with practice, we can learn to
remember more and more. In the same way, if we practice
paying attention to episodes within our waking dreams, our
real Self can learn to remember more and more. Then when
we awaken at the end of a lifetime, we will have learned
more as a result of our experiences.

To know how unconscious we are of the real Self is
the first stage of awakening. It serves us because it focuses

our attention on the nature of our life experiences. We become more aware that we are living in a dream state, which kindles the desire to know ourselves as the real Self and to live in the real world of energy. Endeavoring to know the real Self can lead to the second stage of awakening.

In stage two of awakening we become aware that we are dreaming while still in the midst of a waking dream episode. Marsha is a twenty-eight-year-old expectant mother preparing to give birth to her first child. In her waking dream, like Lois and Terry, Marsha felt like a child. But she was aware of that during the experience. This is an excerpt from her journal:

> Before our recent visit to the obstetrician, I wrote up a birth plan. I was aware that I felt nervous about showing it to the doctor, and I asked that Bob please accompany me to the doctor. (Bob was in agreement with everything I had included in the birth plan.)
> The visit with the doctor started with my examination. I noticed that I was acting friendly and outgoing with her, trying to establish and feel a rapport with her, and, I suspect, wanting her to like me. The friendliness was a little strained and artificial for me because the more prominent feeling in me was nervousness and discomfort about going over the birth plan with her. I breathed deeply and relaxed my body as much as I could.

Marsha was observing herself while she was in the midst of the event she was living. She was not only conscious of what she was doing and saying, she was also aware of her feelings. In fact, she was aware of several layers of feelings and thoughts going on at once. She sought to direct herself in the experience, by breathing deeply and relaxing her body.

Then we went into the doctor's office and showed her
the birth plan. She told us her position on several of the
points which reflected to me a conservatism on her part.
. . . I found myself telling her that if there was a problem
we would be agreeable to certain actions, but I did not
fully state what I believed would constitute a problem. I
seemed to be more concerned with making things right
between us. I also could feel that I wanted her to like me
and approve of me, and that this interfered with my ability to simply express how I felt about things.

Again Marsha, in the midst of the event, was conscious of how things were going. She was aware of the
shrunken sense of self that was undermining her in the
interaction.

I felt like a child who had the audacity to state my preferences to this authority figure, the doctor. Some part
of me still believes that I simply have no right to do this.
Though I have begun to hold in my consciousness that
the doctor is a symbol of a part of me in this waking
dream context, it is still not well-enough integrated to
remain strongly in my consciousness when I am taking
an action such as this one.
Bob, on the other hand, appeared to me to be very comfortable with sharing how he felt, even if it differed from
the doctor's viewpoint. I perceived him to be having an
adult interchange with the doctor without difficulty. I
was very comforted by his presence, and felt that I was
able to risk just a little bit in stating my own feelings
because of what I saw him modeling.

We see in Marsha someone struggling to awaken
while within a waking dream episode so that she could

direct it with more confidence. She observed herself and the dynamic and became aware of the limitations she imposed on herself. She was also keenly aware of Bob and how he was interacting with the doctor. His behavior showed her what was possible. To be aware of limitations and possibilities while in the midst of living an event is the second stage of awakening.

If we remind ourselves throughout the day that we are the dreamer, and stay alert to our senses of self, we can learn to make conscious choices about dynamics that might otherwise seem out of our control. Then we will experience lucid living.[7]

As Ouspensky put it:

> Only by beginning to *remember himself* does a man really awaken. And then all surrounding life acquires for him a different aspect and a different meaning. He sees that it is *the life of sleeping people,* a life in sleep. All that men say, all that they do, they say and do in sleep. All this can have no value whatever. Only awakening and what leads to awakening has a value in reality.[8]

Although the concept of multiple lifetimes is unfamiliar to many of us, it is central to wisdom teachings. According to the Ancient Wisdom, at a certain level of development, we prepare ourselves to wake up during a lifetime. Before we incarnate in another body and personality, we set the intention to wake up and remember that we are the real Self. To have such a realization during a lifetime brings a tremendous sense of liberation. We feel empowered and enhanced.

Studying our life experiences as if they had been dreams helps to prepare us for this kind of awakening. In stage one we begin to realize that we are dreaming. In stage two we learn ways to wake up within our lives, to discover the power of the real Self, and to unleash that power.

But there is a third stage of awakening. *We can wake up from the life-dream while still living.* To awaken and know the real Self and to identify with it changes the sense of self dramatically. When the awakened state becomes a lasting one, some teachings call it enlightenment, *samadhi,* or *satori.* Though few people reach this ongoing state of consciousness, many catch glimpses of it.

Sol is a 75-year-old painter who has been on a lifelong spiritual quest. He suffers from a debilitating heart condition. During an incident brought on by his heart he had an experience of waking up to his real Self:

> It is early evening. Esther is in the kitchen. I am sitting in the recliner in the living room, reading. Suddenly I experience strange sensations. I feel like a part of me has shut down. My breathing is irregular and I feel slightly nauseous.
> I take my pulse and I cannot feel anything. I call Esther who kneels down beside the chair and takes my pulse. Her eyes fill with tears. She lowers the recliner so that my body is in a horizontal position.

Sol made little mention of strong feelings or emotions in describing this experience. Rather, he wrote as the observer, the one who was conscious of the events and present within them, but not overwhelmed by them.

> My eyes go to the painting I had done of Sai Baba.[9] I begin to recite his name to myself. Over and over, I repeat his name. I feel calm, unafraid, carrying the music of his name into my being.

Sol's feelings of calm and lack of fear enabled him to be totally conscious of the events transpiring, and to make choices in relation to them.

> Esther calls the senior physician of the practice where she works and he says he will be over immediately. When he arrives they help me into the car and we head off to the emergency room.
>
> At the hospital there is a doctor on duty in whom Esther has no confidence whatsoever. He wires me to the monitor and begins his examination and some explanations. Esther goes out into the hallway and calls the internal medicine man I saw on regular visits. Although this is his night off, he promises to come over to the emergency room at once.
>
> Through all this I continue to recite the name of Sai Baba. Even as the doctor on duty was offering his point of view, some of which I questioned, I continued the recitation. I recognized that something was going on with my body and that it might die. Yet it did not really matter. There was an intermingling of thoughts, feelings, and sounds; there were no boundaries.

Again we notice how detached Sol was. He was not caught in the events. He did not feel victimized by them. He recognized that his body might die, but he was free in relation to that prospect.

> I could hear doctors speaking, nurses speaking, phones ringing, intercoms sounding, all the sounds of an emergency room, as well as my doctor and Esther speaking beside me. All the sounds became an undertone to my recitation.

Then came Sol's recognition that he had awakened

from the waking dream state of consciousness. He was no longer perceiving the world as made up of discrete objects separate from each other and from himself:

> I became cognizant that I was experiencing another level of consciousness. The ambiance of the emergency room, the different sounds, the thoughts and feelings in me, were not separate in themselves. They were like variations of lights of energy moving in and out of each other, interpenetrating, and at the same time part of a greater whole. It was like the first movement of a symphony with a larger part to unfold.
> I looked at Esther. She was Esther, but also a shimmering, golden light that was interspersed with drop-like shades of bluish purple that fell over the light like a waterfall. I could see her fear, her tears, her terrible anxiety, and I felt a wave of deep love, of compassion for this lovely lady.
> I did not feel a sense of attachment, of my personal ego hanging on, wanting to be with her or reluctant to let her go. Rather I had the wish to impart to her love, strength, and tenderness, and to soften and melt her apprehension, to let her know everything was really OK.

Sol sustained his awareness of his surroundings as he became conscious of his real Self. His words reflect an expanded sense of self that knows total integration in the Whole. In such a state, all boundaries and limitations disappear. We recognize ourselves as the one who dreams the waking dream. The effect of such an experience is profound.

Though we can identify three stages of awakening, they are not necessarily sequential. It is possible to live in all three stages at once.

The Fruits of Waking Up

You might be asking yourself, why would I want to wake up from what I know as my life? Think about your workplace. Do you feel caught in a constant power-struggle, in a ruthless competition, or on a fast-track to nowhere? Does it seem that no one cares whether you survive on the job, let alone thrive? Are you exhausted by constant pressure in a race against time? Do you wonder what your life is really about, since your work is getting you nowhere?

And think about your relationships. Do you have trouble establishing and maintaining intimacy? Does it seem to you, as John Gray suggests, that men are truly from Mars and women from Venus? Do you often feel as if no one really knows you or understands you? Do the smallest conflicts seem impossible to surmount? Does your family life revolve around the television set instead of around meaningful interactions with your mate and children? Could all of these relational difficulties reflect your lack of knowledge of your real Self?

We feel powerless and invisible when we are creating our lives unconsciously, living in a waking dream state. If we can wake up even occasionally, we can begin to see new possibilities. We can learn how to direct the course of our lives. We can feel more hopeful, more at peace with ourselves and in greater harmony with the people around us. And most important, we can begin to feel the deep satisfaction that comes from fulfilling the larger meaning of our lives that until now we have known only as restlessness in our psyches and emptiness in our spirits.

Waking up is not some mystical exercise. It is deeply

human and practical. It gives our lives meaning, quality, and integrity. Moreover, our survival on this small planet requires that we learn to live together as a peaceful body of diverse peoples. That ability must begin within each one of us. It is vital that we each wake up.

When we first begin, we need lots of practice. Initially we focus on waking up *after* a vivid life experience occurs, when we realize that we were asleep within it. In the Life As A Waking Dream method, the primary tool we use at this stage is writing down the experience as if it had been a dream. We examine it carefully, as we would a sleeping dream, to search out its meaning. Such attention to meaning also helps us to stay more awake in future events.

Next we practice waking up *in the middle* of vivid life experiences and changing the course of events. At the first signs of strong feelings, sensations, or intuitions, we breathe consciously and remind ourselves that we are the dreamer. Then we ask ourselves, "What do I really want?" and we make conscious choices about our actions.

When we become more skilled at waking up within our life experiences, we can practice being aware *before* entering into them, holding a clear purpose in mind and consciously choosing a sense of self.

These practices will, in time, lead to the third stage of awakening, for only by waking up can we come to know the real Self. By consciously engaging with our life experiences as waking dreams, we can identify what we are learning, integrate our new awareness into our sense of self, and awaken more frequently to and from our life-dream.

From the Unknown
To What Awaits Us

Working with any vivid life experience provides an opportunity to learn about our state of consciousness and our life purpose. Asking *What don't I know?* is one of the best ways to start. When Lois looked into what she didn't know about her vivid life experience of driving the wrong way down a one-way street, what she discovered was very revealing:

> I don't know a lot of things about this incident and it is bothering me a lot. I don't know how I could have driven so far without knowing where I was. I don't know why my mind didn't adjust more quickly to realize I wasn't where I thought I was. I don't know why I made the wrong turn in the first place when I am very familiar with the downtown streets. I don't know why I didn't bring enough money for the train when I knew I was at my credit limit, couldn't write a check, and had no extra time. I think that driving the wrong way on a very busy street during rush hour is a very powerful symbol, and that having two women help me out of the situation and trust me is very significant, but I am not sure why, and I don't know what it all means.
>
> The whole situation reminds me of some major life decisions I have made about relationships and jobs. The feeling I have often had, in the middle of the decision-making, was that I had no idea how I got there and no idea what to do next. This event reminds me of my lifelong big question: Where the hell am I going anyway, and is there a "right way" for me? My fear is that my choices are all "wrong."

By writing out our life experiences as if they had been dreams, or talking them into a tape recorder, we often naturally highlight what is important by the way we write or speak about it. Lois wrote down, and then realized, that she had a lifelong pattern of having no sense of clear direction. Our class joined her in considering the images that the waking dream offered.

One of the group members addressed Lois. "You mentioned that driving the wrong way on a very busy street during rush hour is a very powerful symbol. What do you feel it symbolizes?"

Lois laughed nervously. "I'm not sure. It just seems to indicate that I am going the wrong way in my life."

I asked Lois to stand back in her consciousness, to identify with a sense of herself as the one dreaming the dream, rather than as the "child" who lived the experience. Working from the idea that everything in the dream was a symbol for something in Lois's consciousness, the group looked first at the symbolism of the one-way street. Someone asked Lois, "What does that mean to you?"

Lois searched for a response. "I don't have as many options if I am driving on a one-way street," she explored aloud. "Perhaps it means I have limited choices available to me."

"And yet you were able, in the dream, to go the opposite direction on the street, the so-called 'wrong way,' without getting into an accident. No one was hurt," someone offered.

"That's true," Lois said, exhaling as though she had been holding her breath. "But all the other vehicles were going the right way. Aren't they also symbolic of something in me?"

We all agreed. An automobile is symbolic of some

vehicle through which we can express our sense of self. It could represent the body, or the whole personality, or a more contracted sense of self. In this experience there were many automobiles, so it seemed that each of them represented some facet of Lois, and all but one were going the right way on the one-way street.

When Lois realized that, she sighed deeply. "Maybe I'm not totally messed up after all," she said quietly.

Someone probed further. "Do you remember the sense of self in which you lived this waking dream?"

"Yes. I felt like a child," Lois responded.

"Could it be that this sense of self feels at odds with the rest of you, as if she is wrong, or going the wrong way?"

"That fits. The pain I felt in my chest that day brought back memories of the months just before and after my seventh birthday, when I was very sick with scarlet fever and then pneumonia. Because I am the oldest of nine children, my mother quarantined me on the third floor of our big house in New Jersey and I spent several weeks almost totally alone, recuperating." Lois was deep in her memories.

A class member followed an intuition. "Did you feel, then, that you were being punished?" he asked.

"It did feel like that. I felt I must have been bad in some way to get so sick and to be left all alone that way. It was as if the other children would be . . . " — Lois's voice drifted off as she looked for the right word — "contaminated by me."

Then she chuckled. "Maybe that's why I felt so furious at the two male drivers. I felt like shouting, 'So you never made a mistake?' but I felt too ashamed and weak to do that. I also thought the policewoman would think I was loaded or crazy or both, so I kept my mouth shut."

Although there was much to explore about the male drivers as symbols, the group's attention went to Lois's strong feelings about the two women who helped her out of the situation, and trusted her. "I'm not sure what it means," Lois pondered. "It just really strikes me that both at the train station and on the street, I was interacting with women, since I rarely see a female ticket person or a female police officer."

The two females seemed to be symbols for yin energy, the feminine force. One of them held the "ticket" that enabled Lois's son, a symbol of an emerging force within her, to visit her estranged yang polarity, symbolized by her former husband. The other yin symbol had the authority to direct the traffic of her own activities, and to remind Lois of the laws, symbolic of the laws of her inner being. Both of the yin forces were gentle, caring, and helpful. They made it easier for Lois to accomplish what she had set out to do.

The terms *yin* and *yang,* which come out of the Chinese philosophy of the Tao, identify the fundamental energy polarities that are intrinsic to the world in which we live. I have found that the use of these Taoist terms avoids associations people have developed with the words *feminine* and *masculine.* Most people have no prior emotional reactions to *yin* and *yang,* and are therefore freer to understand the energy polarities that are at work in everyone.

Lois continued. "It seems like the waking dream says I am connecting better with my yin energies than with my yang, because the only men who stand out in the experience were jeering and angry." Although men do not always represent yang energy in a waking dream episode, they often do.

"Yes," a class member concurred. "Instead of serving to guide and direct you, as yang forces would do when in their right relationship with the yin, your yang symbols seem to have turned against you. And the symbol for your partner yang, your 'husband,' seems at a distance from you and perhaps is not serving you at all."

Lois nodded sadly. "It's hard for me to think of Hank as a primary symbol for my yang energy. I feel so estranged from him, and so angry at him for deserting me for another woman." Her body had stiffened as she spoke.

"Perhaps it would help to tell yourself that the divorce also occurred as part of a waking dream episode," someone else suggested. "It could then be seen as a symbol for some lack of cooperation and communication within you between the yin and the yang."

"I need some time to think about that," Lois said, signaling that she had gone as far as she could in the exploration for that evening.

Where to Begin

When working with our dreams, sleeping or waking, it is important to let our feelings lead the way, not our thoughts. Feelings open us to the unconscious and to the possibility of discovering what we do not know. Dreams should never be initially approached through the intellect. They need to be felt first, because dreams clarify our subjective experience of life. They give us information we haven't paid attention to and open us to what is new.

Feelings indicate the effect an experience has had on us; they are our direct response to the event. As we step back from an experience, as we do when we write or talk about it, we are able to be more objective about it. Then we can bring our feelings into dialogue with our thoughts. Dream work is typically focused on that dialogue.

Dreams attempt to tell us something we don't know. By taking action in response to what we learn from studying the waking dream episode and expressing our feelings, we integrate new information into our waking life, thus changing the way we interact with our world.

You can begin your study of waking dream episodes by making notes on some of your vivid life experiences in a journal.[10] You need to write only a sentence or two that identifies the event and summarizes what happened. These experiences can be as recent as two weeks ago or as long ago as your early childhood. If they come to mind as still alive for you in some way, make a note of them. Subsequent chapters will show you how to go deeper to discover what more these vivid life experiences can reveal to you.

Here am I, my body made of elements that once were stardust, drawn from the far corners of the universe to flesh out, however briefly, the pattern that is uniquely me, my soul, a thing that can breathe in the enormity of such awe-inspiring origins. But who or what is this "I" that I think I am?

— *Danah Zohar*

The chief feature of our being is that we are many, not one. . . . Man in his ordinary state, is a multiplicity of 'I's.

— *P. D. Ouspensky*

I had dreamed once . . . [that] I came to a small wayside chapel. . . . On the floor in front of the altar, facing me, sat a yogi — in lotus posture, in deep meditation. When I looked at him more closely, I realized that he had my face. I started in profound fright, and awoke with the thought: "Aha, so he is the one who is meditating me. He has a dream, and I am it." I knew that when he awakened, I would no longer be.

— *C. G. Jung (c. 1960)*

Chapter Three

The Sense of Self

The sense of self is fundamental to the way we function in the world. We are guided by it, even restricted by it, often without being aware of it. In the following waking dream episode, Bruce's sense of self shifted several times. Bruce was struggling to find a way to relate harmoniously with the yin polarity of energy in his life, and his waking dream reflected that struggle:

> I am sitting at home alone watching television when the phone rings. It is Valerie. I feel delighted she has called. We chat and I feel warm and comfortable.
> She then tells me that she is inviting most of the local Life As A Waking Dream people together for supper on Sunday and would I like to come?
> I feel flattered to be asked, but also torn. I spend the weekends with my girlfriend Betty and I enjoy that life. The particular weekend Valerie has invited me for is more inconvenient than most because I was planning to stay at the Lake through Monday.
> I say, "I will think this over and get back to you, but at the moment the answer is no."

Up to this point the interaction seems an ordinary exchange between adults. If Bruce hadn't reported how he felt, we would have assumed that he made a simple choice between two activities. But his account continued:

> I feel strangely agitated by the whole interaction, for it has endless painful antecedents. I feel caught in a power struggle between two powerful women, both of whom I love dearly. No matter what I do, one of them is likely to feel offended.
> Normally I like to please people. I like to fit in with their plans. I do not know how to deal with conflict - especially conflict between two women.

Bruce has shifted the focus from himself, the choice maker, to the two women. In doing so, he gave his power over to them. That immediately affected his sense of self:

> I feel like a small boy trying to please two mothers. No matter what I do I will be wrong and I will be punished. I find myself feeling totally passive, as if I have no power to resolve this situation.

Bruce's sense of self as a mature adult peer of the women has shrunk so dramatically that he feels like a small boy. The two women have been cast in the role of mothers with the power to punish him — one of the dangers of identifying all women with a given woman known all too well. Bruce felt powerless to take action on his own behalf for fear that if he did, he would offend one or both of the women. Pleasing himself was no longer a priority.

The sense of self lies below the conscious level of understanding ourselves. Most of us have many different ways of knowing ourselves, and thus, many different senses of self. We slip in and out of these various senses of self from time to time, and from circumstance to circumstance. We are usually relatively unaware of our sense of self at any given moment. Nevertheless, it colors our inner world of experience, interpretation, and response.

Components of a Sense of Self

The first component is our *self-image*. Although we may not be aware of it, we carry various ideas of ourselves in our subconsciousness. These ideas are not simple and straightforward, like a photograph would be, but multidimensional. A self-image may be based on how we want other people to experience us, or how we think others *do* experience us, or how we experience ourselves, or it might even be based on what we know, or deny, in ourselves and try to hide from others. A self-image is not only, or even primarily, physical. It includes some of the characteristics that make up our personalities.

Bruce revealed part of his self-image when he reported his experience as if it had been a waking dream. He said he thought of himself as someone who pleased others, not as someone who let them down, told them no, or entered into conflict with them. This sense of himself made it very difficult for him to say no to the women in his waking dream.

The second component is our *capacity for action*. The sense of self may be directly influenced by our ability to take action. When we are unable to act on our own behalf, we feel helpless. Feeling powerful and effective, or powerless and ineffective, influences the choices we make.

In Bruce's case, feelings paralyzed him. He said it was as if he had no power to resolve his conflict. In fact, his feeling of powerlessness may have been the primary component of his sense of himself as a little boy. Children are virtually powerless in many situations because they must do what adults say. It is natural, therefore, that when we feel powerless as adults we often feel like children.

Bruce's feeling of powerlessness may have come over him when he shifted his attention from himself as the choice maker to the two powerful women he was eager to please. By focusing on his desire to please them he put himself in an impossible position, because he could not say yes to both of them. If he had focused on what he wanted, rather than on trying to please them, and remained in his sense of self as a mature adult, it might have been easier to make his choice.

As he worked with the event as a waking dream, Bruce realized that when he reverted to feeling like a child, "I didn't know how to behave, because nowhere in my young life did anyone say to me, you have a right to do what you want. The only thing I was told was to do the right thing! I was to ignore my feelings and do my duty - no matter what the cost." In his waking dream Bruce could see no way to determine what the right thing was, so he felt immobilized and passive in his sense of self.

The final component of the sense of self can be characterized as *relational* or *contextual*. How we feel about ourselves often depends on the context in which we find ourselves and how we are related to the other people present.

In Bruce's waking dream, what was his perception of who he was? Was he primarily Valerie's friend? If so, he might have decided to accept her invitation. On the other hand, if he was primarily Betty's lover, then he would surely say "no" to Valerie. Or, Bruce could have identified himself as an independent man who had the luxury of choosing between two appealing opportunities for his weekend. He might have chosen both. The possibilities of relational or contextual feelings are always manifold, but Bruce's sense of self was so diminished that the only relationship for him to choose was that of child with mother. As he pondered his dilemma, he made a large discovery:

> I recognize a pattern of choosing to go out with the person with whom I am not having a sexual relationship, as if these are more important or more worthwhile people, or as if I am ashamed of my sex partner, or as if I have to "behave properly" and recognize that intellectual discussion is more important than love! Or perhaps it is that I am not supposed to enjoy myself. I'm suppose to do what other people want!

We can see the conflict between what Bruce would have chosen if he had stayed with his own preferences — to spend the weekend with Betty — and what his pattern determined he should do — accept Valerie's invitation. Since the two women had become mother figures to his little-boy sense of self, it was unthinkable that he would put a sexual relationship first! He went on:

> The awareness that at some level I may be ashamed of my sexual involvement - that I try to hide it or minimize its importance - seems to me to be a hang-up from long, long ago. Probably from a time when I was growing up and I was told how bad sex was and how it was only wicked people who got involved with sex. It was as if a parental figure called me away from what I was enjoying doing, and I had no alternative but to obey.

Now it's easy to understand how Bruce retreated to his sense of self as little boy. Unconsciously, he felt as if Valerie had caught him enjoying himself with Betty. So her invitation seemed like a command, calling him to be a good boy. Since Bruce was not conscious of the change his sense of self was undergoing, he felt trapped. Once he recognized the pattern, however, he was able to make a different choice. In doing so, he woke up within the waking dream episode.

> Now that I have written all this I have no doubt about what I am going to do. The awareness of this over-compliant child within my adult body helps me to recognize that I am still reacting to very early training. But since I am no longer a child, I can choose how to spend my evening! I am growing up!

Bruce's sense of power returned as soon as he realized that he could make the choice. He woke up within his waking dream and began to direct the course of it. This ability to feel more powerful in our lives is one of the most significant benefits of learning to see life as a waking dream.

> I am aware that I have all kinds of freedoms - if I take them. It is not my mother or my father who keeps me feeling spineless and infantile, but myself! If I can connect with my initiating force, I can be both strong and gentle!

When we lose the awareness of our possibilities in any situation, we feel disempowered. Instead of looking for alternatives, which would be empowering, we usually project the power onto someone or something else. We believe "they" are doing something *to* us.

In his waking dream, Bruce perceived the two powerful women to be in conflict over him. He said that he felt "caught in the cross fire" between them. However, in his description of the event, it is obvious that the two women did not even know about each other! The women were not interacting with each other; the entire process was going on inside of Bruce. It was his waking dream.

The sense of self is not necessarily apparent to others. They have their own ideas about who we are in a given dynamic, partially according to their own senses of self. The result is that two people who are interacting will experience events as two completely different waking dreams.

In this case, Valerie was relating to Bruce as a member of a group to which she belonged. By extending the invitation to him, she felt like a hostess inviting a peer to a gathering. Bruce's initial response — "I'll think this over and get back to you, but at the moment the answer is no" — triggered nothing more than momentary disappointment that he would not be able to join the group. In fact, Valerie later commented, "I would not have expected him to drop a previous arrangement in favor of this invitation."

Remember, *your sense of self is central to any life-dynamic.* It is the internalized sense of who you are in that moment, and it influences everything you experience. It colors your perceptions, your choice making, your relationships. It determines whether you feel able to take action. *It is the filter through which you live your life.*

Expanding and Contracting

A sense of self is not a fixed state of awareness. It shifts and changes, not only from one period of life to another, not only within a month, week or day, but even within a given interaction with another person. It is possible to feel strong and competent one minute, and inept and weak in the next, though the outer circumstances have changed very little. We saw that kind of shift in Bruce's waking dream. As he put it:

> To begin with I was in my normal adult state, but when Valerie asked me to go out on Sunday night I suddenly reverted to being a compliant child. I stayed in this child state, feeling very torn and uneasy, for a half hour or so. Then, as I realized how upset I was, I decided to work with the event as a waking dream. After writing and evoking all kinds of ancient and largely suppressed events in my life, I suddenly switched out of my child state and into a more balanced frame of mind. As soon as I did so I had no difficulty making a decision.

Such shifts in the sense of self are common. A friend told me this story. She was ill with the flu and feeling very keenly the need to go to bed, to be attended to. She was identifying with herself as one who was sick, the dependent self who looks to others to care for her. Then her husband called from work and asked her to meet him at the train station much earlier than his usual hour. She knew by the tone of his voice that something urgent had arisen. At the station, he told her he had been diagnosed with cancer of the lymph glands and could have as short a time as six months to live.

She did not think about her flu until months later, so instantly did her sense of self shift. She became the caretaker, the loving wife, the comfort giver, the mobilizing mother, etc. There was no place in her new sense of self for her own illness. It fell away. The "reality" of her illness changed with her sense of self.

You can probably remember examples of similar shifts in your own life if you give your attention to them. Some are frivolous; others, like the one mentioned above, are momentous.

If we were totally conscious of our own state of development, we would have a wide scope of Self-knowledge. We would know our real Self. To live in that knowing would be to live in an awakened state. In fact, most of us are not fully conscious of who we are. Consequently, our various senses of self can shift dramatically. Most of us live in an illusion that we are less than we are.

Our false state of Self-awareness determines which qualities and skills we draw on in a given life circumstance, and what feelings are aroused. It is the instability of these senses of self, the way that our sense of self can turn on a dime, that leads to the dreamlike quality of daily life. It is as though we have no solid internal ground to stand on. In a given situation, we plant our feet in what seems to be a firm sense of self. Then, without warning, the ground shifts and we feel uncertain of who we are and how to function. Only by identifying with our real Self can we find solid inner ground.

Debra had an experience of how rapidly a sense of self can shift, which she described as a waking dream.

Mother calls me about 8 A.M. She is having a hard time breathing and her head feels stuffed up. She is afraid to get out of bed and go to the kitchen to make her breakfast.

I am aware of not wanting to jump in the car and go over; I am in the middle of baking a pie. I feel frustrated because this is the same complaint I have been hearing for years and there is little that can be done. Her doctor saw her last week and could find nothing treatable.

In the beginning, Debra's mature adult sense of self predominated. Debra, in her 50's, assessed her mother's situation and her own and decided not to rush out the door.

> I finish the pie shell and call her back. Her voice sounds pretty strong, but she's still in bed. We negotiate breakfast and lunch. "Maybe you can bring me something that'll serve for both," she suggests.
> "What would you like?" I ask.
> "Something good." My stomach knots up.

A simple response like "something good" evoked a different sense of self in Debra. Her stomach knotted up and she "became" the resentful kid who grudgingly gave up her morning to take care of Mother.

> Nothing tastes good to her anymore; this is like finding a needle in a haystack. I tell her I can't guarantee anything will taste good.
> "I try to get the best I can get," I say defensively. She allows that it is not my fault. We agree on oatmeal and a slice or two of ham.
> I get my stuff together and go to the market. I see fresh chicken livers and pick them up. I get the ham and cheese also, just in case.

A pleaser/performer sense of self popped out when Debra discovered the chicken livers and thought her mother might like those, but her resentful kid self reasserted herself when she found her mother's door unlocked.

> I arrive at her apartment. The door is unlocked. She's been able to get to the door to unlock it, even if she hasn't been able to stop in the kitchenette and heat her tea water.

> I say hello and tell her what I have brought. "Cook the
> chicken livers," she says. "Just two."
> She eats, and I clean up and am all set to leave. I want to
> go to the pool before the open swim is over.

Debra was aware of what she wanted, which was
to go swimming. But like Bruce in the earlier example,
she felt powerless to choose what she wanted because she
was operating from her resentful child sense of self. Her
powerlessness awakened strong feelings:

> She says she needs to brush her teeth and take her medi-
> cine and she wants me to stay. Suddenly I am seething.
> Why couldn't she have mentioned this a little earlier?
> "OK, I'll stay," I respond grudgingly.
> She operates in what feels like slow motion. She is, after
> all, 91. "Where is my compassion?" I ask myself. On
> the other hand, I am irritated that she is taking up a day
> when I had planned not to go out, but to write and do a
> little cooking.

For a moment another sense of self tried to emerge,
asking "Where is my compassion?" This was the adult
sense of self speaking, or perhaps even the spiritual aspi-
rant. But the feelings of the powerless-child sense of self
had prevailed as Debra sank into a sense of herself as
martyr. Then a loving caregiver self, both compassionate
and healing, emerged in Debra in the face of her mother's
genuine vulnerability:

> Finally she is done. She climbs back into bed and seems
> very small and very scared. She is frustrated with feeling
> so lousy and not knowing how to fix it. She is aware that
> she is fading away and it frightens her. I sit on the bed
> and pat her leg. She is all bone, down to 72 pounds with

all her clothes on. She wants desperately to die in her sleep and not suffer. It is hard to know what to say. I am ready to let her go, but she doesn't seem ready to let go.

Debra's sense of self shifted once more as she left her mother's apartment and got to the pool in time to swim for half an hour. When Debra sought to name this last sense of self, she was at a loss.

Finally, some part of me which I seem not to have named surfaced and took care of my need to go for a swim.

Six different senses of self appeared over the course of a few hours in this waking dream, each coloring Debra's response to her mother and her mother's circumstances. At first that might seem unusual. As we observe ourselves, however, we find that we have a surprising array of ways of knowing and experiencing ourselves.

It takes a lot of consciousness just to identify and name the various senses of self we have developed. [See Illustration #1, page 61.] In Debra's case, for example, she did not yet know what sense of self enabled her to respond to her own wants and needs. When we begin to study our waking dreams, we must learn to identify the multiple senses of self. Then we can learn to direct them so that they are not unconsciously running our lives.

Just knowing that the sense of self expands and contracts and is therefore not a constant expression of the real Self is helpful. With practice, we can learn to relax into this dynamic. Physical discomfort, strong feelings, and intuition can all trigger our awareness of a shifting sense of self. We say to ourselves, "Hey! Something is going on here that I am not conscious of." Then we can expand the

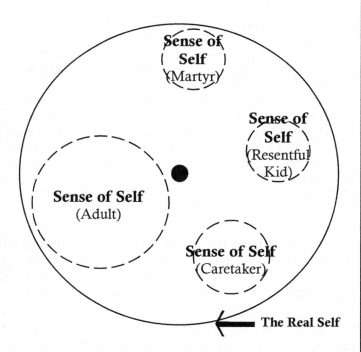

Illustration #1
Senses of Self

Contracted senses of self are identified with only small bundles of qualities and/or life skills and are unaware that the rest of the real Self is available to them.

sense of self to make room for additional qualities and skills available in the real Self. Trusting that there is more to ourselves than we identify with in the moment, we can create our reality more consciously.

Jeffrey was able to catch his sense of self shifting in the midst of an experience.

> I was at an ongoing weekly personal growth group where I act as assistant. Various members were commenting on my phone calls to them and the feelings that came up for them about the content of what I had said or the way in which I had spoken.
> As I listened, I had some flash feelings of "not doing well enough," and of "not pleasing them." It seemed some did not want my help and caring. I had a sense of "how can they say this after how hard I have worked for them?" and "Oh, oh. Here's my old stuff coming up again."
> I had a sense of shrinking down for a small moment as I allowed my inner critical parent to creep in.

Jeffrey was aware that he had been functioning in predominantly yin energy, expanding and opening up to take in comments from the group. As long as what they said felt good to him, he remained receptive. When, however, the feedback ceased to feel good, he began to criticize himself, and immediately he felt himself begin to close down, becoming more yang. He was less willing to be receptive and more inclined to be discriminating and judgmental. As soon as Jeffrey realized he was beginning to feel "picked on and on the hot seat," as he put it, he made a new choice:

> Quickly I affirmed myself by saying silently to myself, "Jeffrey, you are OK. This is good learning for you and you need to look at it." As I said this, I felt myself open-

ing wider to them, going more yin, to take in their feelings about me and also to hold them in my hand lightly
and look at what some said that didn't seem to fit at that
moment.
As we moved to other group work I was aware of the
different feelings that had come up and my responses to
them, and how I moved through them, and I ended by
feeling OK!

The key for Jeffrey was that he remained conscious
of his feelings throughout the interaction. When his feelings were in response to old patterns and shrunken states
of self-awareness, he was able to make new choices and
expand again by reminding himself that he was more
than the characteristics being pointed to by the group. By
remembering more positive qualities, he was able to stay
in the interaction without becoming disempowered by
external or internal criticism.
Cindy had a similar experience opening an envelope she received in the mail:

I know this to be my monthly alimony check. As I pick
up the envelope I become aware it contains more than
just a check. I think it might be a holiday greeting from
my ex-husband and his new wife. However, it is not a
holiday greeting, but more of a business letter. Written
on his business note paper, it reads: "Cindy, According
to my records, this is payment number 114 of a total of
120 payments due to you. Six more checks will be sent
after this one to complete the 10-year alimony require-
ment. If you don't agree with this information, or have
any other questions, please contact me. Jim"
As I read this note, I am feeling tense and frightened.
His tone is a familiar one, lacking emotion. I am a credi-
tor being reminded of our agreement and the status of it.
I try to take in the feelings coming up in me. In the last

few years I have been preparing for the coming end of
these checks by not relying on them to cover my living
expenses. I hoped I hadn't been fooling myself. I wondered if perhaps I have been holding onto some false
sense of security.
I feel myself beginning to fret, to spin my wheels. I
choose instead to go yin and just take it all in.

Cindy paid close attention to her feelings in the midst
of the event. When she began to feel tense and frightened,
she was aware that she was becoming a reluctant yin, on
guard and self-protective. She didn't want to shrink into a
victimized sense of self, so she made a conscious choice to
remain open. Cindy expanded her sense of self by deciding
to receive what her ex-husband had said without taking it
personally. In so doing she affirmed that when functioning
in yin energy we remain powerful if we stay open and take
in what yang offers.

As the sense of self expands, it becomes more yin,
more diffused. As it contracts, it becomes more yang,
more highly concentrated and focused. Were it to expand
sufficiently to encompass our real Self, we would wake up
from our life-dreams. We would know all that is contained
in our consciousness. Then the diminished senses of self
would cease to exist. We would be completely Self-aware.
[See Illustration #2 on page 65.]

Who Are We Really?
The sense of self is the "I" that unconsciously inter-
acts with the other people, places and things in life. It is

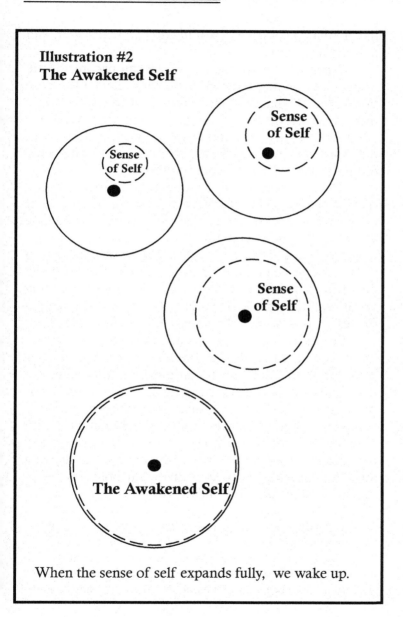

Illustration #2
The Awakened Self

When the sense of self expands fully, we wake up.

the "I" that experiences a waking dream, reacts to it, and tells the story of it.

Wherever we are right now, we can become aware of ourselves in the context of our environment. Our sense of self, the "I" that is seated in the room where we are, in the city where we are, in the state or province where we are, thinks of everything outside of itself, starting with the chairs we are sitting on, as other than itself. This is the ordinary state of human consciousness.

To view life as a waking dream, we change our concept of reality and view everything in our lives as part of one reality, the reality of Self. The real Self is the one dreaming the waking dream.

Hindu philosophy holds that the whole of creation is a dream in the mind of Brahma, or God. We are being dreamed even while we dream, and Brahma is learning about Itself through this process called cosmos. Everything that exists is a symbol of some facet of Brahma.

Such a concept might seem strange to the Western mind, and yet many modern approaches to dream interpretation in the West teach that every person and object that appears in one of our sleeping dreams is a symbol of some facet of our own consciousness, some aspect of Self. And we are quite aware that when we wake up, the dream "disappears." In his autobiography, Carl Jung, the widely recognized dream expert, writes of a remarkable sleeping dream that revealed a similar truth to him, not about sleeping dreams but about our life-dream:

> I had dreamed once before of the problem of the self
> and the ego. In that earlier dream I was on a hiking
> trip. I was walking along a little road through a hilly
> landscape; the sun was shining and I had a wide view
> in all directions. Then I came to a small wayside chapel.

The door was ajar, and I went in. To my surprise there was no image of the Virgin on the altar, and no crucifix either, but only a wonderful flower arrangement. But then I saw that on the floor in front of the altar, facing me, sat a yogi — in lotus posture, in deep meditation. When I looked at him more closely, I realized that he had my face. I started in profound fright, and awoke with the thought: "Aha, so he is the one who is meditating me. He has a dream, and I am it." I knew that when he awakened, I would no longer be.[1]

When Jung realized that he (the "hiker" sense of self) was being dreamed by his real Self, he knew that he, the hiker, had no independent reality. He would disappear when his real Self awakened.

Waking dreams can be viewed as stirrings of our real Self as it tries to see beyond the perspective of a diminished sense of self. As the Russian philosopher P. D. Ouspensky said:

It is a well-known psychological fact that at moments of very intense experience, great joy or great suffering, everything happening around seems to a man unreal, a dream. This is the beginning of the awakening of the soul. When a man begins to be aware, in a [sleeping] dream, that he is asleep and that what he sees is a dream, he awakes. In the same way a soul, when it begins to realize that all visible life is but a dream, approaches awakening. And the stronger, the more vivid the experiences of a man, the quicker may come the moment of consciousness of the unreality of life.[2]

When we become aware of a vivid life experience, we can ask ourselves, "What was my sense of self? Who did I know myself to be?" Often when we tell friends about such experiences, we say things like, "This is so unlike me," or, "I never do things like this, but for some reason that's how I responded." Such disclaimers express our awareness of a shrunken sense of self.

Rachel struggled with her sense of self in this waking dream episode with her grown son, Roger:

> Thursday is damp and dull and depressingly "heavy." I need to put new batteries in the alarm system, but I can't get the cover off, so I phone Roger to ask him how he'd handled the system while I was away. He feels frustrated about the whole experience and gets impatient: his voice becomes loud and angry, and he's not hearing what my question is. Then he says he'll be coming over later about something else and he'll take a look at it then. I feel uncomfortable, an inefficient nuisance, but I don't say anything, and don't really take much notice of my feelings. I just "stiffen the upper lip" and plod on: no feelings, except discouragement.

Rachel was immersed in a waking dream, unconscious of the sense of self in which she was functioning.

> My immediate task is to gather up garbage which has been collecting over several months, and to take it to the dump in my car. I do this very efficiently. As I'm ready to leave, I think I'd better tell Roger I'm going to be out for a while, so that he won't come over while I'm not here. So I phone him and I am surprised to find that my throat is so tight that my voice is hardly audible.

Rachel stirred within her waking dream when she noticed that her throat was unusually tight.

> I tell Roger I'm going out for a couple of hours. He notices the strange voice and asks, "Are you all right?" I

say, "Yes, but I just don't like to be shouted at," and my
voice breaks in tears.
Roger says he wasn't feeling mad at me, just frustrated at
the nuisance of the recalcitrant alarm system, and that
he had not meant to shout. I tell him "OK."

Rachel was speaking to Roger out of a shrunken
sense of self; he responded as if the interaction were "real,"
that is, a straightforward conversation between the two of
them. But Rachel was on the verge of awakening within
the dream:

Then I'm driving along, appropriately enough with the
trunk full of garbage! And I find I'm saying it over and
over as I go: "I just don't like to be shouted at," and
crying helplessly. I keep saying it and I keep crying, and
I know clearly that it's my father I am speaking to, not
Roger; I'm a small child talking to my dad.

Rachel did something very important. Once she became aware that she was in the midst of a waking dream,
she stayed with the feelings that had been awakened, giving
them full life and expression, until she discovered what
was trying to emerge. She kept saying aloud to herself, "I
just don't like to be shouted at," and she continued to cry
helplessly, until the new awareness was sharp and clear:
she was reacting to her father, not to her son Roger.

This ability to trust the process of a waking dream,
knowing that it has something to reveal to us, is essential.
We won't gain any new insights by interrupting the dream.
Rather, it is by giving our attention to what *is happening*
(or to what happened, if we are exploring the event in
retrospect), by listening, watching, and continuing to play
out the event, that we make new discoveries.

Rachel identified her sense of self. Rather than experiencing herself as the mature mother of a grown son, she had shrunken into identification with herself as a small child speaking to her father. Her inner experience was of a different context and relationship from her outer reality. Once she realized this, she was able to recognize what her real Self was trying to tell her:

> In the waking dream I see that the child was never able to say this to her Father. What she had always done was exactly what I'd done that morning with Roger: feel inefficient, stupid, lacking and a failure. And, when he [father] got angry and yelled at me, I'd just battled on, refusing to give in or give up. I had pushed on through the storm, with hatches battened down, feelings bottled up, not permitted, never questioning the rightness of his wrath and judgment, or my own stupidity that had kept me from meeting his standards and pleasing him.

As a child, Rachel's sense of self had shriveled in the face of her father's criticism. Her self-image had been that she was inefficient and a failure. All her other attributes had faded into the background of her awareness. Her capacity for action had been greatly reduced, because she felt unable to speak up to her father, to stand up to him when he shouted at her. Since Rachel had not let herself know what she was doing, her "reality" as this child had remained a bad dream. After this interaction with her son, Rachel seized the opportunity to awaken:

> I never thought that I had the right to say to [my father], "I don't like to be shouted at! It upsets and frightens me. And anyway, I'm NOT stupid about lots of things, and I don't have to be clever at everything!"

Rachel found an expanded sense of self. It included the ability to tell her father how she felt. Rachel played it out as she drove in her car:

> The sense of my father's presence is very strong, and it feels as though I am telling him, at last, how I feel. I have at last uncovered these long-hidden feelings and seen that I have a right to them.
> Later, I get a sense that my dad was surprised and shocked at my upset. That he hadn't realized how severe he had been to the child. I also see how the old pattern had become a habit, and a habit that could very suitably be left at the garbage dump!

Rachel was not only able to uncover feelings she had harbored in a relationship many years ago and claim her right to speak from those feelings, she was also able to see her father in a new light. She recognized that he probably hadn't been aware of the impact he had had on her as a child.

In the aftermath of her discovery, Rachel made a choice to let go of an old pattern of reacting (feeling stupid, a failure, etc.), and of a sense of self that no longer served her (the wounded and unappreciated child). She laid claim to a new self-image as a capable person, expanding her capacity for action.

Rachel was able to function with a different sense of self in the subsequent interaction with her son regarding the recalcitrant alarm system. And her son, who had served as a symbol for the harsh authority figure in her earlier waking dream episode, later manifested different qualities:

> Later still, when Roger came over, we got the battery

situation successfully sorted out, and he was very gentle
and regretful of his earlier roughness. I didn't tell him
that I am now grateful to him for triggering something
so important for me, and that, in fact, the blowup had
very little to do with him at all.

Such an outcome is typical when working with vivid
life experiences. Once we have realized the significance
of the message from our waking dreams, the people with
whom we've been interacting suddenly appear to change,
even though we've said nothing to them about the process.

It is often unclear whether other people *actually*
change after we do, or whether our experience of them is
just different because we aren't relating to them in the same
way. This matter of others who appear to change when
we do remains one of the mysteries encompassed by the
question "What is real?"

Aligning Our Senses of Self

As we examine our waking dreams, we discover that
in many situations the sense of self is not appropriate to the
role we are in or the function we wish to fulfill. Choosing a
sense of self that is aligned with our role and function helps
us to stay awake. Sally wrote of a time when she struggled
to stay aligned with her role as therapist:

Angie and Jerome quit therapy tonight in a huff. Angie
said, "That's not good technique. Three months in
therapy and nothing is accomplished. It's three months
wasted. We are worse off than previously." I wondered

if I should defend myself. After all, it was the second
time she had said that and it sounded as if she was deliberately attacking me. I asked myself, "Is it good therapy
to challenge that, or would I lose control of the session?"

Sally was thinking about what to do while the situation was unfolding. She had every intention of being a
responsible therapist, and also of remaining conscious
and not getting caught in her waking dream. Nevertheless,
she found herself in conflict with herself throughout the
session:

> I asked Angie, "Would you like to talk to me directly
> about what's going on between you and me?" I knew she
> was trying to make me at fault for the pain she felt at this
> second failed marriage, but did I have to take her criti-
> cism?
> She said I have no technique and she wants someone
> who will fix their relationship. I would usually have
> recoiled at those words. However, I had just come from
> a supervision group where we had discussed the use of
> this very technique, so I felt confident. I explained the
> method and said maybe she would like someone more
> directive, and I would refer her.
> My voice cracked and varied in pitch. I was aware of it
> and tried to project, but I associated the phenomenon
> with fear and self-doubt.

Sally was observing herself, but she was not able to
choose her sense of self consciously, so she shrank into
identification with the cracking voice:

> Angie used bigger words and grew more articulate. I
> kept using smaller words and felt an undefined feeling
> welling up in my stomach. I realized that my parents

were just like this couple - lost and hurting and lashing out in anger - and I had tried to "fix" [my parents] and failed.

Sally felt herself slipping into her own waking dream. She tried to pull herself out:

I said, "I'm here as a guide, a facilitator, a witness." I didn't like to do so much explaining.
She said, "That's not enough," confirming what I had feared, to not be enough. I told myself, "She must feel she is not enough. No matter what I said to her, it wouldn't be enough."
It was 8:00 P.M. I reached for my briefcase for referral numbers. The briefcase hit my foot. I thought, "God, I'm clumsy. Can't I even close this session smoothly?"

When Sally explored the experience as a waking dream, she could see that her sense of self had shifted around several times: herself as the therapist, trying to evaluate her intervention and to do what was right for the clients; herself as a child, seeking to protect herself; herself as a clumsy and inept person; and herself as a person trying to remain conscious within a waking dream.

Sally wanted to function as a therapist. When she slipped into her sense of self as a child, she no longer had her skills as a therapist at her disposal. She lost her capacity for action. In those moments, she wanted to deal with her own emotions, but that would have made her nonfunctional as a therapist. Consequently, she tried to find appropriate responses even though her sense of self had contracted.

To fulfill her role as a therapist, Sally needed to remain identified with her feeling of being competent, well trained, and experienced. She needed to remember that Angie was the client. Her own inner child could not become the focus of her attention. She needed to act on her own convictions rather than calling herself into question.

Sally's saving grace was that she struggled to remain conscious during the conflict and thus was able to keep from identifying completely with the child who feared not being enough, and who viewed "failure" with these clients as a confirmation of that fear.

As we bring a given sense of self into sharp focus, we discover which facets of Self are encompassed by it and which have gone temporarily unconscious. We note the qualities and abilities with which we identify, and those with which we do not identify in that sense of self.

As time goes on, we find names and voices for the senses of self that appear most often in our waking dreams. Learning to recognize those voices makes it easier to notice quickly what is really going on in our experiences so that we can make new choices.

We might choose names like: the Slave Driver, the Victim, the Quitter, the Poor Sport, the Worthy Opponent, the Rescuer, the Leader, the Wise Woman or Man, the Peer Friend, the Responsible Adult, the Helpless Child, the Workaholic, and the Couch Potato.

It can actually be fun to name the senses of self that appear most often, to become intimate with their characteristics. The names need to feel true to us and may change as we gather more knowledge of a particular sense of self. But having names to use seems to make waking up a little easier.

The majority of our waking dreams occur when our sense of self is in a relatively diminished state. Only occasionally will an experience stand out because we are in a state of awareness that is more expanded than usual. Danah Zohar, a physicist, philosopher and mother of two, wrote of the profound experience she had when her ordinary sense of self expanded in a wonderful way:

> During the pregnancy with my first child, and for some months after her birth, I experienced what for me was a strange new way of being. In many ways I lost the sense of myself as an individual, while at the same time gaining a sense of myself as part of some larger and ongoing process.
>
> At first the boundaries of my body extended inwards to embrace and become one with the new life growing inside me. I felt complete and self-contained, a microcosm within which *all* life was enfolded. Later, the boundaries extended outwards to include the baby's own infant form. My body and my self existed to be a source of life and nurture; my rhythms were those of another; my senses became one with hers, and through her, with those of others around me.
>
> During all those months, "I" seemed a vague thing, something on which I could not focus or get a grip, and yet I experienced myself as extending in all directions, backwards into "before time" and forwards into "all time," inwards towards all possibility and outwards towards all existence.
>
> I joked at the time that I had lost my "particle-hood" and my husband told me that I was experiencing projective identification with the baby. Freud would have called it an oceanic feeling. Whatever, it was both unsettling and exhilarating and through it I lost my lifelong terror of death.[3]

Danah touched new aspects of her real Self through this experience and was able to identify with them to such an extent that she lost her fear of death. Expanding the sense of self, if we do not get so "fuzzy," to use Zohar's word, that we lose the sense of "I," can be very empowering.

Unfortunately, when the sense of self shrinks we most often feel disempowered, like Sally. In a disempowered state, we appear to feel things more keenly, either emotionally or physically. These strong sensations are like alarms going off, calling us to wake up.

You may want to begin to watch for senses of self as you move through each day. Pay attention to strong physical and emotional sensations, and when you notice them, ask who you are just then. Try to find a name for your sense of self and notice the circumstances in which that sense of self showed up. Notice in which senses of self you feel weak and in which you feel empowered. As you practice, you will come to know yourself much better.

Everywhere in nature . . . the reproduction of any kind of form, emotion, or thought must arise from the union of two polar opposites.

— *Manly P. Hall*

Every event or experience represents a combination of yang and yin, masculine and feminine energies in varying degrees of emphasis. ... On the cosmic level, it is through the interplay of the masculine and feminine aspects of the Divine nature that the universe and its "ten thousand things" arises. ... On the individual level, this same basic polarity manifests as the principles of active and passive awareness, or observer and observed. ... The act of self-reflection is continually ... bringing about the variations and secondary qualities which make up each person's symbolic drama.

— *Ray Grasse*

Chapter Four

The Creative Forces: Yin and Yang

Like most other animals and many plants, human beings are divided as a species into female and male. The fact that two genders enable humans to reproduce reveals a key to the life process: *it takes two polarities to bring a third something into being.* In the Hermetic[1] tradition this was called the law of generation: "Everywhere in nature . . . the reproduction of any kind of form, emotion, or thought must arise from the union of two polar opposites."[2] This is the secret of the power to create.

At the heart of everything that exists, two polarities of energy function in a powerful union — the yin (feminine force) and yang (masculine force). It is the exchange of force between these polarities that causes things to come into being. So it is also with us as individuals. Not only did it take the union of our fathers and mothers to bring our bodies into form, but two fundamental energy polarities, yin and yang, continue to operate within us — physically, psychologically, and spiritually. Without them we would not be able to think, to speak, to act, to love, to feel, or to live.

When we look at our lives as waking dreams, our fathers and mothers, or primary caretakers, can be viewed as symbolic representations of the two forces within us. If life really is a waking dream, then how we remember our parents from our first five to seven years may reveal the state of our own consciousness at the beginning of our lifetime. Katherine's memories of her early life, which she has written as a waking dream, illustrate this approach.

> I was born in a small farming community in the Midwest, the second child of a couple in their mid-20's. It was 1938 and the country was just emerging from a depression.
>
> My father was a business man. He owned a gas station and oil distributorship. He worked hard, long hours, yet he held his family as his highest value. He tried to join us for all our family meals, though often he was called away from the table by something that needed his attention at the station.
>
> My father was young and vigorous. He was full of energy and good humor. He made us laugh a lot. He played games with us in the evenings and took us on long drives in the country each Sunday.

In reporting our memories, it is not important what was objectively true of our parents, but what we remember. When we write of our early life experiences, we describe our parents in order to learn how the formative forces, the yin and yang, were operating in our own consciousness. That our own experience will differ from that of our siblings, or from others who knew our parents, is almost a given since each of us is living a different waking dream.

Katherine remembered the yang, as symbolized by her father, as active in the outer world, yet deeply committed to, and connected with family (including her mother, the yin). This suggests that Katherine would have felt comfortable moving out into the world herself, without losing her sense of being connected with herself and her inner world. She would not easily get lost in the outer.

> I felt safe with my father. I knew he could and would protect me. One time a large dog jumped up on me and Daddy chased him away with a rake. When another dog bit my hand, Daddy held me on his lap while the doctor cleaned the wound. He distracted my attention from the pain and made me laugh.
>
> My father was kind. He listened to me and took time to explain things to me. He taught me how to do things, not only in those early years, but throughout my teens.

Since Katherine felt safe with her father, she would probably feel secure about moving forward with her own initiatives. She would feel she could trust the direction her inner impulses would take her. And because Katherine knew her father as a teacher, she would be able to follow her own impulses to do new things, trusting that she would learn what she needed to know along the way.

When Katherine turned her attention to how she knew the yin force in those early years, she described her mother:

> My mother was a homemaker. I could always depend on her when I needed her. She was a constant presence in my life. I told her all my secrets and experiences and she received me with quiet understanding.
>
> Mother held me on her lap in the evening and read me stories. She was very patient, often reading me my favorite stories over and over again. When I went to bed at night, Mother always came to tuck me in and say my prayers with me.
>
> Mother let me help her around the house and she taught me how to do chores "like a big girl." She was young and pretty and I felt very secure with her.

Knowing the yin, as symbolized by her mother, as a constant presence suggests that from a very early age Katherine felt at home wherever she went, bringing her full presence to each experience. She was probably open and receptive to other people, listening to them and receiving them with understanding. She probably felt comfortable guarding the secrets of others as well as her own.

Because Katherine knew her mother as the one with whom she said her prayers at night, Katherine may have found her deepest spiritual experiences in the quiet of her inner reflections and meditation. That she asked her mother to read her favorite stories over and over suggests that Katherine welcomed learning from her life experiences even when they were repetitive.

Feeling secure with her yin energy, Katherine probably felt confident about taking as much time as she needed to bring projects to fruition without getting discouraged or calling her own ability to succeed into question.

> My parents never fought or disagreed with each other. They worked together a lot around the house and in the yard on weekends, and we did lots of things as a family. They were happy together and always supported each other.
> My parents had many friends and were part of two large extended families. My parents took us to church every Sunday and taught us to be generous and to help those who were in need.

Katherine's waking dream revealed that in her early years she knew the two polarities as a team, working well together in a cooperative and productive fashion. She also saw them as part of a larger network of forces, as symbolized by the extended families, the large circle of friends, and the church they attended. Katherine seemed to feel integrated in that large network. Applying the Hermetic principle "as within, so without," we could say that what Katherine saw in her parents was actually true of her.

From that perspective, it seems that Katherine knew both polarities of energy very well when she entered this lifetime. Moreover, Katherine seemed to understand that the two polarities work together as one, in a union. Based on Katherine's early life dream, we would expect her to be well-balanced and healthy, as well as independent and creative.

Of course not everyone's early life-dream reveals such a balanced and clear reflection of the fundamental energy polarities in their basic nature. Mark's memories of his early life, when considered as a waking dream, disclose a different awareness of the two polarities

> I was born in a small farming community in Wisconsin in 1952. I lived in the country with my parents, older brother, older sister, and younger brother. I dreamed my mother had rheumatoid arthritis which made her hands and feet funny-shaped and caused her to be in pain a lot. She took a lot of medicine, which helped, but she had episodes of illness when she was not home or was bedridden.
>
> My father was a busy man with work all day and meetings many nights of the week. He also had a large chicken barn and when he was home he worked out there.
>
> I remember my father as big and strong and important. My mother was weak, submissive and crying a lot. Yet it was my mother who set the feeling tone of the family. When she was happy and feeling good, it seems we were all happy, but when she was feeling bad we all walked around on tiptoes, helping with household chores, hoping that she would feel better.

In Mark's waking dream, his mother was weak and submissive as contrasted with his strong and important father. This seems to indicate that Mark had not brought his yin polarity into parity with the yang. In his consciousness, the yang force was both more important and more effective in all realms except the emotional. Mark might have been full of good ideas and projects which he undertook with enthusiasm, but without a matching yin strength, he wouldn't be able to bring them to fruition.

Mark's mother's arthritis might represent a distortion in Mark's knowledge of the yin. Whenever our understanding of reality, or the way we look at things, is misinformed, it brings us pain, and Mark remembers his mother as having been in a great deal of pain. From this we can infer that learning how to express the yin force powerfully and effectively is one of Mark's major life challenges.

If this were true, Mark would need to give birth to yin qualities in his personality, such as openness, receptivity, magnetism, and flexibility. He also needs to learn what actions are characteristic of yin, such as nourishing other people, tending to details, giving form to ideas or impulses, and forgiving people's shortcomings. With practice, Mark could strengthen his yin polarity sufficiently to make it an equal to his yang force.

Understanding Yin and Yang

A word of caution as we work with the concepts of the yin and the yang. Generalizing our feelings about our parents or principal guardians may lead to misinterpretations of the yin and yang. For example, Mark experienced his mother as weak and submissive. It would be easy for him to conclude that it is the nature of the feminine force to be like a doormat. Not wanting others to walk all over him, Mark might feel he wants nothing to do with expressing yin energy. However, when yin energy is strong and functioning well, it is not overpowered by yang. In fact, without a balance of the two forces, Mark cannot be a powerful and creative individual.

Pamela, on the other hand, would have good reason to distrust the yang force if she based her understanding of it on her experience with her father. She wrote:

> Mommie was our primary parent during most of childhood. She was reasonable, easygoing and soft-spoken. She was barely five feet tall and Daddy was six foot four. This was not the only point of contrast. My father was a rager and a perfectionist. I feared him in so many ways and was always trying to get his approval. He didn't just yell at us kids, he was critical and angry towards Mother as well. There were happy times and there were times of a lot of fear.

Pamela might have concluded, based on her experience with her father, that the masculine force cannot express tenderness, patience or love. If she wants to be loving, she might believe that she has to express primarily yin energy, not yang. But without yang, Pamela might find that she lacks discrimination and is unable to express her own convictions.

It is important to step back and loosen up from our usual associations with the masculine and feminine in order to broaden and deepen our understanding. In looking at our lives as waking dreams, we seek to understand the forces themselves, and how they function. In response to new understandings, new feelings will emerge, and new insights into our past experiences will almost inevitably result.

During our teen years we learn to differentiate between the two forces. We become self-conscious about being either male or female, and then begin to relate to the opposite sex with a newly discovered sense of mystery. Russell encountered tremendous difficulties when he reached those crucial teenage years. He described his experience as a waking dream episode:

> When I was thirteen I was sent away from my sheltered home environment to a brutalizing boys' boarding school. There I attempted to learn trust and intimacy in a large number of homosexual experiences. With some boys there was a mutual acknowledgment of our softness, vulnerability and sexuality. With other, smaller boys, I was the father force while they supplied the longed-for feminine aspect which was so lacking in our environment. But a good deal of our relating was a sort of ritual act of defiance, a bonding of two rebels who found each other in opposition to a common enemy. Although beatings and canings were an everyday experience, the most extreme social sanctions were reserved for those among us who were unfortunate enough to be caught in some sexual misdemeanor. In such an atmosphere it would have been incautious in the extreme to give the slightest hint of caring for another. We were hungry children grabbing at the smallest crumb of affection.

Russell's sense of self in that waking dream was as "a criminal." He explored his strongest feelings:

It was a time of terrible loneliness and alienation for me. If anyone in authority could have said, "Sex isn't so bad. Of course boys have sexual urges. It is natural!" things might have been different. I might not have felt like such a criminal. My confusion and uncertainty were heightened by the fact that there were a number of masters at the school who were themselves homosexual. Much of my life was colored by my efforts to dig myself out of the well of loneliness and deception I experienced then.

Russell experienced the complete subjugation or denial of yin energy at a time when he needed the yin as a contrast for his developing awareness of yang. These circumstances delayed his natural unfolding in consciousness. Rather than differentiating during his teen years and coming to identify with the yang, he did not accomplish that feat until he was twenty-one. It was difficult for him to identify fully with the masculine polarity of energy when there were no females around to represent the contrasting polarity, as Russell discovered:

While there was some variety in the homosexual relationships I had, there was very little knowing of the forces. These were truncated experiences because there was no true female polarity. While we each had a yang and yin aspect of self, there was too little yin force to bring forth fruit or satisfaction.

Russell was fortunate, however, to form one lasting relationship with a male during that time, which enabled him to have a positive experience of bonding:

My first true homosexual lover . . . was several years older than I, a medical student in his last year at Oxford. He represented culture, intelligence, breeding and sophistication, as well as male energy. He had a beautifully developed body, like a god. I fell head over heels in love with him. The bonding between us was deep and a very lasting relationship developed, which continued in the form of letters and occasional visits right up to his death. In due course both of us married and had children, and I am still friends with his wife and children even though he died several years ago.

In Russell's waking dream he became able truly to love himself as a male when he entered a "true" homosexual relationship. Loving his friend was a symbolic statement of his enduring commitment to himself as male, and to his yang force. When he was twenty-two, he fell in love with a woman and began to explore his opposite polarity.

Same-sex sexual explorations in the teens are natural and uncomplicated when they are balanced by the presence of the opposite sex. We explore the bodies and psyches of our same-sex friends as a way of coming to know ourselves more intimately, and as a beginning of knowing and loving ourselves as male or female.

We explore the bodies and psyches of the opposite sex as a way of bringing into our consciousness the polarity opposite to our gender. Leticia describes this episode from her waking dream:

Warren is a friend. He sits down beside me on the horse-drawn hay wagon as we head off into the fields. We talk and laugh and enjoy each other's company. I feel very comfortable with him and not at all self-conscious until he puts his arm over my shoulders. Then I realize that something is happening that I am not prepared to handle. I had held hands before but this takes on a different energy from the beginning. Soon his hand goes over my shoulder and presses lightly onto my breast. I take his hand and hold it in mine. Later he kisses me and gets very "aggressive," putting his hand up my sweater in the back and moving on around to the front.

In describing an exploration of her body by a boy, Leticia finds the yang, as symbolized by Warren, aggressive and she, representing the yin, is not fully receptive or responsive. In her sense of self, Leticia was just beginning to find out about the yang:

I was "the innocent." That evening I knew for the first time that such things must go on between adults. I felt loyalty towards my body and caring about what I would experience as the maturing process continued.

Leticia went forward in her exploration with new awareness, having been the recipient of Warren's attempts to come to know the yin. Barry reported this episode from his waking dream, when he was the yang "explorer":

I was with my steady girl at a dance. We had been dancing close and I got a hard-on. I led her over to the chairs on the sideline and sat down. I took her hand, which I was still holding, and placed it next to my erection. She did not pull away. I was surprised.
I asked her if she wanted to leave. She agreed. We drove up a mountain road and parked, overlooking the city. We started to make out. I had touched her breasts plenty of times, but I had never been inside her pants. I took her hand and placed it on my erection. She held onto me through my pants. That gave me courage. I lifted her skirt, feeling her legs and her belly. Then I lowered her underpants. I was surprised to discover she was moist. I touched her gently, afraid she would tell me to stop. She didn't. I pressed harder, pushing my middle finger inside her. She was very wet. I lost it in the excitement, but it

was worth it to have touched that most secret place.

Barry, confident in his yang energy, proceeded boldly into the unexplored territory of the yin. His girlfriend allowed and encouraged the experimentation. In the process they were coming to know themselves and each other. Symbolically, they were coming to know the yin and yang and how they interact with each other.

In both of these brief waking dream episodes, the yang force was the initiator and the yin was the mystery being explored and discovered. Yin chose whether or not to receive the yang advances and respond to them. This is a true reflection of the two polarities in interaction.

Symbolically, we learn about yang through interacting with males and about yin through relating to females. But in fact, we learn about both forces in all relationships, because each of us has both forces at work within us. This is perhaps best represented by a symbol from the Chinese philosophy of the Tao, the *T'ai Chi T'u.* [See illustration #3 on page 93.] The yang is represented by the light half of the circle and the yin by the dark half. In the yin, there is a small circle of yang energy, and in the yang, a small circle of yin energy. This represents the knowing that neither force is ever devoid of the other. There is always some yin active in yang energy, and some yang in yin energy. Together they make one whole. And so it is within each of us. In order to express ourselves as whole persons, we must know how to make both the yin and the yang come to life through us. Through countless life experiences, we come to recognize both forces in ourselves, and we learn how to bring balance to our Self-expression.

In this waking dream episode, Nancy experienced the imbalance of her two forces and then made a choice

**THE CREATIVE FORCES:
YIN and YANG
TWO IN ONE**

**T'ai Chi T'u
(Which means "The Ultimate Supreme")**

Illustration #3

to bring them into balance:

> I was to have lunch with a close male friend. He had
> invited me six days earlier. There was no contact in the
> meanwhile except for a brief hello yesterday on my
> answering machine.

Nancy was in a yin modality. Her friend took the initiative by extending the invitation, and she responded. He called to leave a message; she received it.

> This morning his secretary called to say that my friend
> would not be in the office today. I knew immediately
> it meant the cancellation of lunch. I felt irritation and
> disappointment, wondering why he didn't call directly
> and why his secretary had so obliquely communicated
> his message.
> I was functioning primarily in the yin polarity, being re-
> ceptive to an invitation, listening to the information the
> secretary gave me on the phone, and being reasonably
> patient, accepting and initially accommodating toward
> this situation.

Nancy understood the two forces and thus could describe how she was embodying the yin. She also knew that until she gave some expression to her yang force, she would not feel complete with the interaction:

> After reflecting awhile on what was really going on, I
> shifted to a yang mode. While I could not call him and
> confront him about these events, I did not want to wait
> until tomorrow. I wrote him a brief, succinct note and
> mailed it so that he would have it upon his return to the
> office. This act was risking, choice-making, urgent, force-
> ful, and making known (all characteristics of the yang).

It was also a major departure from my usual posture of taking a disappointment like a beating and saying little or nothing, but feeling hurt and abused.

Nancy had empowered herself by taking action in response to her feelings. This is how she described it:

My strongest feelings in this experience were anger, a sense of being conveniently used, offense at the lack of commitment on my friend's part, impatience that I had experienced this situation repeatedly with him, real irritation that while I respect and accommodate his priorities, I do not receive the same treatment from him. Hours later, after acting on my anger by writing a note stating my feelings, I felt elated at having taken action. I noticed that all my tension had been released. I felt like I had reversed a long-standing pattern of hiding my feelings. I had taken charge of my life.

Nancy gave life to both the yin and yang, and in doing so she experienced the power that is released when those two forces interact with one another. In Nancy's case, the balance between the yin and yang was established within herself. When two persons in whom the forces are in balance interact with each other, the result is a free-flowing, cooperative and jointly-shared event which is empowering to both and brings something creative into being.

Craig was recovering from hip-replacement surgery. He lived alone in his apartment, and thus was dependent others for several weeks for both companionship and for help with shopping and transportation. Craig is usually very independent, relying primarily on yang energy to make his way through life. It was a relatively rare occurrence for him to enter into a balanced interaction. Here is his account of a waking dream episode:

> My friend Sarah came to see me, bearing many balloons. After a warm greeting she said, "Let's take off those tight stockings (which I wore to prevent blood clotting) and give you your onetime relief for the day!" I said, "Great," and she pulled them off. Sarah stared at my left leg in horror, saying, "Oh my God, look at that." When I looked, I could hardly see my toes my leg was swollen so badly. I was scared and bewildered.
> Sarah took charge. She made several calls, finally reaching the Saturday Physical Therapist who said, "call the ER." We did, and then went there as fast as possible. Sarah stayed with me the whole time. After three hours in the ER, she brought me home. Then she went to J C Penney's to buy a recliner I badly needed to elevate my legs. Then she helped me rearrange my house. By the time we finished, my leg was virtually back to normal.

Craig's waking dream was about a female friend who came to his rescue — a scenario that was unusual for him. He was used to rescuing others. When he reflected on the balance of yin and yang energies, he saw that there had been a good flow between the two polarities.

> When we first discovered the problem, I was too yin: weak, unfocused, feeble, etc. But I was a positive yin when receiving Sarah's forceful, single-focused directive to "elevate your legs." I trusted her judgment. Then I mobilized myself (yang), got more active, found the phone number of the hospital, had creative ideas on what to do. I was yang in making phone calls and then sometimes yin when Sarah got on the other extension to tell the person "what was going on." Once we got in the car, I gave Sarah directions (yang) to the hospital

ER, and she was the accommodating yin, following directions. At times she probed (yang), asking me "how far to the next turn," etc. Once in the ER, I told (yang) Sarah that I was feeling weak and scared, and I let her concern touch me (yin). I practiced yin patience at the ER, receiving from Sarah and others, waiting in expectancy for test results, etc. I really listened (yin) to Sarah and the doctor and I spoke (yang) when I had something to say. I offered some ideas (yang), but mainly I took in ideas (yin) from the doctor as to how to make sure this problem did not recur.

Craig's waking dream revealed his growing ability to move back and forth between the two polarities in order to be whole in himself and to have a creative and cooperative relationship with another. He was excited about his newly discovered balance.

I felt powerful in the knowledge and feeling that somehow I (and the bond with Sarah) had created this whole experience. Before this waking dream episode, I thought I knew how to take care of myself — a very yang attitude. Now I realize I need to be much more yin — open, flexible, receptive, and detail-tending. Although I need my yang discrimination and need to pursue and be exacting, I also need to be more all-embracing in yin, seeing the bigger picture and asking more questions. I had been unaware of how to create a more positive and effective yin-yang relationship with self, each polarity serving the other in a back and forth, rhythmic way as Sarah and I did most beautifully during what was a difficult, scary day. I see now that I can only take care of myself if I cooperate with the yin and yang polarities in loving, respecting, caring for, listening to, and cooperating with each other.

Primary Characteristics
of the
Creative Forces

Illustration #4

Here are descriptive words that characterize the fundamental energy polarities. They apply "relatively speaking" (i.e., comparing one force to the other). We could say these forces "tend toward" these characteristics, all else being equal, when they are functioning in polarity. Remember that power is released *between* the two polarities; each is powerless if it does not cooperate with (polarize with) the other. The power released is "neutral," in that it can be used constructively or destructively.

Yin	Yang
The primary characteristic of this force is that it gives form to the pattern that it takes into its substance.	The primary characteristic of this force is that it sets the pattern for what will come into being.

Receiving
    sustaining
    holding
    protecting
    yielding
	Initiating
	    catalyzing
	    thrusting
	    risking
	    penetrating

Substance-lending
    accommodating
    all-embracing
    accepting
	Organizing
	    discriminating
	    selecting
	    judging

Continued	*Continued*

Yin *(continued)*	**Yang** *(continued)*
Responding	Directing
offering options	choice-making
detail-tending	goal-setting
permission-giving	standard-setting
reality-orienting	ideal-orienting
offering	demanding
nurturing	exacting
patient	urgent
Obscuring	Revealing
keeping hidden	making known
Dark	Light
mysterious	forthright
diffuse	focused
Paradoxical	Explicit
ever-changing	steady
enduring	eager/energetic
unfolding	evolving
cyclic	progress-oriented
Spacious	Condensed
round	straight-lined
soft	hard
curved	pointed
pliable	unbending
flexible	unrelenting
Expectant	Willful
dispassionate	passionate
attractive	active
magnetic	electric
allowing	forceful

Like Craig, we can all learn about the importance of the balance of the yin and yang as we study our waking dreams. We must remember that the two forces are inseparable. They work together.

As we examine our own vivid life experiences, we begin to have an inner sense for the way the two forces function based on our *experience* of their dynamic qualities, rather than relying only on our *ideas* about those qualities.

An understanding that is basic to the wisdom teachings in all traditions is that *nothing can be known of the yang force except through the yin, for unless yang is given form, it remains invisible.* In examining our life experiences as waking dreams, we look for the invisible purpose of life (the yang) as it is revealed in the form and content (the yin) of what actually happens. Through our waking dreams we discover how to cooperate with the creative energies at work in our lives. Gradually we learn to read the stories of our lives as if they were books of wisdom.

Early Life Dreams

To begin an exploration of the fundamental forces, try writing a description of your first seven years of life as if they were a dream. Then examine what you have written to see what it reveals about your own perceptions of the yin and yang. Here is another early life-dream, very different from Katherine or Mark's:

> I was born in a small rural town in northeastern Pennsylvania in 1948. I was the firstborn. I sensed anxiety around me. We lived in an economically depressed area

and the underlying adage was "life is hard."
The man who was my father worked those early years
at a variety of jobs ranging from driving a beer delivery
truck to working in a large steel manufacturing plant.
The woman who was my mother worked also, usually
sewing in factories.
The world looked dark to me at that time. My memories
are very unclear and in most of them I feel like I am
looking through a tunnel, with very limited access in the
scene.
Thoughts of my father carry fear — of his loud voice
and especially of his anger. The fear of him and what
he might do permeates my memory. I wanted to please
him despite my fear, but he was unapproachable. Mostly
I remember him yelling, "Be quiet" and "Stop crying
or I'll give you something to cry about." He was not an
affectionate man.
My mother was not an affectionate person either, but
there was an aura of love around her. I felt safe when
she was near. I wanted to please her and I could when
I helped her with my baby brother and cleaned up the
house. She acknowledged my help and I felt appreciated.
In general, the beginning of my waking dream is dark
and limited in scope.

Dorothy's early life-dream seemed to reveal that she
had not yet developed much awareness of the fundamental
energy polarities and how they function when she began
this lifetime. Consequently, she reported her memories as
"dark and limited in scope," a description that would apply
to her own grasp of the feminine and masculine polarities.
She apparently had an urge to know and develop these
energies, reflected in her eagerness to please her parents,
but her yang seemed to work against her. It stifled her self-
expression rather than encouraging it. She was afraid of

her yang energy instead of feeling confident of it.

Dorothy felt better about her yin energy — there was an aura of love around it and she felt safe with it. But she does not tell us much about the yin, indicating that it may not have been clearly differentiated in her consciousness.

As you explore your early experiences, remember that you are describing symbols in your waking dream, not the actual persons who were your parents or guardians. Describe them as you experienced them, not as you believe others saw them. This will give you a truer picture of your own understanding of the two polarities at the beginning of your life.

Early life dreams also often reflect our knowledge of and attitudes toward what might be called the Great Yin and Great Yang, polarities of the Creative Force that brought cosmos into being. If we feel connected to the Great Yin we feel we belong on this planet, are at home in our bodies, feel a strong connection to nature, both plants and animals, feel secure in life, trust life, and are comfortable functioning within the limitations of form.

When we have a strong connection to the Great Yang we have a sense of awe and wonder about the grandeur of the universe, we have a sense of purpose for our life, even if we can't name what it is, we trust that we will be guided through our life, we know that we have potential that is not yet realized and that we may not yet recognize, we have a feeling that there is always more for us to know, and we are eager to explore the more.

In the early life dream, these larger creative energies are often symbolically represented by Grandparents. Here is Marion's experience:

My love for my grandparents was unbounded. They
lived only two blocks away from us and I often spent
time with them at home and on their farm. I have countless memories of experiences with both my grandfather
and my grandmother in which I felt very special and
very loved. They took very good care of me and I always
felt safe in their presence. I remember telling my mother
that if anything ever happened to Grandma and Grand-
pa I would not want to go on living.

Marion felt close to both her Grandparents. She felt
loved and cared for, as well a safe in their presence. If we
see the grandparents as symbols for the Great Yin and
Yang, the polarities of the God Force, we would anticipate
that Marion would be confident in her knowledge that she
belongs in this universe, that she is safe here, that she will
always have what she needs, and that she is not only lov-
able but that she is always loved.

Brad's experience was similar:

I was sent to spend summers with my grandparents on
their Illinois farm. I went to ride horses, ride a tractor
with my grandfather, help milk the cows, and eat lunch
with Granddad and the farm hands out in the field.
Grandmother had me help her feed the chickens, collect
eggs in the morning, throw table scraps out to the hogs,
and do other chores. I felt very grown-up while I was
with my grandparents, like I could do no wrong. Granddad taught me how to do lots of things and Grandmother assured me I could do anything I wanted with my life.

Brad was able to feel at home in the natural world
because of his summers with his grandparents. He learned
to have confidence in himself and his ability to manifest
his potential.

It is often the case that the clearest example of unconditional love we have in our early lives comes from our grandparents. The fact that young people today often do not get to spend time with grandparents may help to account for the feeling of alienation and despair that many experience. Fears, hatred, and anxieties about one's place in the Universe are symptoms of not feeling connected to the Great Yin and Yang. On the other hand, trust in the Life Process is the outpicturing of a sound relationship with those universal forces.

Sometimes Grandparents appear in our waking dreams in their dark or destructive aspects. We may experience a Grandmother as judgmental, harsh, or even punitive, and it may seem that nothing we do will please her. When we experience the dark side of the Great Yin we are called to search out those attitudes and qualities in ourselves that keep us from experiencing unconditional love. In Hindu mythology, the destructive side of the Great Mother is known as Kali, who slays the demons of duality, ignorance and fear. A Grandmother symbol in our early life dream who is hard for us to relate to may be urging us to awaken to such qualities in ourselves so that we can move beyond them and know what it is to be loved unconditionally.

If a Grandfather appears domineering, exacting, and unforgiving, he may be calling us to awaken to an inner resistance to the larger plan for our life. Or his presence might serve as a wake-up call not to go off course as we seek to follow our inner guidance. In other words, we would look at Grandparents who seem difficult as invitations to discover whether we are in some way alienated from the Great Yin and Yang.

It is vitally important that we learn to communicate with both the Great Yin and the Great Yang and that we integrate both polarities into our way of knowing ourselves. To do so will bring balance to our Western way of approaching life, which for the last two-thousand years has been almost entirely focused on developing the yang polarity. The Wisdom Tradition has always taught what John Freeman calls the essence of C. G. Jung's philosophy of life: "Man becomes whole, integrated, calm, fertile, and happy when (and only when) the process of individuation is complete, when the conscious and the unconscious have learned to live at peace and to complement one another."[3]

What we call prayer can be understood as a form of communication through which we attempt to reach beyond what we know into the realm of the Great Unknown. When we reach by exercising the yang polarity, we call it prayer to the Father-God. When we reach via the yin polarity, we call it prayer to the Mother-God. Both are essential if we are to live with insight and understanding (yang) and with wisdom (yin).

By lifting our energies to the great yang polarity in the cosmos, referred to as the Father-God, we come to know the natural order of things and how we fit into it. Opening to the great yin polarity, the Mother-God, on the other hand, is a way of seeking understanding of our individual lives and our daily experiences. The yang polarity imparts patterns and ideals, helps us to understand abstract questions, and facilitates the organization of large overviews. The yin polarity reveals cyclic patterns of unfoldment in exquisite detail. Both polarities need to inform our choice-making if we want to function in full consciousness.

People often become frustrated with prayers to the Father-God, in yang energy, feeling that they go unanswered. Perhaps that is because they are seeking guidance with regard to specific decisions they are facing. Such prayers might better be submitted to the Mother-God and answers to those prayers come through our waking and sleeping dreams.

In ourselves, the Great Yin manifests as our bodies, both in instincts and in sensation, as our feelings, intuitions, and knowings. Work with both sleeping and waking dreams lends itself beautifully to awareness of these modes of communication, as do various techniques of bodywork, nonverbal expressions of feeling (through music, the arts, etc.), and other approaches to the uncovering of intuitive wisdom, such as the Tarot, the *I Ching*, and Runes.

The Great Yang, on the other hand, manifests in our thoughts, wisdom and direct perception. Study, concentration, contemplation, and meditation are ways of consciously approaching the Great Yang.

What do your earliest memories reveal about your knowledge and perception of the yin and yang at the beginning of your life? What you discover will provide a foundation for your learning during and after waking dream episodes. You will begin to be conscious of your own knowledge of these fundamental forces.

Over the years, of course, you have been learning about the fundamental energies and growing in your ability to express and embody them even when you weren't aware of doing so. Now you can consciously cooperate with the integration of these two forces in your everyday life.

When you are ready to explore your early life dream, you will find questions to guide your exploration in the appendix.

Sensation (i.e. sense perception) tells you that something exists; *thinking* tells you what it is; *feeling* tells you whether it is agreeable or not; and *intuition* tells you whence it comes and where it is going.
— *C. G. Jung*

Experience is accessible, yes, but the intimate, immediate, 'pure' experience is almost instantly drowned by our thought processes which conceptualize the event and then mistake the concept for the experience.
— *Anne Bancroft on Evelyn Underhill*

Chapter Five

Communicating with Self

We are living a waking dream because we are not identified with the real Self. How can we wake up within that dream? How do we break the identification with a particular sense of self that is smaller than the real Self?

One way is to pay more attention to the body, psyche, and spirit. Each of these components of the real Self has a unique way of communicating the experience we are having. In our waking dreams, we usually pay attention to information from only one or two components of the real Self at a time. This contributes to our limited perspective. As we learn to expand our awareness to include information from all three components, we are more likely to break the spell of a given sense of self and to wake up to the real Self.

Instinct and Sensation: Expressions of the Body

A system of Self-communication was present in us all from the moment of birth (and perhaps prior to birth), permitting the development of a growing sense of self as "I." In the beginning the flow of information was one-way only, from our bodies to our emerging sense of self.

In infancy, we came to know ourselves through the two primary expressions of our bodies: *instinct* and *sensation*. We even knew our connection with the environment and other people through our bodies.

As adults we often forget about our bodies. We move through life asleep to what our bodies are communicating to us. When we have trouble with our bodies, we go to experts to find out what's wrong, not realizing that there may be a message for us in the symptoms we are experiencing. To find the meaning of our waking dreams, we must pay conscious attention to all communication from our bodies.

Instinct represents the accumulated learning of all species. Instinct communicates the body's wisdom[1] by expressing an innate predisposition to behave in certain characteristic ways that satisfy the urge to survive.

Instinct remains relatively unconscious in us, not only in infancy but even as we begin to awaken. It is not that instincts cannot be brought into our awareness. It is, rather, that they are so inherent to life in the body that it takes very careful attention to notice them.

We can learn to direct instinctive urges once they are aroused, and we can learn to evoke them consciously. Their functioning, however, remains the expression of a will much larger than our own and does not usually require our conscious attention.[2]

When I speak of instinctive behavior, I refer to all physical functions that perpetuate the life of the body, including those often called autonomic. This definition serves our purpose of understanding Self-communication. The instincts, as I identify them, are those bodily responses that do not require conscious monitoring. We become aware of instincts only indirectly, through body states and conditions — that is, through sensation, the second

**Illustration #5
Instinct and Sensation:
Expressions of the Body**

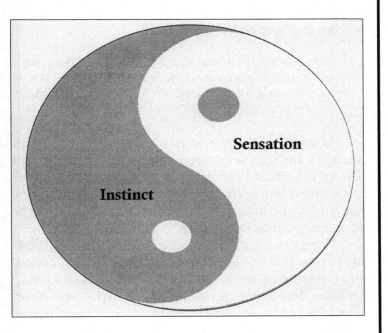

Instinct is the yin polarity of the body's expression; sensation is the yang polarity. Instinct performs its function even if we are not conscious of it. Sensation, on the other hand, requires a conscious response if it is to serve us.

expression used by the body. Instincts can be considered yin (unconscious) when contrasted with sensations. [See Illustration #5, page 111.]

Sensations are energy impressions taken in consciously, through seeing, hearing, smelling, touching or tasting, or registered kinesthetically.[3] Information often comes to us through the instincts, but enters our consciousness through sensation, as Hector discovered through this waking dream episode:

> I am about half an hour into my Feldenkrais[4] class. We are lying on mats on the floor of a large old gym. The air is dry and hot and dusty. My head aches; my nostrils are dry and parched. I feel as if I am in a desert.

You may remember times when your body got your attention through sensations similar to Hector's: head aching, nostrils dry and parched. These were evidence of instinctive responses to the environment. The air was dry, hot, and dusty and the body was trying to cope with the stress those conditions induced.

Struggles often arise between the body, which is trying to take care of itself in the instinctive ways it knows, and the sense of self, which has its own agenda. Hector, for example, was paying more attention to the outer directions of an instructor than he was to the body's instinctive reaction to the environment:

> The instructor directs us to exhale as we move toward the right, and to inhale as we move back to center. My lungs say, "Don't breathe in at all. There is too much dust."

When we don't heed our body's warnings, other

components of Self chime in. Hector's sensations translated into thought, as if his lungs were saying, "Don't breathe at all." He was aware of the communication from his body, but was only willing to do something about it when the instructor called for a break:

> When we stop for a moment's rest, I cup my hands over my face and nose and create some moist air to breathe into my lungs. I feel restless and tense and unable to concentrate on the instructions.

Hector cooperated with his instincts. He responded to his body's need to lubricate his nasal passages and lungs by using his own hands to capture the air coming from within and recycle it. Hector had registered his body's discomfort through the sensations of restlessness and tension. His body was communicating with such urgency that Hector could hardly concentrate on the instructor's words.

Sensation was the first expression of the body that we learned to recognize as infants. Because in the initial stages of our life experience we were conscious of little beyond sensation, we only knew ourselves as bodies. As adults we tend to think of ourselves as personalities (psyches). Consequently, we don't pay as much attention to sensation as we did in our childhood. The failure to attend to sensation may result in health problems because we do not respond quickly enough to our bodies' reactions to their circumstances. Sensations, when we pay attention to them, can make us aware that we are asleep and dreaming by alerting us to what is going on in one component of Self: the body. Just noticing sensations may help us to wake up.

Hector was on a quest to expand his consciousness of

Self. Yet in the specific situation of his Feldenkrais class, where he sought to become more conscious of how he was functioning through his body, he was slow to respond to his sensations. As a result, other components of Self began to communicate:

> I am aware that this is the first time the furnace has been on since we began this course in September.   I feel angry and panicked. I begin to think of leaving.

Perhaps you will recognize the process Hector went through. First he felt panic, a feeling that described his body's urge toward "flight" for survival. When Hector failed to act in response to his sensations and the feeling of panic, he experienced anger. Anger is a feeling that often arouses us to action. His thoughts translated his body's message as "get out of here." Thus Hector's psyche, through feelings and thoughts, had joined his body in offering information about his experience.

Nevertheless, it was not until the instructor urged him to respond to his body that Hector finally did something:

> Then I hear the instructor's voice again, saying, "If you find yourself uncomfortable, feel free to rest before I call for a rest. It is awareness we are calling for here, and taking responsibility for our own body's comfort." I want to scream, "I want out of here. I'm never coming back to this class if we have to be in this place." Then I finally hear what she has just said.
> I look up at the ceiling, discover the radiators are in the ceiling, and that I am directly under several of them. The only others are at the far end of this huge room. I get up, pick up my mat, and move to the opposite side of the room, lie down again, and find I am in cooler air. My throat, sinuses and nostrils are comfortable. I relax

and go on following instructions. I check with others after class. No one else had noticed the dust.

When we ignore body messages as long as Hector did, distress signals will eventually express in many ways. Hector was receiving the signals through instinct, sensation, feeling, and thought. The transmission of information within the Self can switch channels very quickly when we don't respond. As Arnold Mindell, a key figure in the revolutionary field of dream and body work, suggests, "Processes can switch suddenly from hearing to feeling, from feeling to visualization, or from seeing to moving, like lightning. If you can follow processes as they move in and out of the body, you are then able to move with the flow of life, and sometimes witness surprising things."[5]

Later Hector realized how important it is to respond quickly to instinct and sensation:

> At home in the evening my throat and sinuses were clogged and irritated. I did not imagine this irritation, it was there. I sneezed a lot and the congestion cleared. I had no cold the next day, and no problem. The knowing came to me that if I had remained in my victim sense of self, "poor me," I would have created a cold.

Hector's Self-communication moved to another level when he came to a new knowing. He watched his body instinctively clear away the congestion that was forming in response to the earlier dust and dryness. Hector realized that if he had delayed further in responding to his body's discomfort, he would have developed a head cold.

A head cold would have been the intensification of the body's instinctive need to lubricate Hector's nasal passages and clear out the dust in order to restore balance in his body. That instinctive process would have taken much longer than the evening of sneezing Hector experienced. He didn't remain identified with his diminished sense of self as "victim of his circumstances." Instead, he woke up and too action.

When asked to identify his sense of self, Hector said:

> I felt as if I were a distraught parent in relation to my body (which was the child in distress) not wanting the child to suffer, and yet not wanting it to create an interruption in the class, and also knowing that I had brought the body there and paid the tuition because I knew the body would benefit from the experience.

The vivid life experience, Hector discovered, was created by his sense of self as the distraught parent. Hector was caught between two desires: to help the "child-body," and to stay with the flow of the class. He was ignoring the mature wisdom his body was expressing. Because Hector had determined before signing up for the class that it would be good for his body, it was hard for him to receive the message that all was not going well.

He went on:

> At first my sense of self was not hearing my body. It had its own agenda. I am not sure how I let go of the voice of the sense of self, but I heard the instructor. I looked around to see what I could do then and there, saw the possibility of moving, and moved with the Will.

The perfect pattern that guides all life processes is experienced by our real Self as the power of self-direction, or Will. As we identify more and more with the real Self, we find ourselves wanting the Will of the real Self to be done in and through us, rather than the will of any smaller sense of self.

If we remain asleep within our waking dream, the Will of the real Self will continue trying to communicate with us through instinct, emotion, and intuition. But by awakening within a waking dream episode, we can respond to the inner directives of the Will with conscious, reasoned choices. Hector was aware of this process:

> At one point I had been telling my lungs not to breathe. When I let go of that reaction to the distress I was registering, my breathing and my feelings both calmed down. I was finding the pathway from feeling to knowing by moving with the Will. The body data were giving me a direct experience of this pathway, which I have read about, heard about, and thought about. Now I have experienced it in a new way.
> The instructor's words seemed to be the direct words of my real Self. The word "responsible" suddenly became the opposite of "poor me." She tells me I am responsible, so I can't at the same time be "poor me." This was not new information for me, but the way I received it was new. The dust was really there and so were the words, spoken by someone else, and I heard them. The impact of both in this connection was new.

Hector saw and understood how the outer and the inner cooperated in this experience, awakening him to a new understanding of the pathway from feeling to knowing by moving with the Will. He had come to a deeper appreciation of the importance of listening to his body:

> I can begin to give my body more credit for its wisdom and really notice and receive its messages as direct ex-

pressions of the Will. It puts "doing" above just "thinking about" as a priority.

Gathering information from our bodies by bringing
instinct and sensation into our consciousness can help
us to expand the sense of self and provide a stimulus for
awakening.

Feeling and Thinking: Expressions of the Psyche

Even more information is available to us in the real
Self. The body was the first way we became conscious
of ourselves, but as we've expanded our consciousness,
we've come to know Self as psyche,[6] that is, mental and
emotional processes. The psyche uses *thinking* and *feeling*
for Self-communication.

The psyche is made up of the qualities and characteristics in our personalities that make us unique. Beyond
that, it includes memories of both group and individual
human experience,[7] and our private worlds of evaluation,
judgment, beliefs and values. The psyche contains the
knowledge we gain from exercising our faculties of feeling
and thinking.

Feeling is an unconscious or automatic function for
most people. For that reason, feeling is considered yin
when contrasted with thinking. [See Illustration #6, page
119.] Most of us are convinced that feelings "happen to
us" or are evoked or provoked by outer circumstances. We
usually don't know why we feel the way we do. We don't
think we have any choice about what we feel. So it may

**Illustration #6
Feeling and Thinking:
Expressions of the Psyche**

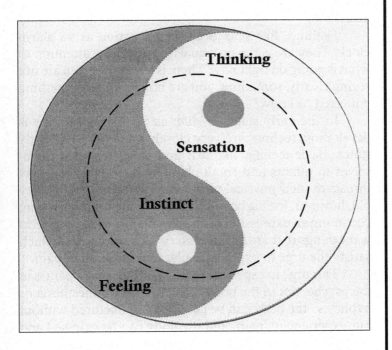

Feeling is the yin polarity of the psyche's expression; thinking is the yang polarity. Feeling is harder to choose and direct consciously than thinking.

seem strange, at first, to think of feelings as messages to the sense of self from the real Self.

Most of us believe that our feelings tell us something about other people or about outer events. We often express our feelings as a way of trying to get others to change their behavior. We need to develop a new conceptual framework in order to think about feelings as an expression of the real Self that gives us information we can use for our own awakening.

Feelings, like sensations, can function as an alarm clock. They are wake-up signals saying, "Pay attention to what is going on right now. There is something you are not seeing clearly, something you are not doing, or something you need to know."

In the early stages of life, as Self-consciousness is developing, feelings are very closely identified with body states. Basic feelings like fear and anger manifest themselves in infants and small children as a result of direct threats to their physical well-being. Before a child is very old, however, feeling begins to differentiate from sensation, becoming an expression of the psyche. The child begins to want things that are not necessary for survival, but which satisfy the urge to experience pleasure rather than pain.

This urge to experience pleasure rather than pain is in the psyche, not in the body. If we are under anesthesia or hypnosis, the body can be cut open or punctured without our experiencing pain, and the body can be caressed and tenderly cared for without our experiencing pleasure.

The development of a personality, reduced to the simplest common denominator, is the result of how we respond to that urge to experience pleasure and avoid pain. Some children learn to pursue pleasure directly and actively, and to aggressively fend off threats of pain. Others determine early on that they are dependent on others for their pleasure; they develop strategies for staying on good terms with others so that they will be rewarded rather than punished. Still others conclude that life is unpredictable and undependable, and resign themselves to be victims of the whims of fate. These and other patterns of response to the urge to seek pleasure and avoid pain are the basis of personality patterns.[8]

This primitive urge is expressed, in a more evolved form, through many different motivations. For example, it brings great pleasure to some individuals to wield power. Others find pleasure in mastering skills, talents, and abilities. Others want nothing more than to love, or to be loved. Others want to be famous. Others prefer to pursue their lives in solitude. What they pursue is what most pleases them.

So fundamental is this urge to experience pleasure that the right to pursue happiness was written into the Declaration of Independence as an inalienable and self-evident right, and psychological textbooks identify the enjoyment of pain and the inflicting of pain as pathologies.

Feelings register the impact of experiences, going beyond the five senses. Feelings tell us whether or not we like something, and whether or not we want something in our lives. As a registry of the impact of experiences, feelings can be immediate or delayed. Maryanne's are both in her account of a middle-of-the-night experience:

> I wake in the night, my whole body throbbing with strong physical pain and with a scene from the evening TV [1991 Gulf War] news replaying vividly in my mind. I experience tides of strong energy pulsing through my body, which register as physical pain. At the same time,

> what I am "seeing" is the TV scene in which a large sea
> bird is struggling, oil-soaked, in a sea of oil, towards an
> already oil-drenched beach. It shakes its head but cannot
> shake free from the coating of oil.

Maryanne was experiencing communication from
both her body and her psyche. Her body was expressing
pain while her psyche showed her a picture held in its
memory from the night before. The sensations of pain in
her body were real and immediate even though the picture
was of an event that was far removed from her.

Maryanne's feelings were aroused.

> I feel huge anger and grief as well as helplessness. The
> night before I had realized there was nothing I could do
> about what I was seeing, so I had switched off the TV,
> changed the subject, and gone to bed. When I woke up,
> I recognized that my pain-filled body was saying, "Wake
> up: you can't just switch that off!"

Maryanne's body was expressing pain. It seemed to
be demanding that she give her attention to an event she
could not change. To address the event as a waking dream
was to ask why her body wanted her to look again. The
images had stirred painful feelings, and her body seemed to
be clamoring for her to complete the Self-communication.
Maryanne's account didn't reveal the sense of self with
which she was identifying, but it became clear that she
was attending almost entirely to the psyche's thinking and
feeling processes.

Thinking evolved in human beings as a second expression of the psyche, enabling the emerging Self to see beyond
the immediacy of the moment. Feelings, like sensations,
can lead to unconscious reactions. But thinking opens up

the possibility of reflection and considered choices about how to respond to both sensation and feeling.

Thinking involves abstraction, and thus is always removed from the energy event. First, an image of the object must be formed in the psyche. The image is composed of sensory data and is often held together by the feelings that were aroused by our first experience of the object.

Imagine, for example, an object made of blue metal standing on four rubber tires. It has windows all around, four doors, internal leather-upholstered seats in two rows, carpeted floors on the interior, a steering wheel mounted before the front, left seat, and an instrument panel beneath the front window. Holding the image in our minds, it is as if we can see it, touch it, hear it, and even smell it. The sensations we awaken in our psyches will depend on our past experiences with similar objects.

Since the image is not the object, but rather a picture of it, it is once-removed from the object itself. Naming the object "car" takes the observer one step further away from the object.[9]

Just naming the people and things in an event is not sufficient for the thinking process, however. We have higher orders of abstraction, such as classification and generalization. For example, we might say the car is a sedan, an American-made automobile, a Ford. There are more abstract qualities still. We might call the car serviceable, safe, comfortable, expensive. In assessing the car's value, we might decide that this is a poor buy, or a good buy, reliable or a lemon.

Even simple thought processes like this are carried out on a sophisticated level of abstraction to facilitate judgment and decision making, as well as to permit communication with others.

When thinking about abstract qualities like safe, comfortable, and expensive and making value assessments, we create our own private worlds. Private worlds are like edited video tapes of our past experiences, and the beliefs, opinions, and preferences we developed as a result of those experiences. Because we usually retreat to our private worlds to do our thinking, thought processes vary from individual to individual and lead us to different decisions. Thinking, therefore, leads to a growing differentiation between individuals and is an activity that helps make each human being unique.

Instinct, sensation, and feeling were already quite evolved in the plant and animal kingdoms before humanity emerged, but *abstract thinking* was fully developed by human beings. It is the expression that makes possible the transcendence of time and space.

Instinct, sensation, and feeling are relatively direct responses to events. If a feeling is not direct, but is evoked by a thought or an idea, it is because a memory is held in the psyche and that memory awakens the feeling. Feelings are secondary reactions when they are colored by the interpretation of an event.

This was the case in Maryanne's waking dream. When her body demanded that she give attention to the pain she had experienced by reawakening it, Maryanne agreed to open up to the communication. She responded, "OK, Body, I'm awake and I'll watch the show again."

Memory held in the psyche is a storage bank of images that we can draw on for our own thought processes and for our communication with others. As our consciousness expands, we find that these stored images are also integral to our communication with Self.[10]

Maryanne used her memory to go back to the event of seeing the oil-soaked bird on television. This ability to let images have new life is one of the gifts of the state of consciousness developed by humanity. As Maryanne reviewed the images, her private world of beliefs, values, and convictions was fully awakened.

> This is an unbearable outrage against a defenseless, innocent creature, against all the wild creatures of the Gulf. It's awful enough that people are murdering people in this wanton, useless war, but at least, as people, in some way we have a responsibility for what's going on, whereas the wild creatures, and this bird, are innocent. He looked so surprised, shocked, and doomed, caught in the oil, as my body is caught in this pain.

Maryanne was thinking her way through her pain as she went over the images in her psyche. She was evaluating and making judgments about the events pictured. She thought about the helpless wild creatures, and she attributed to them her own feelings of shock and helplessness. She was focused on her thoughts, and thus was gathering information from only one component of her Self. The message from her body remained below the surface of her conscious understanding.

The ability to think about the world liberated human beings from the animal state of consciousness, which is bound by the limitations of physical laws. As humans, we can think of things on the physical level that happened in the past. We can also think about things on the physical level that have not yet happened. In that way, we can tie the past together with the future. An animal, identified only with its body and having no sense of "I," cannot connect the past with the future as far as we know.

I remember the time I watched our dog wrap the rope she was tied to around a tree until she was held tight to the base of the trunk. Because she had no memory of her own process of wrapping the rope around the tree, she couldn't undo it. She was dependent on me to free her.

To think through the process by which she wound the rope around the tree, my dog would have had to sustain an image of the event in her psyche. Then she would have had to abstract from it a sense of the "I" who did the winding, of the I's relationship to the body to which the rope was attached, and of the relationship of that body to the activity of winding.

Next, the dog would have had to form an image of the process in reverse in order to see how to get out of her predicament. And finally, she would have had to evoke the Will to put into action the process of unwinding. We humans do this process daily without being aware how advanced it is.

We need data not only from the mind, but also from all other components of Self if we are to make sound choices for our own well-being and the well-being of others. Paying attention to all the forms of communication within the Self is easier to do when we view life as a waking dream. We evoke the thinking process to provide the memory of a vivid life event. Describing the event (out loud or in writing) awakens images in the psyche with all their associated feelings, sensations, and instincts. As we reflect on the event, we can take all this information into account.

Most of us remain unconscious that we hold images in our psyches because *we believe that our images of the world are true to what the world is. That is the beginning of the waking dream, because the world is energy, not image. To relate to the images as if they were real in some objective sense is just as misleading as it would be to attribute objective reality to sleeping dreams.*

Focused on the images in our psyches, we go immediately into our private worlds of interpretation. Most of our choices are based on those interpretations rather than on a response to what is actually happening in the energy of an event. Thus we live in a waking dream state rather than in the real world of energy.

In a waking dream, communication within the Self remains unconscious. We are not aware of it. We behave as though the events *as we experience them* have some objective reality. We don't pay attention to them as information that could expand our Self-knowledge.

Hector's waking dream about the dust in his Feldenkrais class is a good example. When he began to experience discomfort in his body, he immediately focused on the fact that there was "too much dust" in the air. Since in his private world he had concluded that the dust was the problem, he looked to find the cause of the dust. The radiators in the ceiling were clearly the cause, since the heat had been turned on for the first time that year. Having found the problem, the next "logical" conclusion was that he would not come back to the class if it was to be held in that room!

There was, in fact, dust in the room, and the radiators may well have been the source of it. But whether it was "too much dust" in some objective sense can not be determined solely from Hector's experience. In fact, when he asked classmates about it at the end of the class, none of them had noticed the dust.

The message actually being given to Hector was "There is too much dust *for me.*" The difference is small, but crucial. Hector was trying to pay attention only to the instructor. In doing so, he was ignoring information being given to him by his body and his psyche. If he had not brought that information into his awareness, it would have been dealt with on an unconscious level, probably resulting in a head cold.

The message in Hector's waking dream, however, was not merely about that one incident. It was also about Hector's need to pay more attention to the wisdom of his body in all circumstances and situations. He could not have arrived at the understanding he needed by taking action to clear the dust from the classroom.

In Maryanne's case, her waking dream ego was paying a great deal of attention to feelings that were in direct response to her private world evaluations. When she examined her feelings, she found that they were all directed toward people "out there." She wrote, "I am angry at those who have allowed this war to happen and at those who have caused it to happen."

It was not only what they had done or not done that made her angry, however. She had also attributed to them characteristics and motivations on which she passed judgment, and that increased her anger:

> I am angry at their arrogance, at their total disregard for the rights and needs and well-being of individuals, and for the well-being and safety of our earth, our home. I am afraid for us all. I feel great grief.

There certainly were people "out there" who allowed the war to happen and who caused the war to happen. Some of them may have been arrogant. Some may have totally disregarded the rights, needs, and well-being of humans and the planet. But by focusing solely on her images of those people and what they had done, Maryanne was missing the information being offered to her by her body. Her body was in distress as it responded to the strong feelings she was having. What was her body trying to tell her?

Was her body's message that she should go out and try to stop the war? Were her strong feelings indicating that she should take action against those who started the war, or did not stop it? Was the message that she was harming herself by awakening such strong feelings in response to images of an event over which she had no control? Or was her body calling her attention to the effect of her private world judgments? These are questions that cannot be answered by referring to outer events.

Maryanne did not find her way out of the waking dream to new insight, even after bringing into full awareness the data offered by her body and psyche. She needed to be open to still more information if she was to receive the message carried by her extreme distress.

By looking at life as a waking dream, we learn to communicate consciously with the various components of the real Self so that we do not sleep our way through our life experiences. Reminding ourselves that how we experience an event may say more about *us* than it does about the *event* encourages us to be open to more information.

Intuition and Wisdom: Expressions of the Spirit

Knowing Self as a psyche — as a thinking, feeling being — was the second phase of expansion in the sense of self as we human beings evolved. Expanding further to know ourselves as spirit puts us in touch with *intuition* and *wisdom*. These offer us still more information about our experiences and contribute to our waking up.[11] The spirit is an expression of the urge to find meaning in our life experiences, to weave the various events of our lives together into a fabric that makes some kind of sense to us.

As we look at our lives as waking dreams we address this urge to find meaning, and it is for that reason that I consider this a spiritual method.

Our *intuition* is a relatively unconscious, or yin, expression of spirit. [See Illustration #7, page 131.] It is knowing without knowing *how* we know, and sometimes not even knowing *that* we know. It is following an impulse that feels similar to instinct in that it seems embedded in the body, but that connects us to human learning accumulated through the ages.

Intuition sometimes serves us in very practical ways, as is evident in Steve's experience:

> In this waking dream, I am playing golf on Good Friday.
> It is sunny, cold and windy. I am playing with three
> other league members, and this front nine counts toward
> my league score.
> I am feeling tremendous ease on the tees. I have not
> missed a tee shot in the last two sets of nine holes in the
> past week. I begin to talk to the ball in my mind, giving
> it directions to the target. I swing easily and each drive is
> in the fairway and long.

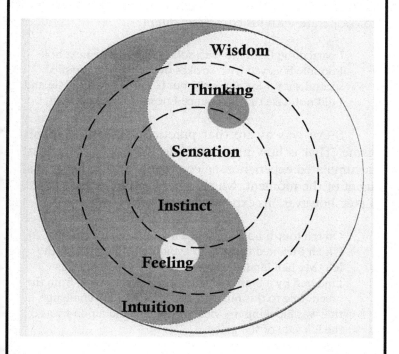

Illustration #7
Intuition and Wisdom:
Expressions of the Spirit

Wisdom

Thinking

Sensation

Instinct

Feeling

Intuition

Intuition is the yin polarity of the spirit's expression; wisdom is the yang polarity. Intuition is knowing without consciousness of how we know; wisdom is an integrated, conscious living out of what we know.

Steve, a young man in his early thirties, was using *thinking* to align himself with *intuition*. By talking to his ball, he was awakening in his consciousness, just below the level of active thought, all that he had learned about golf. He was, in effect, inviting his unconscious functions to cooperate with his conscious intent.

> I parred the first hole with solid putting. The next hole I double-bogeyed [two strokes over par] with a pulled second shot. I hit it cleanly, but it was a down-hill lie and I did not have the experience I needed to set up right.

Steve was aware that practice is essential to his game. That is how intuition is developed. Without that accumulated experience, he could only rely on his assessment of the moment, which turned out to be inaccurate. Later, however, his experience paid off:

> On the fourth hole I crushed my drive with a draw, which I wanted in order to avoid out-of-bounds on the left. My ball landed under a tree and my swing was hindered by a branch. I was only a wedge away from the green (due to this huge drive). To add to the challenge, a tree was blocking my view of the flag and a pond was on the left side of the green.
> My intuition was to use a seven iron and a half swing. I was simply focused on making contact with the ball. I trusted my sense of the distance and hit the shot. I made my swing, hit the ball perfectly, looked up and saw it fly over the tree and land ten feet from the hole. Another par, after a near-birdie [one stroke under par] putt.
> I had such confidence!

Steve was aware, as he looked back on this waking

dream episode, that he was feeling self-confident. He was trusting his intuition as reliable. When he did not, he had quite a different experience.

> I hit the next shot off. I felt like I had the wrong club but did not honor the intuition and went along with the objective mind. A bogey [one stroke over par].

The logical mind relies on the past and functions on a level several times removed from the immediacy of the moment. Consequently, the mind often comes to conclusions that are not responsive to the energy data of the moment. Learning to discipline the mind so that it pays careful attention to the moment, without distorting it by comparing it to the past, is part of the work of learning to live in consciousness. In this vivid life experience, Steve remained awake and alert for most of the round, and the results were impressive:

> I parred both final holes for a thirty-nine and my best score to date on this course! I had such a sense of well-being. No bad putts, no choking on the chips, no out-of-bounds, no missed hits. Just solid golf that was moving towards mastery. I could sense that I had made a shift in consciousness in my game. It was now within my reach to break forty.

Steve was feeling very in tune with himself. Consequently, the flow of communication within the Self was smooth and easy:

> I was in touch with my instincts and intuition and trusting them for guidance. I felt the environment, tested out the energies before making a move. I was attuned to the task. I was in the flow.

> I felt confidence and a growing sense of well-being. My
> bodily sensations were pleasurable. I felt at ease. I felt
> calm and a growing excitement and anticipation of a
> good round. I was playing just to play and to experience
> the "essence" of playing well.
> I remained emotionally calm, directing my mind and
> then letting my mind imprint my emotions. The balance
> was evident in the ease of my actions throughout the
> round.

Steve was in an expanded sense of self that enabled
him to be aware of a wide range of communication from
many components of Self. He paid conscious attention
to his instincts, feelings, and intuitions, which most of us
relegate to unconsciousness. He used his senses to heighten
his awareness of his surroundings, and his pleasurable
body sensations told him all was well. He consciously
directed his thoughts so that they stayed aligned with his
chosen objective for the day, which was "just to play and
to experience the essence of playing well." This enabled
him to avoid comparisons with other rounds of golf, or
other golfers, which would have blurred his focus. Only
once did he fail to honor his intuition, and when he did,
his shot was off and he was one stroke over par.

Steve's experience makes clear how important full
communication with Self is, even when playing a round
of golf. It enabled him to function with confidence and
ease. All his skill and training as a golfer were available
to him, not only through his physical proficiency, but also
through his intuition, which represented the accumulated
experience of years of play and perhaps even the play of
others. Perhaps you have had similar experiences of being
in full Self-communication, thus experiencing tremendous
well-being in your life.

The spirit represents a more expanded state of consciousness than the psyche. As we come to know ourselves as spirit, we also begin to realize that we have access to more knowledge than we could possibly gather as individuals. Instincts connect us with the accrued learning of all species over the millennia about how to survive. Feelings connect us to the immediacy of the moment and to our personal histories. Intuition enables us to tap into human knowledge acquired through the conscious application of skills and techniques for thousands of years.

Wisdom is the conscious integration of learning, both conscious and unconscious, gained over a long period of time. Therefore, to be wise is not only to be aware of our intuitions and to be able to think about our goals and intentions, but also to embody what we know. That is, to bring our accumulated experience into thoughts, feelings, and actions — even affecting our own instincts.

In Lauren's vivid life experience both intuition and wisdom played strong, clear roles.

Several years ago my life had its own special earthquake. My husband had an affair with a married young mother of an 11-year-old. A few days after finding out, I decided to pack a few bags and head for "somewhere."
I began driving down the highway. All the while I was remembering that when I was eleven my mother also had an affair and my father was devastated. The hurt that I had known then was very vivid to me as I drove. I stopped at a McDonald's to get a Coke after driving for some time. When I ordered the Coke, I asked the waitress, "How far away is the Newcomerstown exit?" She replied, "It is the very next one, about fifteen miles."

Lauren's waking dream was a remarkably simple, yet profound experience. Her thoughts turned to memories of a similar event from her childhood. Her instincts enabled her to drive the car safely, and her intuition responded to the events about which she was thinking, causing her to inquire about the Newcomerstown exit. She was paying attention to her feelings of hurt and betrayal, both as an eleven-year-old and as an adult. Lauren was in clear communication with three components of Self: body, psyche, and spirit.

> I drove on and headed directly for my father's grave site. I knew that I needed to talk with him and ask him how I was going to cope with my sorrow.
>
> He had died when I was eighteen and only one time a couple of years after that had I been to the grave site. I was not certain where the cemetery was (nor the grave), yet I drove right to it. As the entrance came into sight, I said, "Daddy, I don't know where you are, but please help me find you."

Lauren's intuition and instincts aligned with her memory to take her directly to her father's grave, though on a conscious level she did not have access to that information. She formulated her request for direction to her father, who was a symbol for her of the knowledge she had not activated for a long time. The knowledge was, in effect, dead to her consciousness.

> About five minutes later, I was sitting on the headstone crying my eyes out. My tears flowed as a release and a farewell to the "little girl" that loved her daddy so dearly. An hour or so later I asked, "Daddy, what should I do?" In an instant the answer was clear for me. I must go

home and not expose the affair to the community and to the little girl, age eleven, that waited at her home with her daddy. This circle must stop with me. I drove home.

Lauren gave full expression to her feelings of grief, and then opened herself up again by asking her father, "What shall I do?" The answer that came was a synthesis of learning, not only by Lauren, but also by her father and her mother: she must go home and keep the information to herself so that the cycle of pain did not begin again. The inner directive came through *knowing*, an expression of Lauren's emerging sense of self as one who is becoming whole, and her wisdom was expressed in her ability to act on that knowledge. She went home and did not reveal the affair to the community nor to the other woman's family.

Wisdom is expressed in how we live, through being and acting on what we know. When Mahatma Gandhi was asked to give a message to the world he responded, "My life is my message." He spoke the language of wisdom. In Lauren's case, as she lived out her knowing, she came to understand more deeply on a conscious level the meaning of her waking dream.

Though the flow of communication within the Self isn't always orderly, it tends to move from the relatively unconscious, to the relatively conscious, to the relatively unconscious, to the relatively conscious, or in reverse. This doesn't hold true in all cases, of course. To characterize feelings as unconscious when contrasted with thoughts, for example, ignores the fact that sometimes feelings are conscious and thoughts unconscious. Nevertheless, it can be useful to see how the flow of communication tends to move in order to be more conscious of the inner process.

For example, if *instinctive impulses* (unconscious) are awakened, we tend to become aware of them through *bodily sensations* (conscious). The **sensations** (conscious) tend to awaken *feelings* (unconscious) and the *feelings* (unconscious) to trigger *thoughts* (conscious). *Thoughts* (conscious), in turn, may awaken *intuition* (unconscious), which might lead to *wisdom* in the form of consciously following the intuition. [See Illustration #8, page 139.]

Or, the process might move in reverse. You might *act wisely* (conscious), which could awaken an *intuitive knowing* (unconscious). How would that intuition become available to your *thoughts* (conscious)? The answer is illustrated by Lauren's story.

She made the decision, at the outset of this experience, to "go somewhere." This was her first act of *wisdom*. There were many alternatives. She could have created a scene with her husband. She could have gone to confront his lover. She could have gone out to have an affair herself as an act of retribution. She did none of those things. Instead, she packed her bags and decided to "go somewhere." That decision was an embodiment of knowledge which only became clear to her later: that she could put an end to a cycle of pain.

The "somewhere" was not yet known to her on a conscious level, but as she got into her car, the inner process of communication proceeded with clarity. Her *intuition* (unconscious) guided her, awakening memories of an event out of her personal past that was directly related. Those memories stirred associated *thoughts* (conscious) and *feelings* (unconscious), which in turn aroused *sensations* (conscious) and *instincts* (unconscious) that enabled Lauren to find her way to the grave site.

The Self was communicating through *wisdom*. Where

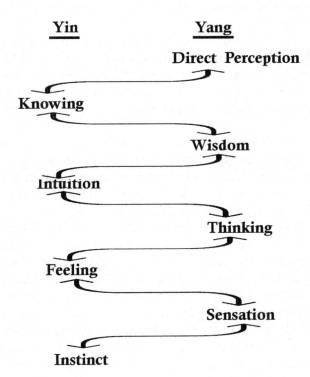

Illustration #8
The Flow of Self-Communication

The flow of Self-communication tends to move from the relatively unconscious to the relatively more conscious, to the next level of relative unconsciousness, to the next level of relative consciousness, etc. Or, it tends to move in the opposite direction.

Lauren went and what she did was all a symbolic playing out of an inner message. That is the nature of a waking dream. In other words, *her own actions were part of her communication with Self, and everything with which she interacted was a symbol being used to awaken her to what her real Self knew about her situation.*

Had Lauren not been willing to set out on a journey without identifying the destination in advance, or had she not been willing to go to her father's grave, the communication could not have been completed in the same way and might have taken much longer.

To understand our lives as waking dreams we must pay attention to the stories of our lives as symbolic communications. The wisdom they represent makes it possible to expand our sense of self and to come to a deeper understanding of the meaning of our existence.

In Lauren's case, daring to live out the impulse to "go somewhere" enabled her to reconnect with a knowing she had come to through an experience with her father. She did not just *think* about that past event. She drove to the grave site, a symbol for something buried in her consciousness. Then she brought her knowledge to conscious awareness through her tears and her inner conversation with her father. She acted in response to her inner dynamic, therefore making the communication with Self more vivid and real.

Knowing and Direct Perception: Expressions of Integration

By looking at our lives as waking dreams, we learn to read and understand our personal stories. As we study our vivid life experiences, we begin to notice that our personal stories touch on universal themes, connecting us with all people everywhere. Our sense of self as spirit expands and we begin to feel connected with, rather than separated from, everything. We feel we intrinsically belong to the Whole.

The Latin roots for the word *individual* mean "cannot be divided." *Integration* means "becoming one." When we become fully integrated individuals, we will be indivisible. We will not feel like many components within one self. Instead, we will experience our wholeness. And we will have come to know everything as an expression of one Self, thus no longer feeling separated from life around us.

Knowing is an expression of this integration. [See Illustration #9, page 142.] It is the fruit of embodied intuition. We confirm our intuitive knowledge through our experiences. We *know that we know*, and we are able to offer stories from our lives to illustrate the truth of each knowing.

Our sense of self as "one who knows" grows stronger even while we are still dreaming. Experiences of waking up within our waking dreams occur with increasing frequency, and we build up our capacity for lucid living. We know that we are becoming whole, but are not yet fully integrated. We strengthen our ability to live wisely and to honor our knowings by taking them more and more seriously. In time, we will be able to sustain an awakened state, identifying more and more with the real Self.

Illustration #9
**Knowing and Direct Perception:
Expressions of the Integrated Self**

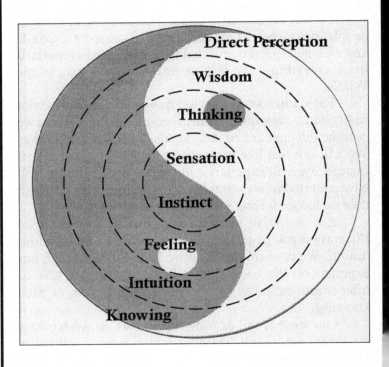

Knowing is reflected in Intuition, Feeling, and Instinct. Direct Perception is reflected in Wisdom, Thinking, and Sensation. The integrated Self is aligned within and functions in harmony with the Whole.

We can only develop and exercise the faculty of *direct perception*, the second expression of integration, during awakened states. Momentary awakenings grant us glimpses of what is to come. Direct perception enables us to see, hear, and sense reality for what it is, namely, an energy world. This also makes it possible for us to align with our Will by conscious choice making.

We all have the potential to become fully integrated individuals and to function with direct perception. Working with our lives as waking dreams supports this individualizing process.

The wisdom teachings were formulated by individuals who were awakened and who, through direct perception, saw and knew the nature of the universe and humanity's place in it. They taught that this state of wholeness and integrity is the most expanded state of the individual sense of self. When the unfolding process of cosmos is complete, the Whole will know itself as one integrated energy body of which each "I" is a cell.

This perception, offered by seers through the ages, can help us to sense the inherent worth of the real Self and the relative value of our senses of self. Senses of self have value because they contribute to the process of awakening. Those who have awakened no longer need multiple senses of self.

When we fully identify with the real Self, we will become conscious that we are a microcosmic representation of the whole cosmos, complete unto ourselves and mirror-reflections, in structure and function, of the entire cosmic process. The physicist Danah Zohar says, "The mind/body (mind/brain) duality in man is a reflection of the wave/particle duality, which underlies all that is. In this way, human being is a microcosm of cosmic being."[12]

Thus, paradoxically, by becoming uniquely who we are, we come to know our oneness with all that is. As Jill Purce expresses it:

> Each person who is integrated, realized and truly individualized becomes universal; and the extremity of differentiation of individual consciousness leads back into the Totality. In this spiral, every one of us all over the globe is like a light becoming gradually brighter, until there are so many and so intense, that there is one light, the light of cosmic consciousness, or what Teilhard de Chardin has called the "psychical convergence of the universe upon itself": the Omega Point.[13]

We live in a symbolic world. We should be reading it all the time, or allowing it to speak to us, because everything we see is speaking to us, telling us something, if we read it aright.

— *Kathleen Raine*

What constitutes growth and development into the consciousness of Reality? To surmount the images and see the Reality. It is right here all the time; you are in it. You are not going to get a thing that you do not already have. Open your eyes and see what you have and what you are here-now. See yourself in life-facts, in livingness. Not the way you create images and then try to chase them.

— *Vitvan*

Chapter Six

Symbols and Meaning

When we awaken from a dream at night, we often say to ourselves, "I wonder what *that* meant?" If we have learned to study our dreams, we will look at various symbols within the dream to help uncover the meaning. Being on a roller coaster might mean our life is out of control, having an enormous black panther move into our house might mean new strength is being released within us, or receiving a large sum of money from an unexpected source might indicate that our luck is about to change for the good.

Learning to interpret symbols in our waking dreams helps us to discover the meaning of our lives. That meaning has more to do with the unfolding of our inner potential than it does with the content of outer events. The "outer" is a metaphor for the "inner," an illustrated message from our real Self asking us to cooperate in our further development. We look to symbols in our waking dreams to see what they are telling us about ourselves.

A *symbol* is, by definition, a term, a name, an image, or an object "that may be familiar in daily life, yet that possesses specific connotations in addition to its conventional and obvious meaning. It implies something vague, unknown, or hidden from us."[1] It differs from a sign, which is an arbitrary convention used to convey a universal meaning, such as the circle with a slash through it, used around the world to indicate that something is forbidden. A symbol calls forth meaning and understanding that is not apparent on the surface.

For example, the form of a pole with a crossbar is very familiar to all of us. It serves to support telephone wires all across this country and others. However, that form is also called a cross, which is an ancient symbol used long before telephone wires came into being. In our Western culture the cross is usually identified with Christianity, but it was used even before the time of Jesus.

The cross means different things to different people. The Romans used it as a form of execution; therefore, for many persons the cross represents death. For others, it is a symbol of suffering, because crucifixion is such a painful way to die. For still others, the cross speaks of the life, death, and resurrection of Jesus, or of the church that was formed in his name.

From ancient times, the cross has represented the coming together of two levels of consciousness, sometimes called the human and the divine. It also has symbolized the intersection of consciousness with embodiment in time and space. And the list could go on. It is because the cross can evoke so many levels of meaning that it is known as a symbol.

Meaning is abstract and therefore not discernible through the five senses, yet without meaning we feel lost and disoriented. Life does not seem worth living. As Carl Jung put it:

> Man positively needs general ideas and convictions that will give a meaning to his life and enable him to find a place for himself in the universe. He can stand the most incredible hardships when he is convinced that they

make sense; he is crushed when, on top of all his misfortunes, he has to admit that he is taking part in a "tale told by an idiot."[2]

Symbols have an evocative power. They act like forceful magnets that pull up related feelings, thoughts, instincts, sensations, memories, and intuitions into our consciousness. Symbols affect all levels of Self-communication. For that reason their role in our waking dreams warrants careful examination. [See Illustration #10, page 177.]

Common Waking Dream Symbols

Certain symbols occur frequently in our most vivid life experiences, but the same symbol will have different meanings in different contexts for different people. Cars, for example, often serve as symbols for our bodies, since bodies are the vehicles that enable us to move around in time and space.

Carla was having trouble turning the key in the ignition of her car, and the tumbler needed to be replaced. She wondered how to interpret this experience. She was looking at the car as a symbol for her body and the key as the starting mechanism. She wondered if there was something wrong with her heart or lungs.

It turned out that Carla wanted to lose weight, but had not been able to get started on a program. Her waking dream seemed to offer a symbol for the connection between Carla, the driver, and her body, the car. The key seemed to be a symbol for her will, which she needed to activate to get her weight loss program going. The broken tumbler reflected her many false starts at dieting.

Carla was aware that she, the driver, needed a more powerful sense of self. She was unhappy with her body and didn't really believe she would ever be satisfied with it, like a customer who bought a car that turned out to be a lemon. She knew she could not engage her will effectively until she changed her sense of self. As the philosopher Ouspensky once said:

> Will can exist only in man who has one controlling 'I', but as long as he has many different 'I's which do not know one another he has just as many different wills; each 'I' has its own will, there can be no other 'I' or other will. But man can come to a state when he acquires a controlling 'I' and when he acquires will. He can reach this state only by developing consciousness. . . .[3]

Carla realized that she had been trying to diet while asleep in her waking dream. One sense of self wanted to lose weight; another felt the effort was fruitless. She needed to wake up and take control with one empowered sense of self. Carla chose to be "the conscious choice-maker" so that she would not fall into unconscious patterns. This sense of self enabled her to undertake a successful weight-loss program.

For others, a car may symbolize the personality. Brenda felt she had taken a large step forward in her sense of self when she turned in her 1983 Volkswagen for a Limited Edition Mercedes sedan. About the Mercedes as a symbol, Brenda wrote, "The car represents the outer personality which I show to the world. I am now willing and eager to 'put myself out there,' not being shy, but courageous." She felt that moving up from the VW, the "people's wagon," to a Mercedes symbolized her new feeling that she and her life were beautiful.

Harvey was leaving his apartment complex when another car backed out of a carport into his path. He swerved as far to the left as he could, but crashed into the right rear fender of the other car, which was driven by a woman. Harvey's own car was severely damaged.

As Harvey examined this waking dream episode, he saw his car as a symbol for himself, body and personality. He felt his waking dream was about being on a "collision course" with women. He received his vivid life experience as a warning and looked at his behavior with women to determine how to change his course before he, or a woman, was seriously hurt.

The meaning of a symbol in our waking dreams is often indicated by our feelings about the symbol. Harvey felt angry at the female driver of the car he hit, and he recognized that he often wants to "smash" women to "get back at them" for what they have done to him. Carla felt frustrated by her key when it would not start her car, like she felt about her failure to lose weight. Brenda was excited and happy about her new Mercedes, as she was about her new personality expression.

The symbol of a house appears often in waking dreams. A waking dream about our home may be about how we most consistently know ourselves. If our waking dream involves a new house or the remodeling of a house, it may symbolize a change in our consciousness, or an expansion (or contraction) of our awareness. We must keep exploring possible meanings until something feels right on as many levels as we can touch.

Elvia had moved into a different house. She was full of joy about it and spent time and energy settling in and making it hers. Within a short time the house began to fall apart. There were problems with the roof, the plumbing, and the foundation. She became aware that this waking dream episode was the repetition of a familiar pattern. Elvia saw the problems with the house as a wake-up call to pay attention to some flaws in her own character that she had been unwilling to attend to and change. She decided she needed to make some fundamental "repairs" in her house of self.

A house could also represent a structure held within our consciousness: a pattern of behavior, a belief system, or a complex of feelings in which we often take refuge. For several years Sharon had been dissatisfied with the condominium she shared with her husband Royce. When no one was around to hear her, she would shout, "I hate this place. It is a dump. I'm tired of this old stuff. I want something newer and nicer."

One day she looked at the condominium as a symbol for the state of consciousness in which she was living. She realized she had become a chronic complainer, "like a needle stuck in a record groove playing the same sound over and over again until the needle is physically moved." She decided to move the needle. "As I began to clean out, discarding or giving away timeworn or unwanted items, I decided to see each item as a symbol of an aspect of myself I was releasing. I wanted to come at this old issue from a new perspective to learn what it said about myself."

Sharon felt exhilaration and determination when she took charge of changing her condominium. Royce began to cooperate with her, and that made the effort easier. In the end she was no longer complaining; instead, she was expressing gratitude for all she had not fully appreciated in their condo and for all the changes she had made in herself.

A house can also represent a sense of self. Renee lived in a three-story town house, which she saw as a symbol for the house of self: body, psyche and spirit. Renee sought to refinance the mortgage on her townhouse so that it would not cost so much. She was denied the mortgage.

As she studied her vivid life experience, Renee realized that she had applied for the new mortgage in her sense of self as "victim." She had proceeded "with trepidation," feeling "at the mercy of the bankers' whims. I felt impotent, subjected to an authority that said, 'you are not good enough.' I felt I was in an utterly losing battle, an effort destined to fail."

This pattern, Renee discovered, was what was "costing" her. Her sense of self as "victim" was a tremendous drain on her energy, just as the mortgage was on her finances. Renee had not yet developed a powerful sense of self to make things easier for her in the world. Until she did, her house of self would continue to feel like a burden.

There are no fixed meanings for symbols; it is their nature to evoke our intuition. It is important not to be too narrow or literal in our interpretation of symbols. We need to go beneath the surface meanings to a more personal and subjective interpretation.

Harry recently took a new job which required him to move from New York to New Mexico. He decided to view this change as an opportunity to change his sense of self. His identity had been completely wrapped up in his previous job in New York, and he wanted to feel that he was more than a job description. He chose to view the state of New Mexico as a symbol for a new state of consciousness, and his new job as a symbol for a larger sense of self. As he prepared on the physical level to make his move, he prepared inwardly for a major shift in awareness.

There is no guarantee that the inner shift will come for Harry. However, turning his attention to it and inviting it to emerge makes it more likely that the shift will occur than if he had simply moved from New York to New Mexico with no awareness that his consciousness could also change.

When we examine a waking dream episode, we always try to figure out the meaning of the symbols for ourselves, looking for clues to their meaning in the experience itself. If we get stuck and are unable to discover a meaning, we might look at a list of suggested meanings in a dictionary of symbols or in a book on dream interpretation.[4] But we take those interpretations only as suggestions that might help spark our own intuition.

Frances took some clothing in for alterations. The seamstress engaged her in conversation. On her way home, Frances felt very energized, "the way I do when I am aligned within self. I realized that I felt totally genuine and very focused, totally unencumbered by fear. The feelings made me realize I was in a waking dream."

As she sought to understand her vivid life experience, Frances looked up the word *clothes* in a dream book. It mentioned "attitudes in which I clothe myself," and that seemed to fit. She realized that she had adopted many new attitudes over the past couple of years, and her outer clothes needed to be adjusted to reflect the inner changes. Her new attitudes made it possible to present to others "the person I know I am rather than what I don't want to be." It was her awareness that she had done just that with the seamstress that caused her to feel exhilarated.

Connie had a dream about clothes which brought her a very different realization. While packing clothes for a trip, she took a jacket, which she had never worn, from its plastic bag she noticed an antitheft device still attached to the back of it:

> I have had this garment for several months and know I do not still have the sales slip for it. I feel if I return it to the store without proof of purchase, they will think I have shoplifted it. I decide to remove the device myself. I grab the two sides and apply force, and am surprised how ungiving this device is. When I try to pry it apart, it breaks, and to my horror I see a blood red stain spreading at the attachment point onto this snow white garment. I take a close look at the still attached device which, on the underside, in fine print says: If device is forced and broken, **permanent dye** will emerge, may be toxic, etc.
>
> Then I realize I am adding real blood (further staining the jacket) from my thumb which I have injured in the process of prying the device open.

Connie became aware that in trying to remove something hidden from her clothes, she tapped into the energy of her commitment "to search out hidden patterns and programs which no longer serve my life purpose."

She felt the dream suggested that these hidden issues could escape her attention, just as the antitheft device had. And if she tried to free herself of these old patterns without the help of someone who had greater insight than she did, she could be as ineffective as she was at removing the antitheft device. Connie made a commitment to seek help in her growth process.

Money is another symbol that appears frequently in our waking dreams. Vincent, who was struggling during a "financially unproductive period" in his life, wrote:

> I have scrutinized my feelings, approaches, failures, successes and the roles money plays in my life. I am winding down an entrepreneurial effort with real estate. I have a lot of good ideas and ability for what is next. But I am stuck! I rationalize, procrastinate and justify what is going on.
>
> I associate money with my self-worth. But if money is an outer manifestation of my sense of inner worth, *why* do I feel unworthy? I keep associating money with evil, like a good protestant teaching I got from somewhere.
>
> I have had a varied career path, but I have never made big money. I put the brakes on each time. The goal in my family when I was growing up was to "pay the bills." My father was defiant around obligations and did what was needed in the moment to get by, like write a bad check knowingly. Then the sheriff would come and arrest him. My father was indicted on federal charges of fraud and check forgery. Now that I think of it, "money" is associated with a sheriff's red rotating stop light atop his car. These are very old issues for me, dormant and unresolved.

Vincent worked with several vivid life experiences that had money as a central symbol before he came to the awareness that he could see money as a hidden treasure waiting to be released from his unconscious. That was a turning point for Vincent. He decided to cultivate an entirely different awareness of money, planting new seeds in his subconscious mind which was fertile with possibilities. He said, "It is cleanup time. I will turn the soil over, remove the stones, plant new seeds, and watch them grow."

Darcy's struggle with money was intense.

> My financial situation had reached a crisis. I began to
> sell my plasma twice a week in an effort to cope. I finally
> succumbed to bankruptcy, but found myself still unable
> to manage financially due to lawyer's fees, debts not dis-
> charged, and various requirements of the court. I contin-
> ued selling my plasma and began to count on that $35 a
> week. In the back of my mind I knew this was somehow
> "blood money" and I was uncomfortable with that. But
> the money seemed more important, in the moment, than
> my health or the disapproval of others.

Darcy felt trapped, a feeling that was familiar to her.
She had often felt trapped by poor choices made in the
past, financial concerns, indebtedness, and a background
of poverty. She wanted her constant battle over money to
end. When she looked at the symbolism of her vivid life
experience, she saw money as representing "my resources,
my energy, and what I have to trade and exchange with the
world." She was aware that she had strong beliefs about
money: "That I don't have enough resources, or maybe I
am not enough." She realized that she had been willing to
trade her current life force (her blood) for commitments
made in the past that she had not been able to keep (her
debts). This, she felt, was an attempt to ease her guilt and
showed that she valued other persons over herself. Therefore, Darcy's issues with money seemed to be similar to
Vincent's, having to do with self-worth.

Darcy finally decided that bankruptcy represented
the utter depletion of her energy and the total exhaustion
of her resources. She chose to see it as a chance to forgive
herself for the past and to begin again:

> I attribute a lot of power to money. I think I really do
> believe that money would solve all, or at least most, of

> my problems. It is hard to change this belief, because it
> feels so real to me.
> But I can stop telling myself I'm trapped and have few,
> if any, choices. I can replace the *feeling* of being trapped
> with the *knowledge* that I'm not. I always have choices,
> even about how to feel. I will consciously practice
> choice-making every day.

Darcy needed to alter lifelong patterns, but recognizing that she could change her beliefs about money and see it as a symbol for her own energy helped her to get started in a new direction.

Melinda had gone to a football game with her friend Jim. She did not fully understand the game and felt more like an observer than a participant. The home team was winning and the crowd was wildly enthusiastic, but Melinda felt like an outsider. She commented, "My sense of self was diminished. I felt out of place. I felt uninformed and stupid. I even felt rejected by Jim."

As Melinda worked with her vivid life experience, she realized that the football game was a symbol for how she feels about her life.

> While at the game, I had an image of the Roman
> Coliseum with the gladiators facing the lions and the
> spectators cheering them on. People felt a morbid fasci-
> nation when a player was injured. The TV announcers
> speculated on the nature of the injury and the effect on
> the player's career and on the team's chances for victory.
> It seemed there was little concern for the player himself.
> The crowd wanted a win at whatever cost to the indi-
> vidual.
> Being a trial attorney I am a warrior in the courtroom/
> stadium. The jury is like the spectators, observing in a

participatory way, affecting the outcome. The courtroom deputies are the enforcers, as is the judge. Just like the game, winning is what the event is all about.

I am not comfortable being a spectator. I prefer to be a warrior, but one who puts herself in an arena worth performing in and for a cause worth winning. I can resonate to the concept of "at all costs" but not if the cost is paid by someone else. I am also not interested in performing before others. Any reward I earn for my work is personal and internal.

Melinda decided this vivid life experience was asking her to reexamine her life to determine whether she was investing her time and energy in causes she deemed worth fighting for. She did not want her life to be about winning or losing, but rather about making a valuable contribution.

Learning from Waking Dreams

Because even the most common symbols can mean very different things to different people, we need to trust our intuition as we work with our waking dreams. Each vivid life experience reveals ways we need to grow, or confirms that we have grown, calling into our awareness our unfolding process. We need to act on what we uncover in order to change ourselves and our life experiences.

In the Life As A Waking Dream method, we pay attention to the people, places, animals, objects, and numbers as symbols that can evoke meaning. Learning to interpret symbols helped Peter, a professor of languages at a state college, as he sought to understand this experience:

It's part of my assignment as a language teacher to

supervise the language lab during specified periods of the day. On Fridays my student assistant and I need to leave the lab at one minute to eleven in order to be on time for our eleven o'clock classes. My colleague and his assistant who succeed us in the lab are often late, and the lab and the students in it can't be left without assistance or supervision for administrative and legal reasons. Last Friday my colleague Ezra and his assistant were late again. I was anxious because I had to leave the lab unattended. I hoped these guys would show up quickly. As I hurried to my next class, I found Ezra in the hallway talking to a student. I told him that no one was in the lab, which is our way of saying that the lab is without supervision.

My next class had just gotten under way when the door opened. Ezra stuck his nose in and blurted out in German, "You are crazy, you are crazy, you are crazy!" Now, I know Ezra to be a pretty crazy, emotional guy, but I felt offended and was puzzled as to what was upsetting him so much. After a split second's hesitation, I stepped out of the classroom to ask him what was wrong. He said that his assistant was present in the lab when he got there. I told him that his assistant had not arrived when I left.

On the one hand, Peter recognized that this was a fairly predictable series of interactions, knowing his colleague as he did. On the other hand, a strong feeling had stirred in Peter that caused him to pay close attention:

The next day I encounter Ezra in the division office. I tell him that I don't appreciate being called crazy in front of my class. As I set out to speak, I feel for only a split second a slight tightening of my upper lip. Ezra retorts that my class had been a French class, implying that no one understood what he had said. I tell him that he could not assume that, and besides, that wasn't the point.

I hear myself speak clearly and deliberately. I don't mind having an audience. Mario, another colleague, is in the room. With a hint of a smile I fill him in on the reason for our dispute. Addressing both of them, I say that I would not have mentioned the incident at all if it had not been for the fact that I was in the process of learning to express my feelings, to which Mario replied, "Why didn't you do it right away?"

Peter was involved in a conflict with a colleague. This experience could have been addressed strictly on the level of interpersonal relations and clear communication. However, Peter chose to go deeper by looking at it as a waking dream episode. He wanted to discover whether there was a message here that would enable him to know himself better. First he examined his sense of self:

At first I felt like the victim of Ezra's emotional outburst; I felt exposed before the students. When I finally confronted him I felt a little like a teacher who admonishes, who is in control, who wants to restore order and clarify the situation. I felt very open when I admitted that I was learning to express my feelings.

Although Peter told his colleagues that he was learning to express his feelings, he did not, in fact, do so directly. He said, "I don't appreciate being called crazy in front of my class," rather than, "I felt offended," or "I felt abused (a victim)," or "I felt exposed." And his "hint of a smile" when he told Mario what was going on belied how upset he really was by the event.

When Peter looked deeper, the symbolism helped him discover what the episode was all about.

Ezra is the symbol of my unexpressed emotions. He allows his emotions free reign: I sit on mine.

Mario symbolizes reason and emotion working together, with no hang-ups, because he is always very direct and responsive in his interactions with me.

The college setting symbolizes the school of life, or the process of learning and maturation.

The hallway connects places, is the symbol of accessibility and communication.

The language lab is a place to practice communicating in ways that are foreign to you.

As Peter looked at the symbols, he could see that his unexpressed emotions (symbolized by Ezra) were demanding that he wake up. They got his attention in this experience by shouting at him in his native language, German: "You are crazy!" That aroused sufficient discomfort to cause him to reflect inwardly.

Peter had been trying to learn how to express his emotions, a life skill he both needed and wanted to develop. This experience seemed to say that when he was practicing this skill (symbolized by being in the language lab) he was still not in direct contact with his emotions. Ezra, who represented the emotions themselves, always arrived late, after Peter had gone, implying that the true feelings surfaced in Peter's consciousness only after he had completed his practice in communicating them.

This life event seemed to say that finally Peter and his feelings had met "in the hallway," the corridor of awareness between Peter's communication skills and his feelings. His feelings were becoming more accessible to him. He noticed, for example, when he began to confront Ezra in the division office, a tightening of his upper lip, which occurs "when I become self-conscious when a strong emotion surfaces." Peter was aware of feeling abused and exposed. He also took action, by going into the hallway to ask Ezra what was wrong, and by telling him later that he didn't like being called crazy in front of his students. So the event seemed to reveal that Peter was making progress in his ability to express his feelings.

Sometime later, Peter remembered a sleeping dream he had had over ten years earlier:

> I was lying in a huge open cardboard box. Around the top edge of the box I saw the faces of the members of a group. About a dozen of them were looking at me rather congenially when the leader said with a smile, "We will get him when he falls asleep." I knew in my dream that I had to stay awake at all cost because I did not want to get "gotten."
>
> I was the dreamer who wanted to make contact, who wanted to awaken his feelings. The theme was resistance, hanging on, not wanting to let go, determination, self-reliance, as revealed in my vigilance to "stay awake at all cost." I felt safe only when I was awake because I could remain aloof, protected from my feelings. The box symbolizes my protection: I am hidden, confined, and separated from the others.
>
> My childhood experiences, some of which were rather threatening, have left me with a need for security and a considerable amount of self-reliance and independence which have led me to maneuver myself into a huge brown cardboard box whose shape and symmetry suggest a retreat into isolation and sterile rationality. What is missing are the feelings I was to get in touch with, as symbolized by the people who want "to get" me.

Peter interpreted his waking dream with Ezra as a message telling him that he had made some progress:

> Over the past ten years the box has been tilting more and more because I have gotten up and I am leaning into the tilting side. Maybe the guys on the outside are pushing, too. It has been suggested that I might already have a leg over the edge.

Yet the waking dream was also saying to him, through Mario, who was his symbol of reason and emotion working together without hang-ups, that he could do still better. Mario said to him, "Why didn't you do it right away?" Therefore, Peter took his waking dream both as an affirmation and as a stimulus to greater growth, a common experience for many who look at life as a waking dream.

Other vivid life experiences encourage us to get on with a chosen course of development, as in Ellen's waking dream. Ellen had just come home from work to find her son Josh and his girlfriend Cathy in the computer room:

> I go in, say "hi," and make some comment about playing computer games. Josh says "hi." Cathy's first words are, "Did you see the note I left for you on the blackboard? Did you know Rex (my dog) has a big lump on his side? It doesn't look good. I think it's something serious."
> I immediately begin feeling very angry and annoyed. I acknowledge that I was aware of the lump. She makes some comment about whether I was going to do anything about it. I don't recall if I said anything else or not. Josh tries to convince Cathy that it is probably nothing because the dog doesn't seem to be in any pain. Cathy

goes on with something about lumps being serious even if they are not sensitive. By this time I have gone out of the room. I am furious and wishing Cathy would just mind her own business.

Many of our life experiences do not seem very important on the surface. But when events evoke very strong feelings, as this one did in Ellen, they are worth looking into as waking dream episodes. Perhaps you can recall situations in which your emotional reaction seemed out of proportion to the event and in some way misleading.

How we respond to people within a given waking dream does not tell the whole story of our relationship with them, nor is it necessarily a true representation of our primary feelings about them. In this case, Ellen said she felt like a child being attacked by a woman she didn't like. But if we had asked her in another context how she liked Josh's girlfriend, Ellen might have said that she found Cathy a lovely girl. Or, she might have told us that she did not know her very well.

When we find ourselves in situations like Ellen's, symbols can help us find clues as to what is really going on. Ellen identified the symbols in her waking dream:

Josh: a yang who was trying to reassure an upset yin

Cathy: an hysterical yin

Rex (the dog): a powerless victim at the mercy of his disease as well as his mistress.

As a general rule, males who appear in our life experiences represent yang energy. That is, they are symbols for a pattern-setting force that seeks to initiate, guide, direct, and inspire. Females, on the other hand, usually stand for yin energy: a form-giving force that is receptive, responsive, spacious, and nurturing. This will not always be the case, but we can begin with this as a possible interpretation and then see if it fits for us.

Having characterized the symbols, we need to look at our own behavior to discover what they represent in us. Symbols reflect something that our sense of self does not recognize or identify with. When Ellen looked at her behavior she observed:

> When I entered the house I was already a resistant yin, because I was not in the mood for company. I didn't seem able to shift, and the resistance went from bad to worse. There wasn't much flow or shifting of energy within me.

Ellen recognized that she was not feeling open or receptive to begin with. Her feelings communicated this. She labeled them as anger, annoyance, and powerlessness. And most of that energy was directed at Cathy. Now Ellen was at a crucial point, because she needed to use the symbols to come to a new awareness about herself. Ellen came to this realization:

> I see that Cathy represents the yin I am trying to grow beyond; the yin who hysterically demands that something has to be done instead of either accepting what is, or waiting to see more.

Yin is the force that has the patience to bring things into manifestation in their own time. When yin is functioning well, it trusts the process rather than being focused on the goal, or the product. The hysterical yin that Ellen saw reflected in Cathy seemed to have a lot of yang activated, but not in a helpful way. By spurring Ellen on, urging her to do something, the yang energy within Cathy only made Ellen agitated; it didn't empower her to take action.

Just because this is the meaning Ellen saw in her waking dream, it is not necessarily the meaning another person would find in the same event. Each of us must interpret our own waking dreams on our own terms. Carl Jung makes this point strongly:

> It is plain foolishness to believe in ready-made systematic guides to dream interpretation, as if one could simply buy a reference book and look up a particular symbol. No dream symbol can be separated from the individual who dreams it, and there is no definite or straightforward interpretation of any dream.[5]

What is going on in our life in general often determines how we respond to symbols in our waking dreams. Ellen was trying to develop her own yang force, her ability to see what needs to be done and do it. So naturally she got angry at what she saw as Cathy's hysterical expression of yin energy because she was seeking to move beyond that in herself. She didn't want to be reminded of it because she had not yet found a way either to accept what was going on with Rex or to take some action to help him.

In a waking dream episode, the feeling response we have to another person is not so much a commentary on that person as it is an opportunity to recognize something in ourselves. Cathy might not have felt that she was being "hysterical" at all. She might have perceived herself as calm and rational, or as appropriately concerned.

To awaken more awareness, we can look at what we

don't know about our waking dreams. Ellen realized:

> I don't know what would have happened had I con-
> fronted Cathy with what I was feeling. I don't know why
> I dislike Cathy so much. I don't know why my dog is
> sick. And I don't know why I had an hysterical yin in my
> house!

The final question seemed the most important to Ellen. Recognizing that an hysterical yin was "in her house"
was a way of discovering that she still had the pattern of
the dysfunctional yin, even though she had tried to change
it. Ellen's next question was "why?"

To answer the question "why?" in relation to our
waking dreams we do not try to simply think it through.
As Carl Jung said:

> A word or an image is symbolic when it implies some-
> thing more than its obvious and immediate meaning. It
> has a wider 'unconscious' aspect that is never precisely
> defined or fully explained. Nor can one hope to define or
> explain it. As the mind explores the symbol, it is led to
> ideas that lie beyond the grasp of reason.[6]

We keep returning to the story as we have written it.
The story reveals the meaning. In Ellen's case, the question
why there was an hysterical yin in her house of self was
answered easily: Cathy was expressing concern about Rex.
Ellen saw Rex as a symbol of herself in her victim role:

> Stepping back, I see how powerless I feel, not only over
> Rex's condition, but over life in general. I see how often
> I live life as a victim or potential victim.

To live as a victim is to inhibit the instincts for self-preservation that are inbred in all of us. In denying the basic instinct to look out for herself, Ellen was blocking a powerful force. It appeared that the accumulation of that energy was symbolized by the growth on Rex's body, since animals often represent our instincts.

Viewing Rex as a symbol here is not to deny his independent existence. He was a real dog with a real tumor. However, when Ellen looked at the *meaning* of the tumor on Rex's body, she looked beyond Rex to what he represented in her own life and consciousness.

This point is basic to understanding life as a waking dream. We cannot know from Ellen's waking dream what Rex's tumor meant to anyone but Ellen, since she was the one examining her waking dream. And Ellen is the only one who can tell us. "The dreamer's individual unconscious is communicating with the dreamer alone and is selecting symbols for its purpose that have meaning to the dreamer and to nobody else," as John Freeman says.[7]

As a result of her work with her waking dream, Ellen took steps to act on her own behalf in direct and powerful ways. Her new consciousness helped her to activate more yang energy within herself, making decisions about what she wanted to bring into her life and what she needed to release. She had her dog Rex put to sleep when he began to suffer pain from the tumor. And she chose to view that action as a symbol for putting an end to her own pattern of living as a victim.

As we reflect more consistently on life as a waking dream, we begin to notice that certain themes keep recurring. Sometimes we do not identify with qualities (such as directness, reliability, compassion, and honesty) or skills (such as making conscious choices, focusing attention, managing time, loving unconditionally, and setting goals) in any of our senses of self. Since the potential for these qualities and skills lies within us, an urge to develop them may present itself to us in the form of waking dream episodes that have common themes. Our real Self speaks to us through these situations and people. Christopher had this experience:

> I stopped for gas at a Texaco Mini-Mart station. I was in a hurry, being late to a birthday party. I was parked behind a flat-bed truck in line, and I wasn't sure if the hose from the unleaded pump could reach my gas tank. I had taken my credit card to the booth, as was required, and was listening to a football game as I waited. When the BIG! man with the truck finished, I asked him (quietly and timidly at first, feeling both irritated and somewhat intimidated) to please move the truck forward before going to pay.

Chris had unwittingly prepared himself to live out a life theme in this experience. He was in a hurry, which meant that his attention was spread from the gas station all the way to the birthday party. Consequently, he did focus his full awareness focused on the present; if he had, he might have handled this situation differently. Instead his old patterns took over, and this episode, like many others, revealed a message Chris had spent a lifetime ignoring.

Chris was both irritated with and intimidated by the large driver of the truck. He saw the driver as more powerful than he was and his sense of self shrank. His feelings might have alerted him to his waking dream if he had paid attention to them, but he did not:

The truck driver didn't hear me, so I beeped my horn twice. He didn't turn around, so I tried the hose and by golly it did stretch to my gas tank. I filled my tank and went in to pay. I was right behind my "friend" with the truck. (I wasn't aware of my irritation at that moment, but I must have been irritated as subsequent events proved.) I was trying to think of something to say to him, but he looked unapproachable, grim and impassive.

In retrospect, Chris realized just how "asleep" he was during this vivid life experience. He was not aware of his feelings, not receiving communication from an important part of himself. He was totally attentive to the outer events rather than receiving direction from within.

Finally he finished, and I couldn't resist. I opened my (BIG?) mouth and said, sarcastically, something like, "It wouldn't have hurt if you had moved your truck forward to make it easier for me." He didn't turn around, nor acknowledge that he heard anything.
I was paying my bill, when all of a sudden "he" came back into the store with his green-blue eyes flashing and said, "How would you like to have your lights punched out?" He had heard, all right, and was he angry! And was I scared! Stomach tight, legs weak, perspiring, feeling queasy, plus thinking, "It's all over for me," and "He wouldn't hit a guy with glasses, would he?"

Chris's body told him in no uncertain terms that he was in danger. He registered the message through his feeling of fear and his thought, "It's all over for me." Trying to extricate himself from the situation, he made excuses for his behavior:

I started apologizing like mad, telling him how stressed I

was about driving several hours, and that I was late to a birthday party, etc. Then he told me his story of how he couldn't reach his truck with the hose, etc. The attendant working at the place was very "cool" and finally convinced the guy (Thank God!) to leave, somewhat peacefully.

Chris examined this experience as a waking dream because it felt all too familiar to him. He thought it might be a life theme. When reflecting on his sense of self, he wrote:

I was the Victim, but also the Agitator, since I threw out the sarcastic comment.

As a victim, Chris felt powerless to do anything about the truck or the truck driver. He could not move them out of his way so that he could finish his transaction more quickly. But it was not Chris's victim sense of self that enraged the driver. The irritation and sarcasm that colored Chris's words got the reaction. This agitator sense of self was not unknown to him.

I have opened my mouth at the wrong moment a number of times. I can recall twice when I said things to women in earshot of their men who then threatened to get me. Another time a group of "White Christian Crusaders" were talking about getting rid of the Jews, and I said, "Sir, are you advocating murder?" They said, "Get him! He's a Jew!" and this big henchman came towards me. Somehow I have always regained myself, recovered and gotten away "free." I can also think of many agitating things I have said in personal relationships with men and women that have triggered others off! I must like to do that at some level, and I really "ask" for what I get.

Chris relived similar waking dream episodes because there was something he had not yet brought into his awareness. To find out what the dream was saying to him, Chris looked at the primary symbol within the dream: the driver of the truck. He described him as uptight, muscular, overly serious, insensitive, uncooperative, and aggressive. He labeled him a bully.

When people appear in our waking dreams symbolizing qualities or abilities with which we aren't, or don't want to be, identified, we experience them as different from us. In this case, Chris projected his bully sense of self onto the large truck driver. When he spoke to the driver, he saw himself as an aggressor, but not as a bully. What did this mean?

One thing that stands out is that Chris's primary, if not only, strength seemed to be verbal. He honked his horn (using the car's voice) and attacked the truck driver with words. On the other hand, he described the truck driver as big and muscular, identifying "bullying" with physical attacks. Chris commented, "I was actually bullied (beat up) by kids in the third and fourth grade at a private school." When he felt trepidation arise, Chris thought, "He wouldn't hit a guy with glasses, would he?" hoping that the truck driver could restrain his aggression, and at the same time fearing that he was exactly the kind of target a bully would choose.

Since Chris's dread was of physical retaliation, the bully in his waking dream probably symbolized Chris's masculine polarity on the physical level. This vivid life experience seemed to point out that Chris was afraid of his own physical strength. Even though he verbally assaulted the truck driver, he didn't have confidence that his words could overpower a physical aggressor. He continued to feel powerless and frightened.

Other symbols in this waking dream support this interpretation. The big bully was driving a flatbed truck, which is a significantly larger vehicle than Chris's passenger car. Since vehicles are often symbols for the body, and trucks are usually associated with more yang energy than passenger cars, it would seem Chris's waking dream was trying to awaken him to the fact that he did not identify with a strong, yang body. Another man in a larger vehicle represented those traits in his waking dream.

The experience also suggested that when Chris communicated directly with his yang qualities on the physical level, they listened ("He had heard, all right!") and they responded ("Then he told me his story . . ."). This implies that if Chris would get to know himself in his physical masculinity — "man to man," verbal yang to physical yang — he could integrate the two, or at least establish a cooperative relationship between them. Both the verbal and the physical aspects of Chris were being fully energized by his life force. Each was able to "fill his tank" even though each, at first, feared he would not be able to get close enough to the source (the pump).

As a result of fearing his physical strength and not identifying with his ability to initiate forceful action through his body without losing control, Chris had never developed the muscles or the confidence to defend himself physically. Nor had he formed an image of his physical power that he could comfortably integrate into his sense of self. This vivid life experience pointed out his need to let go of his fear of his physical strength and get to know it.

How could Chris come to know his physical strength?

If he were to work on the challenge objectively, in a predominantly yang way, he might start weight lifting or learn a martial art. In the course of those studies his sense of self might expand to include physical confidence and the ability to direct his physical expressions of strength, and he would have accomplished his goal.

Using the Life As A Waking Dream method, Chris would start subjectively, with a more yin approach. He would allow an image of the primary symbol to form in his mind. He might remember how the truck driver looked when he came back into the mini-mart with his eyes flashing, remember the sound of his voice and what he said, and awaken a kinesthetic sense of what it would be like to have a big body like the truck driver. In other words, he would fully awaken his memory of the muscular essence of the truck driver.

Chris would hold this image in his memory, trying to sense the image rather than actively think about it. If he could imagine himself merging with the vivid image of the truck driver, and sustain that sensation for several minutes, feelings would arise in response. The initial feelings might be associated with the past (such as fear, or discomfort), but gradually, if he repeated the process over several days or weeks, Chris would be likely to touch positive feelings about his own physical strength, feelings like power and self-confidence.

This yin process requires patience (a yin quality) but it can have profound results. It is a conscious way to engage instinct and sensation, which usually influence our sense of self unconsciously. Such visualization can change our affective connection with an image and make it possible for us to form a new sense of self.

Both symbols and images in our consciousness mediate between the world in which we actually live and our private, edited videotape of reality. Holding an image in our consciousness, or contemplating a symbol, invites communication between the various components of Self. Because the images in our psyches are based on past experience, they arouse instinct, sensation, feeling, thinking, and intuition. Symbols held in our awareness are images that also have the power to awaken wisdom and knowing. Images and symbols, because they put us in touch with body, psyche and spirit, can greatly enhance our Self-communication. [See Illustration #10, page 177.]

If Chris were able to form a new sense of self that incorporated feeling good about muscularity and physical strength, he would probably be motivated to do something to bring his body into alignment with that new sense of self. He would begin to feel that he could be as powerful physically as he is verbally, and that feeling would help him sustain the effort to develop his muscles.

Some people prefer to take a yang approach to change; others find a yin approach more natural. No matter which way we begin, eventually we need to communicate the change to all the components of Self through all the forms of communication available to us. Both polarities of energy moving within us need to carry the news that change is occurring. Otherwise the change will not be fully integrated in us, and it won't last.

It is helpful to remember that others will often relate to us as if we were symbols in *their* waking dreams. If someone responds to us with strong emotion that seems out of proportion to the interaction we have just had, we can remind ourselves that this person is probably caught up in a waking dream.

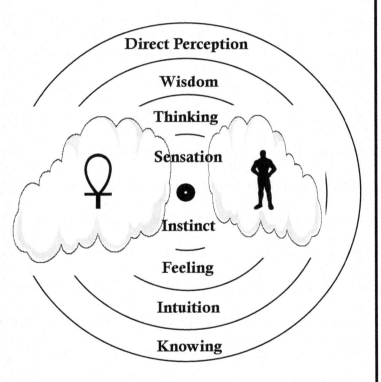

Illustration #10
Images and Symbols
Used in Self-Communication

Direct Perception

Wisdom

Thinking

Sensation

Instinct

Feeling

Intuition

Knowing

Images held in the psyche can awaken instinct and sensation, feeling and thinking, and even intuition. Thus they facilitate Self-communication. Symbols are images that also have the power to awaken wisdom and knowing.

Arthur went into the post office to buy a large quantity of stamps for office work he planned to do at home. The post office was busy and Arthur waited twenty minutes to get to the window. When he presented his order to the clerk, the woman behind him began to shout: "You inconsiderate s.o.b.! Can't you see I've been waiting in line for an hour, and now you are going to keep me waiting another half hour? My kid is standing on a street corner waiting for me, and you're buying enough stamps for an army!" The woman's face turned beet red and her eyes were flashing.

It was clear to Arthur that the woman had not been waiting as long as she claimed, and that he was not the cause of her wait. But even more important, Arthur knew, because of his work with life as a waking dream, that the woman was not really yelling at him. He was clearly a symbol in her waking dream for something going on within her. Though Arthur could not know what he represented to her, he could make the choice not to take her attack personally. He chose not to be a participant in her waking dream, and he made no response.

Most parents have experienced a teenager's rage when they have set limits on the youngster's behavior. If parents could remember that the teenager sees them as a symbol for authority in general, authority that the child has not yet developed enough to exercise over self, they would not be so offended by the rage.

To recognize ourselves as symbols in other people's waking dreams does not mean we do not interact with these people. It does mean that we try to remember that we do not have to accept the role in which they have cast us in their waking dreams. We can make our own choices about what to say and do based on our own values and sense of self.

It is equally important to remember that other people exist independent of our waking dreams. For the time being we might relate to them as symbols of some unrealized potential in us. But as we wake up within our waking dreams, we will begin to relate to them as who they really are. That is one of the most compelling reasons to awaken — to know the true nature of others, as well as of ourselves.

When you begin to examine your vivid life experiences, write down the stories of what occurred, or talk them into a tape recorder, as if you were recording dreams. Close your eyes, breathe slowly and deeply, and call into your consciousness all your sensory impressions. Remember what you were wearing, the colors, sounds and scents in the environment, what the other people in your waking dream looked like, etc.

Tell the stories in the first person and in the present tense, as if you were reliving them. Record each story from the perspective of the sense of self you were identified with when you lived it.

The meaning of the experience is hidden in the relationship between your sense of self and the rest of the story. How you felt about what went on, how you perceived other people and your relationship to them, and the actions you took will provide clues. So will the symbols. It is as if you are living out a mythical play about how you see yourself and your relationship to the world around you. This myth, which is your life story, is full of hidden meanings. Discovering those meanings will help you to know the purpose and intent of your life. You will then be able to live far more consciously, creatively, and powerfully.

What follows is an example of finding the meaning of a vivid life experience by decoding the symbols and then retelling the story in a way that reveals the message it holds.

Title: Yin and Yang at Play

Summary Statement: A recurring dream in which my husband and I go on vacation and have a miserable time.

Description of the Event:
I dream that Phil and I plan to go on vacation. We are excited about getting away and we are looking forward to our destination. In this dream, our vacation is planned as a reward for getting through something hard. It is something we don't do very often because of the expense involved, and money, or the lack of it, often becomes a central theme of the planning, the doing and the aftermath of the vacation.

I am the one who initiates the idea. "I've always wanted to go to San Francisco," I say. "There's a sale on right now. What do you think?" To which Phil says: "I thought we didn't have the money for extras like vacations. If you had trouble paying the bills this month, where do we get money for a vacation?" To which I reply: "We'll take it out of savings."

Our savings consist mainly of the money I have inherited from my parents and grandparents. Phil has always deferred to my judgment about how and whether to spend the money. "After all," I say, "we haven't been on a vacation for three years. Life is short." Phil replies, "It's your money. If that's what you want to do, that's what we'll do."

But in this dream, the money issue is not put to rest. We do go on vacation. I make all the reservations, arrange for child care and attend to all the other details. Phil takes no initiative to contribute to the planning, but goes along quite willingly with whatever I decide. The day comes, and we fly off to San Francisco.

Within a day or two of our arrival, things start to go badly. I notice that Phil is spending a lot of money on food. He orders big, expensive meals. He has several drinks with dinner. He always orders dessert. He seems to require three square meals a day and a snack mid-afternoon. He isn't drawn, as I am, to just a light, inexpensive bowl of soup at a deli; he wants to go to a sit-down restaurant and order from the menu.

In my dream I mention that we are going through our cash pretty quickly. I say, "The reason we can go on vacation is because we are frugal. You are careful about what you spend at home. Why are you so uncontrolled now?" He says: "I don't like to go on vacation and count pennies. Either I have enough money to go on vacation or I don't. I don't want to do it half way."

When we are not eating, we are disagreeing about how to spend the time between meals. His idea of a vacation is to lie around reading, getting up only to eat. My idea is to go out and do things — see the sights, take walks, soak up the local culture. He does those things with me, but really finds the pace frenetic and unrestful. I find reading a waste of opportunity when the weather is good and I'm in a new place and could be out exploring.

We reach an uneasy truce with all this, but I find myself deeply resentful by the end of the experience, as does Phil. I tell him we are going to have to figure out a better way of going on vacation together, that he will have to make his own money in the future, but in various forms the dream recurs.

The Sense of Self:
My sense of self is the Practical Sensualist. I want to see,

hear, taste, feel and smell what a new place has to offer while not spending a lot of money. There's another sense of self I can't quite define but it is disapproving parent of out-of-control child, or something like that.

Polarity:

This dream is about my waking dream ego, the yin polarity, and my yang force trying to play together and finding it hard work indeed. In this dream, the yin and yang are disconnected. There is no flow of energy between the two. Also, the energy polarities are confused. Phil, who represents my yang force, is actually very yin in this dream — passive, yielding, accommodating. I, supposedly a yin force, am actually mostly yang in this dream — initiating, imprinting, developing (although also yin in taking care of all the detail work).

Strongest Feelings:

At first I felt hope that things would go well this time and we would really enjoy ourselves. Then I felt anger and resentment about excessive eating and spending; then sadness that we are further apart emotionally than when we started; then hopelessness that we can ever vacation successfully together. I find myself more and more quiet, less spontaneous, struggling to lighten up and just go with the flow, struggling to enjoy myself no matter what else is going on, but failing to be able to do so.

Symbols:

The vacation period: a space and time in which the rules of daily living don't apply.

Phil: my spendthrift, lazy, undisciplined, self-indulgent inner child

My savings account (money): energy bequeathed to me by my formative yin and yang forces and the universal One.

Retelling the event (using the symbols to translate to the inner what was first perceived as outer):

I give myself a reprieve from the rules of daily living. But from there my warring sides of self take off in two opposite directions. For the indulgent side, the new rule becomes: Eat, drink and Be Merry for tomorrow we can go back to peanut butter sandwiches and penny pinching. For the self-disciplined side, the new rule is: See as much and do as much as you can, but frugally, for tomorrow we will be back in the old routine and the bills from this vacation will start rolling in.

The energy I am living on during this "vacation" from my usual rules was a gift; I didn't have to earn it. Yet it seems I (the sense of self living the dream) am saving this energy rather than spending it or using it, and when I do spend it, I worry about how much I am spending, as if there is a limited amount of energy in the universe and I don't want to use up my share too soon. My "shadow," or opposite side, would use all the energy freely, living for today with no thought of tomorrow. I can't seem to reconcile these two parts of self, and therefore I can't really enjoy any "off" time from my usual frugal approach to living.

Not known?

I need to know more about this ongoing dispute between sides of myself. I don't know how it began or how to resolve it.

Theme?

It seems to be something about controlling my impulsive, indulgent self.

Past Experiences?

It reminds me of how I approached my grand tour of Europe when I was a student. I roamed Europe for three months on ten dollars a day, including airfare over and back. I was the Adventurous but Frugal Student.

The Message?

This dream seems to be about energy and the gaining and losing of energy. I have money, which is energy; Phil eats food, which is energy. In order to increase his energy (eat food), he/we deplete my energy (money).

My yang force depletes my yin force of energy. They are not mutually reinforcing.

This dream seems also to be about my inner struggle between the side of me that is sensual, self-indulgent, lazy and the side of me that is ordered, energetic, productive and self-disciplined. In this dream, the two aspects of self cannot find a way to co-exist. When I indulge my appetites, I can't really enjoy myself because my judgmental parent — my father, I think — tells me I am bad or wrong for my behavior. When I want to do something purposeful and energetic, my lazy side comes along but resentfully. Why all this work, it says, when we are on vacation.

Perhaps the message is that I need a conflict mediator instead of a travel agent!!

Questions and Comments:

What does it mean when the polarities seem to be reversed in a relationship as ours are?

It was helpful for me to write this out. I see the conflict more clearly. Now I just need to figure out what to do about it!!

Try and see your ordinary daily life as the medium through which God is teaching your soul, and respond as well as you can. Then you won't need, in order to receive lessons, to go outside your normal experience.

— *Evelyn Underhill*

Life is a sacred text, to be unlocked through the key of metaphoric knowing. Thus understood, life events yield information about our personality, our karma, and even our future potentials, pointing the way toward greater levels of awakening.

— *Ray Grasse*

Chapter Seven

Realizing Our Potential

There is an ancient law attributed to the Egyptian sage Hermes that says "opposition builds strength." As we face difficulties in our lives, we draw on resources at the core of ourselves. The strength of character we develop through these experiences adds depth and meaning to our lives. It is the real Self that unfolds in the process. And the fruits of this learning — life skills and qualities of being — are what we take with us when we die. Jesus spoke of them as treasures laid up in heaven.

Our daily experiences speak to us of what we have developed and of what lies within us undeveloped. To approach each day with that awareness helps us look at life as a learning adventure. One way to think of our potential is in terms of the balance of our yin and yang energies. These polarities are essential to the development of a well-balanced and highly creative expression of Self.

Almost daily we have vivid life experiences that can help us to identify what we need to develop in ourselves. Heather was expressing too much yin and not enough yang in her life when she went to the doctor for her annual checkup. She arrived twenty minutes late for her appointment, and lost her place to another patient. Fifteen minutes later, she was ushered into an examination room by a new, young intern who was to do the routine preliminary physical examination. Heather wrote:

The assistant is young, relaxed, and pleasant. She listens carefully to my answers to her questions, and makes notes. Then she asks me to undress and roll up in a sheet and lie on the examination table. She pulls the drapes and says, "It's rather cold here," and leaves.

I undress, shivering. It is very cold, and so is the leather table, covered only by a thin paper sheet. I put my sweater back on, also my socks and slacks, and huddle under the cotton sheet. I get colder, and when, as time passes, she does not return, I get angry. I begin to look at the alternatives I have to indicate I am angry.

The first signal to Heather to awaken was communicated through sensation. The body said, "I am cold." Cold is a yin quality. In this case, there was too much yin.

When Heather did not awaken, the message was expressed through feeling. She got angry. Anger is a "hot" emotion; yang energy is characterized by heat. Heather's feelings were saying, "Go more yang." It was only then that she began to consider her alternatives.

Perceiving alternatives is a yang function. However, Heather did not fully express yang initiative. She looked for ways to "indicate" that she was angry rather than focusing on what she could do about what was bothering her, which would have been far more effective.

One thing that feelings communicate is that energy is flowing between the two polarities within us. When we are conscious of our feelings, we have an indication that something is about to be created from within us — an idea, an insight, or an action. As the renowned philosopher Rudolf Steiner put it: "Feeling is the life and activity of the soul within itself."[1]

In this instance, Heather was receptive (yin) to the

doctor's instructions. She undressed, as she was asked. Her anger at being left in the cold signaled a shift within her from yin to yang, which might have empowered her to set something new in motion, to change the pattern. However, Heather focused on making her feeling known, rather than on taking direct action. That left her dependent on someone else to change the situation. Here's what happened:

> I practice deep breathing, both to warm myself (which does help) and also to fully experience what I am feeling. I could go out to the waiting room and get my warm down coat and bring it in. I could ask her if she would have left me here this long if I had been sick and had a temperature. I could ask if they could keep a blanket handy, etc. I discard these and decide to register very clearly my discomfort, and I do this when she returns ten minutes later.

The first alternative Heather perceived was something she could have done for herself, sparked by her yang energy; had she retrieved her coat and wrapped up in it, she might have gotten warm. But she didn't. She kept trying to think of things that she could do from a yin perspective, things she could ask someone else to do rather than things she would initiate herself.

Finally, Heather decided to tell the doctor how she felt. That seemed to satisfy her yang urge to express herself, but in fact she didn't ask for what she really needed. She just reported her feelings to the doctor, whom she had already decided was inattentive and insensitive. Consequently, she remained in her yin position, feeling disempowered and ineffectual.

The doctor responded to Heather's discomfort by

asking the secretary for an auxiliary heater, which never appeared. She took Heather's blood pressure, examined her ears, eyes, chest, etc., then told her to put her clothes back on and go to a technician for a blood test. Heather wrote:

> There was no need at all that I can see for the undressing or the long wait. By the time the technician has begun to take blood samples I am feeling invaded, and a victim.

Feeling victimized was the inevitable result of Heather's failure to act on her own behalf. Her energy began to move toward creative self-expression but got bogged down by her feelings of powerlessness. Heather put herself at the mercy of others. If they didn't do anything, nothing was done. Heather went on:

> The technician keeps asking me if I am all right, because I have my eyes closed. She thinks I am sick, asks if I want to lie down, takes a long time to fill four or more vials with blood, and finally leads me to the secretary who asks me what is wrong.

This is the same secretary who was unable to produce a heater when the doctor requested one. So the secretary becomes a symbol in Heather's waking dream of the ineffectual yin side of herself that doesn't carry through on details. Nevertheless, Heather put herself in the secretary's hands, remaining a victim.

> I tell the secretary that I am angry at being left there in the cold for ten minutes and more. She says she will speak to someone, and I leave.

People who haven't developed their yang ability to

initiate action often have experiences like Heather's. They find it very difficult to set something specific into motion. In her journal, Heather called this theme, "Charting the path of the creation of a victim." She was aware that no one else made her a victim. So the task was for her to look at how she had brought that sense of self to the fore. Heather was all too familiar with feeling like a victim:

> Who was I? I was, once more, a victim. I used the circumstances to create this role. They were all laid out like pieces of a jigsaw puzzle designed for a small child. They just fell together to complete the perfect picture. First, I was late, so I felt rushed. Second, I had been told to have no food for twelve hours, so I was hungry. Third, I was left in the cold for an inordinately long time, I felt, and the undressing ritual seemed to have been unnecessary for such a short, routine examination. Finally, I chose to see the blood test as also unnecessary, and went in for it with increased resentment and mistrust of the whole system which was going to take three visits, whereas, ten or fifteen years ago one visit would have done it all.

Notice that by the end of her account, Heather had spun off from the immediate circumstances to an abstraction called "the system." There is no way to take action in relation to "the system," because "the system" is a mental concept. Action must be taken in relation to someone or something that is identifiable and accessible.

Heather looked at the various symbols in her waking dream and saw a clear reflection of the facets of herself that perpetuate her victim posture. It was significant that all the people in the dream were yin symbols, and all of them were ineffective in finding a way to address Heather's dilemma.

Here are the symbols as Heather interpreted them:

the young doctor: a yin facet of self that follows a preexisting pattern designed to save time even when it wastes time;

the examination table: my own unyielding, cold, slippery intention to be victim, to slide back into my old pattern;

the technician: my yin bewilderment, confusion, and inability to speak clearly and effectively;

the secretary: an ineffectual yin facet of self that is responsible for carrying out details but does not manifest them;

the waiting room (in which carpenters were at work making alterations): a reflection of the beginning of alterations within me, pulling down old walls and supports regarding my victim pattern.

Heather learned a great deal from this vivid life experience. She discovered just how tenacious and subtle the pattern of the victim is. A victim could be understood, in the context of this waking dream, as yin energy that is deserted by its yang polarity. Without yang energy, yin is powerless to make choices of any kind, to decline to accept what others do when she doesn't agree, and to shift into action. In her victim sense of self, Heather is almost entirely yin. The only evidence of yang was in her search for alternatives and in the two times she asserted herself to tell others what she was feeling.

Heather realized that her yang was often reversed, turning back on herself with negativity and criticism rather than thrusting forward in powerful self-expression. She began to see that when she didn't consciously use her yang energy, her yin energy wasn't able to work for her either. What Heather needed to develop was the ability to take action on her own behalf, and to do that she needed to activate yang energy to balance her yin.

Heather's experiences will not change unless she actually practices taking the initiative. She will need to act on her feelings rather than just talking about them. She will need to see herself as the source of her solutions, rather than relying on others.

Wayne, on the other hand, often activated too much yang energy and forgot to go yin. One day Wayne was driving on the expressway. He pulled out to pass a truck that was traveling about sixty miles per hour. Moments later another truck pulled out and followed him close behind, trying to pass him while he was passing the first truck. Wayne described his reaction:

> I became anxious as I proceeded to pass the first truck. I was furious that trucks were allowed on the road, and that they were speeding, and that they use their size to intimidate me, to go faster, etc. I was hating both of them.

Wayne's anxiety indicated that he had a lot of energy moving around in him. The energy was there for Wayne to use in dealing with the situation. But his feeling of anxiety indicated that the energy was not being directed into the activity of passing the truck. Wayne's attention was focused on *symbols* of the yang force - the trucks - rather than on the expression of his own yang energy. Then another feeling arose: Wayne's hatred of the trucks.

We often think we have no choice about what we feel

about a given situation, but if we are conscious within it, we can choose. Some feelings interrupt the flow of energy between the polarities, cutting off communication within and putting a stop to the process of Self-expression. Anger, hatred, and fear, especially in their extreme states, are three of those feelings. They can cause us to dam up that energy, energy that will resurface at some point in a less constructive, and possibly harmful, way.

Anger, hatred and fear can also serve as powerful alarms, urging us to awaken and to make choices that will empower us within a given interaction. When they do, our energy circulates between the polarities, empowering our choice making. Here is how Wayne's process unfolded:

> My anxiety accelerated as I began to fear losing control of the car, or more accurately, my faculties to operate the car. I began to think thoughts that disengaged me from my natural driving consciousness and thus were threatening my safety. I felt less grounded and very much aware of the strangeness of driving in a "can of metal" at 65 miles per hour with huge cans on both sides of me. One mistake and I could easily be killed. I felt light-headed, my hands were sweating, and my body was tensing everywhere, particularly in my neck and shoulders.

Wayne began to pay attention to his own internal communication. He noticed his feelings of anxiety and fear, the thoughts that were threatening his safety, and his sensations of light-headedness, perspiration, and tense muscles. He even used a powerful metaphor to express his overall experience, that of being in a can of metal traveling at 65 miles per hour. These observations permitted Wayne to function more lucidly within the dream:

I drew on my "adult self" to take control of the situation. I reminded myself that I have often experienced anxiety passing trucks and that on an open stretch of road, when I am tired, I often feel more vulnerable to anxiety, and that I could pull over at the next rest stop. After accelerating past the truck, I quickly pulled in front of it and got off at the next exit to rest. I then decided to go more slowly and avoid passing trucks for the day.

Wayne shifted his sense of self to "adult." In that sense of self he was able to change the waking dream from a nightmare to something tolerable by making the choice to get off the road. This was an immediate action in response to the messages being sent to him through several facets of Self. It was as if his real Self was saying, "Watch out!! You are placing yourself in genuine danger!" Although Wayne did not wake up to the deeper meaning of the event while he was living it, he was able to change the course of it. That was a step in the direction of lucid living, of waking up within his waking dreams.

As Wayne reflected on this waking dream, he realized that he had slipped into a lifelong pattern of expressing too much yang. Yang is the energy of initiation, but it is also characterized by a heightened intensity that pushes toward immediate resolution. If more yang is called up than is needed in a given circumstance, instincts and feelings will sound a warning. Both expressions had gotten Wayne's attention.

In such a circumstance, we begin to feel enormous pressure from yang. In this case, the symbols were powerful: two large trucks and one smaller vehicle, all with yang drivers, were exceeding the speed limit and crowding into three lanes side by side, as if in a race. If we see all of these as symbols for Wayne's yang energy, it is clear that he had called up far more yang energy than could be creatively utilized.

Wayne discovered what was undeveloped when he asked himself what he didn't know about this event. He wrote:

> What I don't know is how to not create the anxiety in the first place, or how to identify it and respect it before getting into the denial and struggle. I don't know how to give myself the security I need to make my own decisions without worrying and doubting my judgment about it afterwards.

Wayne was not just dealing with this single incident of speeding on an expressway. He was considering a life theme, which until now he could identify only as "suffering anxiety attacks." He knew some of the circumstances that increased the likelihood of such attacks, but he did not know how to forestall them.

It is impossible to "not create" something. Wayne needed to discover how to create something other than anxiety. He needed to know how to create calm, quiet confidence and inner security - characteristics of yin energy. Wayne needed to develop his ability to function in the yin polarity.

Yin energy moves more slowly than yang energy. It expands in spirals whereas yang energy moves rapidly in a straight line. In yin energy, our awareness can encompass far more. When driving a car, yang would focus on the truck ahead and on the intention to pass that truck. Yin would look at the truck immediately ahead, at the truck approaching from behind, and at other traffic in the lanes to the left. When pulling out to pass, yin energy would enable us to hold other options as alternatives. If we needed to, we could change our minds and drop back again behind the truck, move into the far left lane, or go even faster in order to overtake the truck. In yang energy we can be too single-minded to evaluate our options.

To become more grounded in yin energy, Wayne can practice deep relaxation. This will help him to slow down his inner processes of thought and feeling as well as his outer actions. As he moves into the natural flow of his life, he will not call up the excess yang energy that awakens anxiety. It was that excess that caused him to panic on the expressway.

Although we might expect women to be more comfortable with yin energy because they are females, some women find it difficult to integrate yin expressions into their sense of self. One evening Marilyn was grocery shopping in a large market. She had spent a day in which everything seemed to go wrong. She was looking for a way to change the way she felt.

> As I walked up with my cart towards the checkout stand, I noticed a woman with a cute baby. She was holding the child and trying to put groceries on the conveyer belt. I asked her if I could hold the child while she loaded her groceries. She gratefully handed him to me. As I held him and talked to him, I noticed he wasn't smiling or showing any emotion at all. He just looked at me, as if he were sizing me up. His mother kept telling him it was okay, she was right there.
> When she took him back, he smiled and gurgled. I felt relief, but a little hurt. I missed my connection with that warm little body. I felt very alone. My previous problems

surged back into my awareness and I experienced a lack of energy. As I walked my groceries to the car, it was as though I was walking into the night.

Marilyn recounted a simple incident, yet she was alerted to her waking dream when she became aware of a shift in her sense of self:

I started out in the experience as the rescuer: warm, caring, happy, comforting. But a shift occurred and I became the Mother: unsure, uncomfortable, questioning. Then I seemed to switch to the one who is alone with self/Self in the dark unknown.
What upset me the most was not being able to get that baby to respond to me.

Marilyn's waking dream was full of yin symbols. The grocery store is a place full of provisions for nourishment. This would seem to represent a place within Marilyn's consciousness where she had the resources to nurture herself, and she had gone there "to get supplies."

She met a mother there (who symbolized the nurturing yin force in Marilyn) who had a good relationship with her little boy (who symbolized something new that was emerging in Marilyn). But when Marilyn took the child into her arms, as though consciously assuming the role of nurturing mother, she was not able to get the child to respond to her.

Marilyn's waking dream seemed to be revealing two things. First, the experience seemed to say that she had a well-developed nurturing yin force that had access to all she needed to bring forth creative expressions of self.

Second, the experience seemed to say that Marilyn did not recognize that nurturing force in herself. So when she moved into the role of a mother, she immediately felt unsure and uncomfortable, questioning herself. Marilyn lacked confidence that she could express the mothering force.

Walking away from this situation, Marilyn felt like she was going out into the night, which seems to symbolize that she felt overwhelmed by yin rather than identified with it. As Marilyn comes to know herself as someone with the capacity to nurture, she'll be able to develop the new that is emerging in her, as a mother would nurture a child until it grows up.

Generally speaking, if we were born into a female body it is because we have much to learn about expressing yin energy. Wearing the outer "form" of yin is a reminder to develop qualities that enhance yin energy and skills that express yin energy. The challenge is to know ourselves as confident, competent, and comfortable in the yin polarity.

By the same token, if we were born into a male body we have more than likely taken on the task of learning how to express yang energy more effectively.

Eventually, however, we will want both polarities to work together. Lowell's experience points to that need for cooperation:

> A couple of months ago my friend John broke off his relationship with Doris, with whom he had been in relationship for about a year-and-a-half. Doris did not want to talk about what had happened; she just wanted to close the book on it. But John had been writing her letters.
>
> When John and I talked and he told me of his attempts to contact her, I felt angry. Sometimes I would mention

things I knew were going on in her life. John was like a puppy, eager for any word she might say about him. This also made me very angry. I didn't know why.

Lowell was especially aware of the feeling of anger that arose whenever he thought or wrote about John's behavior toward Doris. Lowell knew he was having a waking dream because of the strength of these feelings:

> It seemed like John's behavior was saying, "Take me back." I, Lowell, felt I would rather hurt her than give her the satisfaction of knowing that I felt like a victim. (As I write these words, I feel anger, and pain in my rib cage on the right side.)
> Ruth, a friend of mine, has become close to Doris in her crisis. I feel anger when they talk of John and his stumbling, hurting, and pain, like he is a wild beast they have wounded and are now stalking to make the final kill.

Lowell's waking dream was about the relationship between the two polarities, as symbolized by Lowell and John, on the yang side, and Doris and Ruth, on the yin side. It seemed that Lowell's real Self was trying to convey a message to him about his own relational dynamics, both internal and external.

Lowell considered the symbols:

> *Doris* seems to reflect somebody who was non-communicative with me: my father, my yang. She angers me because of her unwillingness to communicate, to just explain. (As a teenager I would always ask my Father why he didn't love me. He never had an answer.)

> *John* seemed to be licking up to somebody who abuses him (just as I do). I have always had trouble commu-

nicating. Maybe my father didn't trust his ability to communicate. When I say hi to women and they don't return the gesture, I feel angry, put off and pushed away. I refuse to believe any woman again. I refuse to be imprinted by them; I refuse to be yin. You can't trust them. (Having said this, the knot in my neck feels better.) I can't trust my wife; she might hurt me. I can't trust the feminine in me . . .. In sex I feel I am betraying myself. I am making myself vulnerable to something I don't trust in myself, my yin.

When Lowell tried to sort out the symbolism, he was unable to do so. Doris reminded him of his father who didn't know how to communicate. John reminded Lowell of his own difficulty with communication, as well as his father's. Lowell was finding his way to an understanding of relationships. In doing so, he was developing his yin by trusting the process, and his yang by learning to discriminate between the two forces.

Whenever we work with waking dreams, we must make room for the chaos of not-knowing. If we can make room for the process of discovery by activating yin energy, then our yang will lead us to new levels of understanding.

Lowell had identified communication as the theme of this waking dream episode. As he looked at it his experience, he could see that communication between his own yin and yang was almost nonexistent due to an innate lack of trust. Without trust between the two forces, it is almost impossible to set a creative dynamic in motion.

John's breakup with Doris became a symbol for Lowell of the gap within him between the yin and the yang. He struggled blindly in the waking dream for a clue as to what had gone wrong. Was it Doris' fault because she refused to talk about what went wrong? Was it John's fault because he wanted Doris back? What had happened?

Lowell lacked a basic understanding of the two fundamental forces. He needed to learn to identify the qualities and characteristics of each, and how they function. Then he needed to understand how the two forces cooperate in bringing something new into being, or what happens when they don't work well together. Only then will Lowell figure out what he could do to develop communication between the two polarities within himself.

Expanding the Sense of Self

When we are dreaming our way through life, we don't consciously expand and contract the sense of self. Instead we "find ourselves" in one sense of self or another. During our most vivid life experiences we are often unconscious of a large portion of the real Self. Not only do we temporarily lose sight of the many skills and qualities that we would use in other situations, but there is unacknowledged potential waiting to be discovered. It is the sense of self, at the given moment, that determines which qualities and skills we draw on and whether or not we awaken our potential. As we become conscious within our waking dreams, we learn to choose the sense of self.

Tatiana had worked a great deal with her waking dreams and was able to awaken within a vivid life experience and change it by changing her sense of self:

> It is Christmas Eve, late twilight. I am alone. Nobody is here. Sandra is too ill with pleurisy and flu, so had to cancel our Christmas Eve and Day. I am doing fine with

being alone on Christmas. I don't have the old heavy Christmas stuff from the past any more. Everything has been going well and I am telling myself how fortunate I am. For days I have been experiencing waves of gratitude and really counting and enjoying my blessings.

Tatiana was focused on her feelings of gratitude and on counting her blessings. When she was identified with being the "blessed one" she did not mind being alone on Christmas. Then her sense of self began to shift:

The twilight deepens. I feel tired, and now just the hint of All-Alone-On-Christmas-Eve comes in. There's nobody here. I begin to turn pale gray. I sit in my chair and find my ease with the present seeping away. I think that "everyone else is having together, happy times." The familiar feeling of being abandoned, left out, orphaned is mounting.

The sense of self as a "lonely, orphaned child" robbed Tatiana of her feelings of gratitude and of her awareness of her blessings. Her sense of self now encompassed different characteristics. She felt "cold, small, gray, lonely, and sad." In that self she could not enjoy Christmas.

Tatiana noticed what was happening and made a conscious choice to change her sense of self:

Then the thought "waking dream" comes in. At first I want to reject it and continue the downslide, but something stops me. I become interested in my situation. I clearly see my choices. I can just keep sliding down and create a miserable, lonely, unwanted, unloved Christmas, or I can look at the truth of my situation.
The truth is that I am not alone. It is not true that nobody is here, because I am here, and I'm someone who

knows me well, cares about me, even begins to love me.
I am not alone. I do not need to be miserable. I am not
unloved and unwanted. Several people love me and care
about me and often want to be with me.
I decide to thoroughly enjoy myself, and I do. I play my
many musics and sing mightily. I sit quietly contemplating my many gifts, inner and outer: my home, my
involvement with life, my beautiful friends, my growing
connection with Reality, my everyday pleasures, my cats
and dog, my increasing health and strength, the won-
drous help I receive from so many people and substances
to help me get well, and the clear knowledge that I have
a right to live and that I have a place on this planet. I
know that I really exist. I am filling out — dark and
light. And I am able to feel love in ever greater measure.

The shift was dramatic. Tatiana identified the new
sense of self as the "dreamer awakening." The "awakening dreamer" was identified with a whole different array
of qualities, which she labeled: warm, gay, humorous,
singing, expansive, cozy, and loving. In that sense of self
she could, and did, celebrate Christmas.

Notice that all of the qualities that appeared in this life
experience were already developed in Tatiana. However,
the "orphaned child" sense of self did not identify with
the positive aspects of her life. She could not feel happy,
because she did not recognize that she had anything in her
life to be happy about.

The "dreamer awakening," on the other hand, realized that she had been alone on Christmas in the past and
that she had felt abandoned and lonely on many occasions.
But she also realized that she didn't need to live in that
past. She identified the theme of the experience as: "Living
Christmas in the present, and feeling how I really feel, not
a fictionalized version of the situation."

As the "dreamer awakening," Tatiana told herself the truth as she knew it about her life at that moment. That was something she could not have done while identified with self as the "abandoned child."

When qualities and skills are undeveloped in us, waiting as our potential, we need to form a new sense of self that can express those qualities. We can begin to recognize our own undeveloped potential by observing ourselves in waking dream episodes. When we see what we would have wanted to express but could not, or wanted to do and didn't, we can ask ourselves what qualities or skills we would need in order to express ourselves more fully in those situations.

By reflecting on what she wasn't able to express in an interaction with her boss, Evelyn discovered that her yang polarity needed to be more fully developed:

> Dr. Koch sat quietly at the desk. I stood at the corner of it, still and stiff, and told him that the patient was a few minutes late because she had been at the lab having her blood drawn. Dr. Koch's face flushed a little and his eyes sparked as he looked straight at me. He said, "Mrs. Thomas, I want you to accommodate me and what I want. Do not accommodate the patient."
> I felt my body tightness intensify, my face burned with heat, and the skin tightened. My gut knotted and my neck stiffened.

Evelyn was conscious of her real Self seeking to communicate with her through bodily sensations. All the sensations were yang. Her body tightened, her gut knotted, her neck stiffened, and her face burned. These were all indications of yang contraction. But Evelyn wasn't able to respond to these physical messages:

> Dr. Koch spoke again, more calmly, saying that in the future I should schedule all the patients' labs and other appointments after they have seen him. I agreed with him and left his office, the tension and burning still in my face and my gut knotted and churning. My chest was tight and my throat clogged.

When Evelyn later reflected on the incident as a waking dream, she looked to see what she had left unexpressed:

> I was not assertive in telling the doctor that I did not believe I had made an error in scheduling. Many of his patients go to the lab before seeing him. I was not conscious of how unsure I felt. I thought it would have been inappropriate to differ with him. I did not express my anger at being spoken to so loudly and angrily. At this point in our interaction my sense of self was almost out the window.
> What seems key to me in this situation is my inability to express my feelings in the moment. Also key is my lack of definition of the secretarial function and my not knowing how to balance my service to the patient with my service to the doctor. I was caught in the place of being the patient's advocate. I am afraid to express myself in the face of another's anger.

What seems most important for me to do is to be clear about my functions as a secretary, to develop my knowledge of the doctor's needs and wishes, and to hone my skills in directing the patient's path through the clinic. Then I would feel in charge of my job as a first class professional just as the doctor is a first class professional in his field.

Evelyn identified several qualities that she needed to develop. She needed more assertiveness to express her point of view, more discrimination to determine what was appropriate or inappropriate in a given situation, more clarity about her job, more knowledge of the doctor's needs and wishes, and more skills in directing patients through the clinic. All of those qualities are characteristic of the yang polarity of expression: assertiveness, discrimination, clarity, knowledge, and skills in directing.

Evelyn also realized that in order to give life to those qualities she needed a more clearly defined sense of self through which to express herself. She needed to be clear about the qualities and skills that belonged to her role as medical secretary. Should she be an advocate for the patient, for example, or was her role to please only the doctor? Only with a clear sense of self as secretary would she be able to be more assertive and courageous, and more discriminating.

The work Evelyn would do to form this sense of self would also require that she bring forth more of her yang force — developing a clear pattern and then setting it in motion.

Any of us can study our waking dreams to discover how well-integrated and how well-developed the yin and yang polarities are in us. We can notice what qualities and characteristics would serve us well as we develop each polarity further. And finally, we can define a sense of self that would enable us to develop and express more of our potential.

The Balance of the Forces Within

As we become more conscious of the operation of the yin and yang within us, we are able to bring them into greater balance. That balance is established in two ways. First, by developing both polarities so that they are equally strong. And second, by practicing our expression of both forces so that they are equally active.

The balance of the two forces within stimulates our creativity. Only when the two polarities come together in a dynamic union can anything new be brought into being. The yin and yang move within us on many different levels and in many different ways. We learn to identify the yin and yang by their qualities and by their symbolic reflection in our waking dreams.

Relationships provide us with an ideal context for developing the two forces and bringing them into balance. Joyce, a woman in her fifties, had found her independent identity in mid-life through goldsmithing just at the time when her husband, nine years older, was preparing for retirement. The challenge to their pattern of interacting within their marriage was real:

> Until recently, the nine year difference in our ages hasn't been an issue. Now my husband is making retirement decisions at a time when my goldsmithing creative work is expanding. He is slowing down physically, and I want to be more active. He is content with hours of TV sports and computer games; I want to be more involved with people. . . . I sense the retirement issue will pose some problems for us that are unexpected.

Joyce was shifting toward the yang polarity, and her husband toward the yin. Concerns about the changes occurring within them and between them were surfacing in Joyce's awareness:

> As is our custom on the weekend, my husband and I were sharing a bottle of wine, having enjoyed a nice dinner for two. We were discussing the topic of retirement. At one point I said that in my experience perhaps 20 women had said that their biggest problem was loss of the use of a car. Only one car was affordable in the reduced financial situation, and the husband preempted it. The woman invariably found her life compromised in not being able to conduct her life, meet with friends, etc., as she had done before.

Joyce had wanted to discuss her growing fears about her husband's forthcoming retirement, and the moment had seemed opportune. However, she spoke of a problem friends had mentioned to her rather than speaking directly of her own concerns. Though probably only eight or nine women had told her about this problem, she was afraid her husband would discount the whole subject if she said "a few" had spoken to her, so she exaggerated the number to impress him. His response took her by surprise:

> My husband's reply was that many husbands are henpecked, don't get access to that car, and that none of *those* women would talk to *me*.

Though Joyce didn't know what her husband meant by "those" women, she was very upset that he felt "they" wouldn't speak to her. She knew women's problems to be real and felt that her husband diminished them. She got angry:

> I responded by saying that was equivalent to my reporting on twenty battered women and his counteracting with a defense of battered men. I explained that I hadn't solicited the information, but it was forthcoming from women of my age whose husbands were retired or about to. Some of these women I didn't even know.

Joyce had become involved in a conversation she never intended to have. She had wanted to discuss her own fears about the future she and her husband were facing together. Instead, she was caught up in an argument about men and women she did not even know! It was a disconcerting turn of events, to say the least.

> My husband continued to defend the henpecked husband. I was even more angry and left the table in tears. He followed, explaining that it was his job/duty to defend the other side. I agreed that might be true at work, but that at home his duty was to listen to me.
> He replied that in our situation I would get the car.
> Thinking that he was implying that he was henpecked, I said I could divorce him over that issue.
> He asked me not to shout. He went through an explanation of the relativity of the problem and the percentile difference for those in low, mid and high income levels. We would probably have two cars and therefore no problem. Perhaps the problem in our discussion was the wine, implying that I had had too much.
> He said he was a feminist and often defended women in conversations with men.

Joyce wanted to resolve the differences with her husband at the time, but she did not see a way to do so. She decided to work with the experience as a waking dream and see if that would give her some insight. She hoped that she could wake up within the dream:

> When he said that I would get the car, I felt he implied
> that he was henpecked. I was shocked that I used the
> word "divorce." I've never even thought it before. I've al-
> ways felt we had an equal marriage, and I was suddenly
> feeling all that to be a sham.
>
> I'm becoming more of a feminist as I get older, as I see
> my three daughters struggle with sexist discrimination in
> the workplace and at school. I believe that the standoff
> between men and women can be changed with love,
> understanding and empathy. I know that we all have to
> begin "at home." I want to be listened to and to have
> my opinions valued. I, like everyone else, have a unique
> experience in my life.
>
> I feel heart heavy. After 31 years of marriage, I actu-
> ally said to him, "I could divorce you over this." *Wow!*
> I thought we had worked out an understanding about
> how husbands and wives relate best to one another. Now
> he seemed to be implying that we were just like all the
> others, and I felt if that were so, then all the work we
> had done was for nothing.

After several pages of reflection in her journal, Joyce realized that the content of the discussion had concealed more than it had revealed: "He didn't hear me speak about retirement, but about who should get the car!" She knew that she needed to take a very different approach if she was to communicate to him her deep desire that their relation-ship, even in retirement, be an equal partnership.

She decided to try to improve her communication with her husband by setting a new pattern in motion im-mediately:

> I need to talk to him more about noncontroversial issues

so we have a pattern of dialogue in place when issues arise. I asked him to talk with me tonight before dinner and will continue doing that.

Learning to carry on a genuine dialogue when there were no strong issues at stake would make it easier to address difficult questions in the same manner. Joyce also saw that she needed to gather information from him ("I need to sound him out on the 'henpecked' issue"), and to share more of her thoughts with him so that he would know "where I am coming from."

Joyce became aware that she needed to find her courage and strength even in the face of the yang logic which she often found overwhelming. "I need to learn how to handle myself when discussion turns to argument." Learning how to express her strong feelings without resorting to anger would be to change a lifelong pattern that had been reflected in her parents' relationship. And learning to ask her husband what he meant by his words would help her stay clear of her own interpretations and misjudgments. She needed to build relational skills that would support her objective, which was to have better communication with her husband. Joyce looked again at her part in the dynamic:

I have never found a way to discuss unpleasant issues with him. I'm usually inundated with photocopied documents on issues, but no conversation. I think he feels he can pay for anything I need, so I shouldn't have any problems in life.

I have learned to pay attention when my emotions are aroused. The issues are usually important to me. But I do need to learn how to handle myself when discussion turns to argument.

A synchronistic phone call while I was working on this

waking dream alerted me to a radio program called "The World According to Women — the Woman's Voice." It outlined that at about age eleven, a girl learns not to speak out but to internalize her words along with her feelings in order to be popular, to fit in, or just to survive in some cases. I survived. Now I have to learn how to speak out.

Retirement will be an issue for us. I will probably have to take the lead in discussions and planning. It will be difficult for him in that for the first time in his life, he will need me more than I need him.

The process of dealing with the experience as a waking dream worked. The anger is gone. I didn't have to go through it all with him again. I do have to be more aware in the future.

In the months that followed, Joyce was able to build a genuine partnership with her husband. She continued to initiate conversations when there were no big issues to deal with. She invited him to support her in her growing goldsmithing business. She practiced speaking out when she felt strongly about something, but without calling up anger.

The result was that Joyce felt more confident as she awakened her yang energy and noticed her husband supporting her with more yin energy. A new balance had emerged between them that represented the equality Joyce had longed for in her marriage and the growing balance of the two forces within. It had been important for Joyce to wake up so that she could set change in motion in her primary relationship and in herself.

Whereas Joyce had needed greater balance between her own yang and her husband's yin, Janice was seeking to develop a closer cooperation between her own inner yin and yang. She had lost confidence in her yang force through a series of events and had not felt able to provide visionary leadership for her organization. Over a period of months, she practiced trusting her yang and bringing it forth with greater strength. Then she had this experience:

> I was having dinner with my husband Bryan and with Jerry and his wife Kathy. Jerry and Kathy are psychologists who specialize in consulting work with companies and organizations. I approached them to assist Bryan and me with getting the Personal Development Center back on track, that is, functioning well and in the black. Jerry and Kathy had offered to help us at no charge. Jerry said, "It's like this . . . life has been very good to us and we have no trouble giving back. We think you are doing something of value in the community and we see this as our community service."
> We had a cohesive meeting. It felt like we were all in deep rapport, highly respecting each other. At one point Jerry said, "We will be your support team now."

Janice interpreted this vivid life experience as a confirmation that she had made great progress in bringing her forces into balance. In describing her sense of self she said:

> I felt centered, strong, capable, supported. I felt equal with the others in the dream, like we are going to do something wonderful together. I felt safe.

This sense of self enabled her to take in the affirmation the waking dream offered her. When reflecting on Jerry and Kathy as symbols, she wrote:

Jerry and Kathy represent perfectly balanced yin/yang energy. They do a dance with each other and they are in perfect step. Furthermore, they are dancing with Bryan and me, teaching us how to give and receive, receive and give. Bryan and I know something about this and we do it to a certain extent. Now our dance is being refined.

In this experience, Janice recognized the two couples, Janice and her husband, and Jerry and Kathy, as symbols for the growing balance of the forces within herself. As a result, Janice felt renewed hope:

I want a fresh start. I want to leave the past behind. I want to learn how to be an effective leader. I will put everything I have into refining my "dance steps" [that is, the creative dynamic between the yin and yang forces]. I will do it with love. I will be open and willing to learn.

It is important to have a balance of the two forces within ourselves. With a well-developed yang force we feel capable of moving forward, initiating the new, imprinting others with our ideas or insights, setting patterns for interactions, spurring people on, and offering guidance and direction. With a well-developed yin force, we are capable of responding to what comes into our lives, of being receptive to the initiations of others, of lending our energy to bringing the new into being, and of patiently nurturing what is emerging.

Not only do we express these forces in our interactions with others, but they are active in the creative process within us. We register insights that provide the yang impulses for projects, and in yin we are receptive and responsive to those insights and ideas and bring them to fruition. The two forces in cooperation enable us to give form to what began as an intangible idea or image.

Balancing the driving forces in our lives — the forces that determine how we live on a daily and weekly basis, and through the cycles of our lives — rounds out our experience. In our lives we move through seasons, like nature moves through seasons. And we are likely to discover that the balance of our own energies shifts from one season to another. The balance also shifts from one part of a week or month to another.

We need to adapt to those changing rhythms. If the work by which we are earning our living is predominantly yin, we will want to consciously adopt hobbies that are yang. We can do this according to the overall characteristics of the work and the hobby, or we can do it according to the components of the Self that are activated. If our work is yang on the mental level (requiring a great deal of intellectual activity) and yin on the physical level (demanding that we sit at a desk for hours at a time) we might choose a yang physical exercise program (such as running or weightlifting) and a yin mental activity (like reading fiction or meditating) to occupy our free time.

Life is a waking dream because the real Self, represented by the most expanded state of our energy fields (yin) and the invisible guiding pattern within them (yang), is seeking to awaken. *Each vivid life experience is a wake-up call asking us to expand our sense of self, to incorporate more aspects of the real Self into our consciousness of who we are,* the aspects that have remained undeveloped in us or are not yet fully integrated into our sense of self.

Our current state of unfolding lies somewhere between the various senses of self from which we act in any given situation and the potential represented by the real

Self. Our challenge is to merge into one integrated whole three ways of knowing ourselves — as senses of self, as observers of our own life processes, and as the embodiment of qualities and skills. As we do this we will become increasingly flexible in our ability to function in the world without losing our sense of who we are in Reality.

As we awaken, we will learn to hold both the yin and yang of self-awareness in the focus of our consciousness at the same time. The yin awareness is the most expanded way we know ourselves, including all the skills and attributes we have developed and come to know as "ours." The yang awareness is the focused, functional sense of self that we take on for specific contexts and interactions.

Having developed a way to hold that dual focus, we will be able to consciously interact with others without falling into identification with a shrunken sense of self. Our waking dream experience will be one of cooperation and harmony with people we encounter rather than of alienation, separation, competition, struggle, and pain.

The awakening process will affect the way we live our lives, and the living of our lives will facilitate the awakening process. The way we express ourselves will change the nature of our waking dreams. As the Sufi Kabir Edmund Helminski so eloquently puts it:

> Spiritual attainment is a fundamental transformation of the "I" from a separate, limited, and contracted identity into a rich and infinite one. It is a movement from separation to union.
>
> One of the first steps in this process is to observe and understand the chaotic and fragmented nature of the ordinary self and to understand that a very practical integration and harmony can be achieved. This integrated self is the drop that contains the ocean. At the dimen-

sionless center of our identity is the creative potential of Cosmic Mind.[2]

Kabbalist thought holds that individuals possess their own spiritual destiny, or *tikun*, and can learn to discern the hidden patterns and workings of the divine wisdom through a careful observation of events in ordinary life.

— *Ray Grasse*

It is a vast dream, dreamed by a single being; but in such a way that all the dream characters dream too. Hence, everything interlocks and harmonizes with everything else.

— *Arthur Schopenhauer*

Chapter Eight

Life Themes

When we are awake and conscious, we can function with purpose and a sense of direction. If we know why we are here, we can live our lives in the ways that will be fulfilling.

When we are asleep and living life as a waking dream, we are not acting from a conscious sense of purpose, so patterns emerge that have been imprinted in our psyches. We give them life through our self-expression. These patterns fulfill purposes and objectives of which we are not conscious. They may either conflict with our fundamental life purposes or unconsciously fulfill them.

As we reflect on our waking dreams, we can uncover many of those unconscious patterns. It is helpful to name the theme of our waking dreams, to capture the principle focus in a word or phrase. Often, themes will reveal the unconscious objectives being played out in the event. These themes can help us discover what we were unconsciously trying to accomplish. Repetitive themes often reveal overall patterns, eventually showing us a unifying purpose that has determined the course of our lives.

Identifying themes in waking dreams is crucial for those of us who want to live more meaningful and Self-directed lives. Uncovering a unifying life purpose gives us a compelling reason for living. A life purpose is large enough to give meaning to everything we do from birth to death. It reveals the nature of our deepest longing, what we are here to learn. Life purposes are profound, such as to know God, to know the truth, to be of service, and to love and be loved. They reflect our orientation to life's biggest questions.

Life objectives contribute to the fulfillment of life purposes. They are more specific aspirations, but are large enough to infuse periods of our lives with deep meaning. Life objectives are building blocks, such as to balance the yin and yang within, to learn to love unconditionally, to develop creative expression, and to trust the life process.

We often team up in life with people who are working on complementary life purposes or objectives. We get caught up in the same experiences yet dream different waking dreams. We find that more than one lifelong theme can be played out in a shared experience.

Julie described a vivid life experience she had with her close friend Rose:

> At 3:15 P.M., a phone call came from Rose who was speaking from a phone booth on a downtown street. The background noise was so strong I had difficulty hearing her, and she, me. We were both shouting to be heard. Would I meet her and give her a ride to the class we were to attend that evening?
>
> She had made a similar request the week before and I had found the rush hour traffic of downtown very difficult and stressful. I did not want to do it again, and yet the difficulty of communicating and the suddenness of the request led me to follow an old pattern and say, "Yes." We agreed to meet at the west entrance of the Royal York Hotel, where the buses depart for the airport.

Julie ignored a communication within herself. Had she followed her feelings, she would have said no. But as she acted out an old pattern of saying yes, she set the theme for her waking dream: "The Rescuer becomes the Victim." She observed later, "I knew that I wanted to say no to the invitation to meet. I knew I was receiving Rose's message as more of a demand than a choice. To have refused would have felt more like 'disobedience' than a right to do what I had previously planned."

Julie had inadvertently fallen into a waking dream by saying yes rather than no.

> I was there early, before 4:30, and I waited until 5:45 P.M. The sidewalks were packed with commuters and there were buses pulling in and out, so that I could not leave the car for long, because I was parked illegally. Twice I walked to the front of the hotel, but there was no sign of Rose. I thought she might have been delayed, because there was a partial strike of transit workers. I thought she might have been in an accident.
> Finally I left, with very little time to grab a bite of supper and reach the class on time. As I drove past the restaurant where we were to eat, to my surprise, Rose and Robert, a classmate, were sitting near the window, waving me to come in.

Rose's description of the event reveals her different perspective:

> I was in the subway, on my way to a Voice Workshop, and wishing I could have some time beforehand with Julie. Why not phone her and ask if she'd like to pick me up downtown, as she had done the previous week?

> She agreed, but altered the meeting place. I got there
> and waited - and waited - and waited. She didn't come.
> Somehow we'd missed each other.

Rose was unaware of Julie's stressful experience in
traffic the previous week, and was simply eager for some
time to share with her friend. That gave Rose's waking
dream a very different tone from Julie's:

> I stood waiting until my head was swimming with diz-
> ziness: rush-hour crowds swirled past as offices closed
> for the night. I felt lost and upset and anxious: What
> had happened to Julie? How would I ever find her in the
> huge, rushing crowd? The only thing I could think of
> was to get on a streetcar and go along to the destination:
> the little restaurant where we often have a snack before
> the class, and hope that she would be there.
> But she wasn't there. Robert, one of the class members,
> was there, and I sat with him and told him of my misad-
> venture and upset.
> At last I saw her coming and felt relieved: she was okay
> and we could work out what went wrong.

Rose described an almost identical experience of traffic and confusion, and concern about her friend. The two
were living the same vivid experience, but what it meant
to each of them, as they revealed, was very different.

Rose said this about what happened next:

> Julie came in and attacked me furiously, taking for grant-
> ed that I had stood her up purposely, and that it was all
> my fault by deliberate intention. On and on, accusing
> and scolding. She was not interested in finding out what
> happened, only in punishing me for her discomfort.

Rose felt attacked. She had a history of trying to please her mother and of fearing that she would not "get it right." When Julie began to express her feelings, Rose took them in as judgment and felt attacked. She felt like a child being punished for being deliberately troublesome and difficult. She commented later, "I saw my mother's face and heard her scolding voice."

Julie described the same moment like this:

> A wave of hurt and anger enveloped me. I felt betrayed and used. My first words to Rose were, "There's got to be a good explanation for this." Rose replied that she had waited and waited, how cold she was, and how much she had suffered, and I had not come.

Julie's pattern could be described as a rescuer-victim-persecutor triangle.[1] She said "yes" to Rose's request, acting from her sense of self as rescuer. Yet when Rose didn't show up, she moved into a victim sense of self, feeling used and betrayed. Then when she saw Rose in the restaurant, Julie instantly became the persecutor, lashing out to put Rose in her place. To Julie, Rose was not a belligerent child, but a cruel adult who had "done her in."

As the scene unfolded, layer after layer of miscommunication and misunderstanding occurred because each woman was deep into her own waking dream. They were relating to each other as symbols, not as real people. How they each perceived and heard things was quite different. Rose reported:

> As Julie went on I realized that the mistake had been mine: I had waited at the wrong corner. I told her this and that I was truly upset at having made such a silly mistake. Julie did not want to hear that either. Her rage

continued and she appeared not to believe what I had said.

In her waking dream, Rose was the child trying to placate a raging mother who did not hear or believe her. Julie remembered it like this:

> When Rose realized that she had mistakenly waited at the front of the hotel, and not where we had agreed, she did not apologize, or say she was sorry. She said she was not going to be made a victim. My little self felt that if there was to be any talk of victim, she deserved that spot, and I began to cry, deep wracking sobs, in the restaurant. I covered my face with my hands and couldn't stop.

In her waking dream, Julie did not want to be displaced as the victim. She quickly slipped back into that sense of self to safeguard her perception that Rose was the persecutor.

We do not need to know the end of the story to get the point. These two friends had to wake up from their individual waking dreams before they could even begin to sort out what had happened in reality. Julie was caught in a repetitive pattern of experiencing herself as a victim. Nothing Rose could have said would have changed that. Julie the victim could only have viewed her as a rescuer or a persecutor. When Rose tried to play the victim role, Julie would not allow it. Being victim was Julie's specialty.

Rose, on the other hand, was playing out a childhood pattern which she had never resolved to her satisfaction. Whenever she made a mistake, she immediately felt like the child who had displeased her mother. The theme was: "It's all my fault." So Rose of course felt responsible, and made every attempt to make amends, as if to placate her mother. Rose's pattern was similar enough to Julie's that they could dream their waking dreams together very compatibly, for according to Rose, "My mother operated in the victim mode. That was how she manipulated and controlled me, by appealing to my pity and my desire to help."

As the two women unraveled their waking dreams, they discovered that the messages each needed to hear from within Self prevented them from listening to each other. Julie needed to develop a sense of herself as a person of strength who could make her own choices, saying yes or no to others according to her own purposes and objectives. Rose needed to learn to love herself when she made mistakes, and to realize that love is not earned by being perfect; it is a gift from another. While they were busy building these qualities, they went on to have many other vivid life experiences together, each woman living her own waking dream. This is a common occurrence in close relationships.

When Julie and Rose become sufficiently conscious of their repetitive waking dream episodes and clearly identify the themes, they will be able to restate the themes as life objectives. For example, Julie might restate her life theme "becoming the victim" as the life objective "to respond to inner directives rather than react to outer stimuli." Such an objective would enable her to make choices based on what she wants, rather than trying to second guess what other persons want, need, or demand. By focusing on her inner motivation she can stay in contact with her power to choose, and she will not fall into the rescuer-victim-persecutor triangle.

Rose might change her life theme "it's all my fault

and I must make amends" to the objective "to trust others to deal with their own feelings." This objective would enable her to let go of the feeling that she always needs to make things right for other people. Instead, she would be able to act according to her own feelings, to acknowledge her own pain and distress, and to take action on her own behalf. Rose was able to live out most of this new pattern in this interaction with Julie, but she wasn't able to stay with it. She slipped into feeling like a child.

Jason, like Julie, had lived many vivid life experiences in his sense of self as victim. Through his waking dream work and other spiritual practices, he had been chipping away at the patterns of thought that caused him to identify with the feelings and characteristics of "victim." One day he determined to make a change:

> I woke up on a Saturday morning feeling tired, in conflict, angry, and depressed. I wanted to shake it off, but at the same time I wanted resolution to my feelings. Obviously, work had once again crawled with me into the weekend, and I felt determined to let it go.

Jason awakened within his waking dream. He recognized the feelings that accompany the victim sense of self and he resolved to change the course of the dream. By consulting his wife — who was a symbol for his inner yin — he initiated cooperation between his fundamental forces. We was looking for a creative change that would not only free him from his feelings, but resolve his inner conflict:

> I told Kimberly that I was obsessing about my relationship with Carl, an employee who had been working

closely with me for the past two years in setting up our Center. I was angry at him for "flexing his muscles" in my office on Friday with his concerns and criticisms. I had had enough of his pressure, his pushiness, and his constant comment on how I was running the agency.

Jason was expressing his thoughts and feelings, which was an acknowledgment of the internal communication going on between the real Self and his sense of self of the moment. His relational struggle with Carl was long-standing, and he had tried nearly every approach he knew to make things work between them. He hoped that his wife could help him to see a way out:

> Kim suggested that I see our therapist with Carl and see what could be done. It didn't feel right to me. I crawled back into bed with my thoughts still pounding away in a circular fashion.

Jason was still listening to himself as he consulted his wife. He was not asking her to decide for him what he needed to do. Rather, he was hoping she could help him discover his own right action through the mirror of her suggestions:

> Kim then returned and said, "There is another option, you know. You could just call it quits with him."
> *Yes, yes, yes.* That is just the suggestion I wanted to hear. I had had enough! Kim had given me the affirmation I obviously was seeking to go ahead and honor my feelings and act upon them.

Kimberly's words resonated with the feelings Jason was having. His energy moved from the yin polarity (represented by Kim), in which he was being receptive to the various messages within himself, to the yang polarity which would enable him to initiate something new to replace his victim pattern:

> I decided to take action and ask him to leave the organization. I was both frightened and excited. I felt a deep resolution within me. This felt right for me.

Jason had found a way out of a repetitive waking dream. He had empowered himself through conscious choice-making.

> I was in a contracted sense of self in the beginning of this waking dream. I was the young child needing permission to do what I wanted to do, even though it seemed like a bad thing, an impossible thing for me to do. I was being the victim of powerful feelings that I was not owning, of a relationship that felt out of my control, and of the fear of doing what I wanted to do in spite of the consequences.
> By the end of the dream, I felt very expanded, as if everything was possible. I was an adult again. I was ready to honor my feelings, act on my best judgment, and take whatever action was necessary to move beyond my difficult feelings and into resolution.

Jason described the theme of this waking dream episode as "taking charge of myself and realizing I am not a victim and can make decisions based upon what seems right to me." Jason could actually adopt this theme as an overall objective for his life as a way of obviating any return to his victim sense of self. He might state his objective as "to take charge of myself."

Once Jason had written up this waking dream, he saw

that he had, in fact, "taken charge of himself" at several cardinal points in his life:

> Leaving my college girlfriend; telling my mother I was not going to Christmas Eve services; leaving to go out West via my thumb; leaving Catholic Charities; leaving the agency before that; deciding to get married.

Examining his experience as a waking dream helped Jason to consciously claim a new sense of self as "capable adult." He was then free to embrace his ability to experience and identify strong feelings and to respond to those feelings by taking creative action on his own authority.

Tracing a Life Theme

Identifying the major themes that run through our lives can help us to live more consciously. Aware of our life themes, we can begin to cooperate with objectives that express the yang pattern in the real Self. And this will help us to discover more quickly the lessons we are here to learn.

Kourtni was just beginning to walk a spiritual path. She had longed to live more consciously, but had been focused on building her career and establishing her family. She signed up for a class in Life As A Waking Dream, intent on learning as much as she could as fast as she could. When she heard the story of her early life dream up to the age of seven read to the class she was deeply moved:

> It is 1:00 A.M. I am listening to the class tapes as I drive home from work. I am weary to the bones from a long and full day. Finally I am home. I choose to stay in the

car to listen to one more of the waking dream reports.
My head drops back against the headrest and my body
relaxes heavier into the car's seat. Half awake, half
asleep, I realize that I am hearing my own story.
Tears fill my eyes . . .

In her weariness, Kourtni had gone very yin while
she listened. In her receptivity, she heard her own story as
if it were someone else's waking dream. She opened her
consciousness wide enough to allow a new awareness:

[As a child] I had needed to be held and enfolded, but
my brothers had needed it more. This need to be enfolded still surfaces. It is not a comfortable feeling for me. I
was tearful for the little girl who has grown up and is still
afraid of "not being good enough," and of burdening
others. . . . Weakness [had always been] dangerous.
What I don't know: Could I let my mother or father
enfold me? Could I hold and comfort them? Am I still
afraid to need another, afraid my needs will be draining
to another? Am I afraid that my needs will reveal that I
am weak? . . .
I have often been reluctant to ask for help from my
intimate friends or my husband - not wanting to burden
them, not wanting them to think that I need them, or
that I can't handle it myself.

Kourtni realized that she had uncovered a life theme
in her first waking dream report! The theme was "Denying
my own needs." She tried to translate it into a life objective, and these were her first attempts: "accept my needs
for affection and attention;" "acknowledge my needs;" and
"make my needs known to self and others."

Only a month later, Kourtni fully lived out her life
theme of "denying my own needs" in a major waking

dream episode. As she explored it in her journal she saw
how many things she needed to learn in order to accept,
acknowledge, and make her needs known.

> I dreamed that my father-in-law, known to my children
> as "Big Daddy," called from his home in Texas and
> announced that he would arrive that very evening to
> stay five days. He was contemplating leaving his very
> stressful job and he needed "to get away, to play with his
> grandchildren, and to rest."
> My husband, Wes, was delighted, for it had been three
> years since he had been with his parents. I, too, was
> delighted. Yet, I also felt the air become heavy and press
> down on me. I was in the middle of a difficult work
> schedule of thirteen days without a day off. Further, I
> had to cancel Wes's and my plans for our only night out
> in four months.

Kourtni was only vaguely aware, at first, of the onset
of her life theme, of denying her own needs. She felt "the
air become heavy." Then she noticed signals from her body,
and she immediately responded to her old family message
that "weakness is dangerous:"

> I felt my facial muscles tighten. I felt as though a rock
> were sinking down through my mid-chest and abdomen.
> I tried to stop the feeling, afraid my husband might see
> it. I confronted myself with the question, "Why can't
> you be more flexible and easygoing? Why can't your first
> reaction include the fun and warmth and sharing of his
> visit, rather than the work and disruption and exhaus-
> tion of his visit?"

Kourtni's sense of self was interfering with the communication from the real Self. Her physical sensations were

trying to snap her out of her role of "Polite Hostess." She needed to accept that she had needs, and make them known to her husband and father-in-law. But a critical voice within lulled Kourtni back into her waking dream:

> Sunday, his first day here, I worked a thirteen-hour day at the hospital. Wes took his dad and our children to my brother's country home for a birthday party. . . . Apparently they had a great time.
> They arrived home shortly after I did at 7:30 P.M. When I was informed that they had not eaten dinner, I again felt the internal tightening as a confirmation that this visit was going to be exhausting for me.

Kourtni's body was sending her a strong message: It was time to make her needs known. But she stayed in her shrunken sense of self:

> I launched into high gear. Wes remained his usual steady-paced self through dinner, children's baths, two loads of laundry, bedtime stories, lullabies and hugs. Then after the kitchen was cleaned up, lunches were made and clothes folded, we transformed our two-desk study into a bedroom, removing all books and papers needed for tomorrow's work. Big Daddy comfortably sat in his chair and read magazines.
> In my dream, each day seemed the same. He relaxed in his chair, dozing, reading, talking with the children when they went to him. He did not offer to help, nor did he come into the kitchen area to visit with me, nor did he initiate interaction with the kids.

Naturally, Kourtni's resentment began to build as she poured out her energies on behalf of everyone else without acknowledging her own needs. Finally, her feelings spilled over:

Finally I asked Wes to help me a bit more, even though I knew he was also exhausted physically (maybe not emotionally, however). I asked him to help his father show more attention to our daughter to help balance his obvious pleasure with our son.

This latter request came bursting from me when we had a brief moment alone in the laundry room. I had a split-second warning to censor it or soften it, but I was so upset by Big Daddy's unconscious bias of attention to our son that I let my concern and feelings stand on their own. Wes heard it with equal concern and stated, "I will try to get him more involved with Marcia."

Kourtni had actually spoken of her own needs, but only in the guise of asking something for her daughter. She did not express the remainder of her real feelings:

I wanted Big Daddy to acknowledge me; yet I didn't know for what. I had been dutiful, hard-working, and a great organizer. I had taken him around town, to lunch, and even to the airport to arrange his ticket so he could stay an extra day. Though I wanted to be acknowledged as the loving wife of his son, loving mother of his grand-children, and as a caring daughter-in-law, I felt he may have only seen my organizational skills and my endur-ance for a nineteen-hour workday.

When she stepped back to examine this waking dream, Kourtni saw her life theme shining through. She had been worn down by the circumstances until she was forced to acknowledge her needs. She wrote:

I was awakened to my anger and distress (partially ex-pressed to Wes, in regard to Big Daddy's little attention to our daughter).

> I was disappointed in myself that I was revealing my
> sense of stress. I did not want this mild, sweet, gentle
> man, father of my husband, to feel he was a burden, an
> inconvenience, or an imposition.
> I was overwhelmed by all that I needed to manage and
> accomplish. I wanted to give Wes the gift of being with
> his father in the evenings, but finally exhausted, I had to
> ask for his help.

Kourtni's request for help, however, was minimal
and indirect — she asked for only a fraction of the help
she needed from Wes, and only on behalf of her daughter.
Wes (who symbolized her own yang) was responsive and
took action on her behalf. But, more importantly, Kourtni
knew that she had much more to learn. She reflected on
how her understanding of the fundamental polarities might
be of help:

> Big Daddy may be a mirror for my potential for burnout.
> During this visit he was in yin energy, and I was in yang,
> which could have worked well if I were less pressured.
> Is this yin [of which I was so judgmental, represented by
> Big Daddy] part of my fear and reluctance to more fully
> embrace my own yin?

There was much to reflect on. Kourtni was critical of Big Daddy for many things - "I wanted him to be
more sensitive to his son's needs for work-time, to show
more initiative with his grandchildren. I wanted him to
acknowledge me."

She described him as "unassertive, exhausted by
his high-stress work, unhelpful, uninitiating, quiet, unin-
volved." Some of these yin qualities were also Kourtni's
qualities, but her sense of self wouldn't allow her to manifest them. She was also exhausted by her high-stress work,

yet she identified with being organized, directive, judging, and willful, qualities that are far more yang.

Kourtni also realized that she couldn't utilize the qualities she most needed, because she couldn't admit to needing them in the first place. She wanted to be able to relate warmly to Wes's father, but instead she felt taken advantage of.

In fact, she took advantage of herself. Kourtni drove herself unmercifully from her yang polarity, not acknowledging her yin at all. Her words about Big Daddy's inattention to her daughter were another attempt by the real Self to wake Kourtni up to her own need — she needed to go more yin, to give herself more time and attention. All her energy had been poured into her yang.

To seize this learning opportunity, Kourtni needed to translate her life theme, "Denying my own needs," into a life objective. She might have restated it: "To respond to my needs with the same sensitivity I show to others, and to ask for and receive help whenever I need it." To live out this objective, Kourtni needed to learn how to go yin, to become receptive, and to allow others to wait on her the way she had waited on Big Daddy.

Urgent Messages Regarding Life Themes

Doris, a thirty-eight-year-old back in school to earn her degree as a school psychologist, was helping to pay her tuition by giving massages. She had a vivid life experience that not only revealed a life theme, but also constituted an urgent wake-up call:

I had to attend an all-day workshop, from nine A.M. to ten P.M., to renew my massage license. Arriving at the school at 8:55 A.M. I found a note with a change of location and a map. I had vowed to practice patience that day, so I calmly set off for the new location.

Doris had set out with a conscious intention to be patient. An unexpected turn of events quickly threw her off her conscious course and into a familiar pattern of reaction that was threatening to her health and well-being:

I knew the building by name, but followed the map anyway, which turned out to be incorrect. Finally, I parked near the building I know with that name, but the workshop wasn't there. Walking to the address itself (five blocks away), I found another building with the same name. It was now 9:30 A.M. and, patience aside, I was mad. The title of the workshop was "Breaking the Cycle of Stress," and I even imagined the whole experience was a setup.

Doris's first wake-up call was the strong feeling that arose in her. She did not, however, see what the anger was calling to her attention. Instead, she imagined that the workshop planners had somehow "set her up" to facilitate the theme of the workshop on stress.

This kind of imagination, which attributes motives to other people with no basis, puts us into a deeper sleep-state instead of helping us to awaken. As long as Doris focused on the content of her waking dream - on the events, and on the workshop planners and what "they" were doing or not doing - she wasn't able to see what the experience was revealing to her.

I couldn't contain my anger while registering. I wanted
to calm down quickly (to practice patience), but when
I found out everyone else had been called about the
change of location and I hadn't been, there went that
idea! Of course I eventually settled in (after some deep
breathing), but was not happy with the workshop. With
thirty people attending, demonstrations were tedious,
complicated, and almost impossible to remember.
Though I wanted to renew my license, I begrudged
spending my time and money on what this day was offering me. It was a very long day.

Doris went through the entire day in her disgruntled
state and got very little out of the training. This she also
ascribed to "the workshop." Thus far she had been living as
if life was happening *to* her, as if she had little or no choice
about her experience, an attitude which characterizes the
waking dream state of consciousness.

Doris did not awaken within her waking dream. And
perhaps because the real Self had an urgent message for
her, the day ended dramatically:

When I reached my car at 10:30 P.M., I discovered the
driver's side window had been completely smashed in. I
stared at it a few minutes finding it very hard to believe
what my eyes were seeing. I yelled for the security guard.
He came and very apologetically told me two men had
done it about two hours before. I experienced a brief
moment of anger. I demanded the security guard call the
police *now* and got mad when he couldn't, at first, get
through. A whole day had been wasted and now I still
couldn't go home.
Then I realized one of my psychological test kits was
missing. When I mentioned it to the guard he said they
had carried off two bags.

By now Doris had received a strong warning. Her experience seemed to be saying, "If you don't pay attention and wake up, I will have to break through (the window) to you (the car) in a way that could harm your physical body." Even the security guard (perhaps a symbol for her own immune system) was not able to prevent the break-in by two yang forces taking for themselves what belonged to the yin.

But still Doris didn't awaken. She was too caught up in the content of the dream, focused on everything as external to Self, and busying herself with her private world thoughts about it all.

> I began to think about what this experience would cost me in time: getting home even later tonight, cleaning up the glass inside the car, getting the glass replaced, dealing with the insurance company; in money: deductible on insurance, replacing the test kit; in anxiety: telling the director [of her internship program] I had lost a test kit.

Doris perpetuated her dream-state by expecting to feel anxiety over telling her director about the test kit. In stepping up this anxiety, for the first time Doris *appeared* to take responsibility for some of her waking dream by planning to say she lost a test kit. However, the truth was that she wasn't responsible for losing it! Thus, her dream went on:

> As I waited for the police, I began to cry. The tears just poured out of me. They weren't angry tears; I wasn't sure what was behind them - frustration and sadness, perhaps. They just streamed out of me. I was not thinking at all, I was only crying. When I did begin to think

again the thoughts were, "What am I supposed to be doing, what is this all about? I know this is a waking dream, but what should I be doing? I can't think of what to do." So I just kept crying. I felt something was being released in me, but I didn't know what.

At last Doris began to break through. The real Self was speaking to her through her instinctive tears. Those tears were so powerful, that they forced Doris to ask herself what she was supposed to be doing. At last she recognized she was caught in a waking dream, but she didn't know what to do about it. At least she was living out her confusion, and thus communicating with herself.

After making my report to the police (it was about 11:30 P.M.), I decided to take the quick way to the expressway. I guess I was still upset. I became disoriented and got lost in the worst section of the city. There have been many car-jackings in that area and with no driver's side window I was completely vulnerable. I found myself on an almost traffic-deserted street with men milling about in the street and on the sidewalks. I tried to be invisible, but some saw me, called out to me, and approached the car. I seldom experience fear for my physical safety, but I was scared. I drove (slowly) through a red light and then mistakenly turned down a one-way street the wrong way. Finally I shouted at myself to stop panicking, to look closely at where I was, and to think about the choices I had to make to get where I wanted to be. I finally found my way.

Doris's waking dream turned into a nightmare. It seemed that the real Self was making an all-out effort to awaken. This can be seen as an act of love, even though Doris didn't view it that way at the time. The real Self needed to break free from its identification with the stress-filled sense of self that was endangering Doris's health. Nightmares are anxiety-producing, but they are hard to ignore, and usually cause the dreamer to wake up because of the extreme discomfort.

Doris did fear for her physical safety, attributing it to her outer circumstances. But finally she shouted a message out loud to herself: *"Stop panicking, look closely at where you are, think about the choices you need to make to get where you want to be!"*

Externally, the message was about Doris finding her way to the expressway so she could get home. Internally, Doris was trying to tell herself that anxiety was blurring her vision, confusing her. If she had looked closely at where she was, and thought about the choices she needed to make about how she wanted to live her life, she could have changed her approach to many things. In the process she might have found her way to the path (expressway) of awakening.

Later Doris looked to see what the real Self was asking of her through this waking dream:

> I've been aware of needing to change my pattern of eating to handle the stress in my life, but I just keep putting it off because it's connected to so many other issues in my life, and it feels so powerful.
> The anxiety that I seek to dispel with the food seems so uncontrollable and overpowering that I have to try to quiet it down, put out the fire, cover it up, or "who knows what" will happen. How do I tackle a problem that is so large that it seems monstrous?

Doris felt her anxiety was so large that she could not address it. Her waking dream reflected this in several ways.

First, the group in her workshop on how to break the cycle of stress was very large. Second, the demonstrations of how to break the cycle of stress were tedious, complicated, and almost impossible to remember. Third, her test kit was a symbol of how Doris could measure her true state and assess what was needed to make changes. It was stolen, just as her aggressive reactions to anxiety, fueled by her anger and impatience, had been robbing Doris of her ability to change her patterns.

Once Doris realized she was caught in a waking dream from which she could awaken, she began to look for the "how." She was motivated to recognize new possibilities, even though her problem seemed "monstrous." Not to look for a way to change would be to let the cycle of anxiety and stress continue.

Doris could, from within her waking dream, learn to reduce her stress and rechannel that energy now being expended in anxiety. Or she could awaken from her ongoing stress episodes to realize that she is not a prisoner of their content:

> In the last two to three weeks of school I had twelve projects due. They were planned out, most were started, and I was confident I could complete them, but I found it hard to admit that. I saw myself sitting on a fence, wanting to be "crazy" with the situation (like usual) and at the same time wanting to acknowledge my plans and sense of control. To admit I was handling the pressure and stress seemed almost impossible.
> I felt that old feeling: "If I admit I'm doing well, people will hold me to it; I can't then lose it later and receive any help or comfort from them." I did tell M., finally, but I continued to be pulled between the old pattern of losing it and a new one of holding my own.

Breaking old habits within waking dreams is hard work, but it can be done. Doris took on the task and stayed awake as she did. She observed herself and noticed the power the old habits had to pull her back:

> An extension was given on a paper originally due last Saturday. With an eye toward the five things due this week, I decided I needed to finish it by Saturday. On Friday I heard myself thinking, "I hope I get this done tonight." Alarms went off. What is this hope business! Either my purpose is to finish this tonight or it isn't, but hope has nothing to do with it. Fully awake, I finished it that night. It was a very empowering experience.

Doris could have easily gone back to sleep. She could have allowed herself to give over the power to finish the paper to something or someone "outside" herself. "Hope" implied that the power did not lie within her. But she noticed that seductive thought and woke herself up with the reminder that whether or not the paper got finished was entirely up to her. She felt empowered because she claimed the power that was hers.

As she stayed awake within her vivid life experiences, Doris observed another pattern that was debilitating. In her life, she was placing all the value on end results, and none on the process that brought those results:

> The force of my desire to change finally led me to the idea of finding/creating some referents in my life to depict the importance of process. As I turned my attention to that choice, I started thinking about the newest Life As A Waking Dream classes and what good work I seem to be doing. I realized that I hadn't just, one day, begun to magically write good reports; the process had been

cooking in me through the introductory course, and only now, after this cooking, was I able to process my waking dreams more deeply and meaningfully. It made sense. I could see the value in the time spent groping (or, rather, growing) in the dark, and felt this was a good example from which to build a new perspective.

Then I saw how the structure I had used to plan out and work on end of term projects in small increments was part of the same process. It was becoming clear I couldn't expect projects to blossom in a day or two. I needed to plant the seeds and tend them over time to achieve a good harvest.

By finding examples of the change she wished to make in her life, Doris made her desire more tangible. Nevertheless, she was still not confident that she'd be able to translate those examples into specific new choices:

These referents felt and sounded good, but they were still fairly abstract.

Last Tuesday night I had two projects due and a final examination. I finished the second project Monday night, worked Tuesday morning, and then headed down to school at noon to study for my 5:00 P.M. final. I stopped at the bank (drive-in, of course) and planned to catch a drive-through lunch to eat, in the car, on the way to school, leaving me three-and-a-half hours to study.

On the way to grab lunch I heard a voice say, "You really should sit down and eat lunch." Almost losing control of the car, I replied, "You have got to be kidding. Not today! Look, I know I need to slow down and get some balance and learn to enjoy the process, and I will. But I can't make the change today. I'm right in the midst of it!"

The voice softly yet firmly responded, "Right in the midst of it, is exactly where you have to make the change."

> I had no reply. The truth was larger than anything I could say. I *knew* that I had to change exactly then; so I did.

Doris had come to a crucial turning point. The urgency of the need to change was finally clear to her. Either she would change or she wouldn't. There would never be a better time.

> I went in and sat down for lunch. I even left my study notes in the car. I journaled a bit while I ate, because I was so moved by the experience. Tears even came to my eyes as I acknowledged what I had been doing to myself, and I began to own the desire, power, and love of self necessary for change.

Doris came into an expanded sense of self, about which she later wrote, "I felt open to the new, capable of change, and responsible for my experiences."

> When I walked outside I felt the warm sun on my face, smelled the clean breeze, and saw the true blue sky that Miami sports every day. I felt physically touched, as if nurtured by nature.

Doris had found a way to stay awake within her waking dreams. She paid attention to her inner communication with Self and opened up to the reality of her surroundings. She nurtured herself and felt the reflection of that in nature. Doris had begun to change some lifelong patterns that had lulled her to sleep over the years. She discovered that she had to have the *desire* to change, she had to identify with the *power* to change, and above all, she had to *love* herself enough to take action and embody change.

Fulfilling Life Objectives

Most of us are not able to identify our life purpose after examining only a few waking dreams. We need to gather considerable data before our fundamental reasons for living become clear to us. But many of us will uncover some of our life objectives — those more specific things we want to learn — after looking at just a few waking dreams. In fact, we may already know, even if only unconsciously, some of the themes that have been running through our life experiences. Working with our lives as waking dreams will help us become more conscious of the qualities and skills we have already developed.

Tessa had long recognized a strong theme of "death of beloveds" running throughout her life, starting with the death of her father when she was only a few months old. Her response to that theme had changed over the years, but the theme itself reappeared with considerable frequency.

After she began looking at her life as a waking dream, another of her loved ones died. Because she was able to awaken within the experience, Tessa altered the nature of her waking dream. She felt that she had moved into conscious alignment with one of her overall life objectives, which she might have called "to know death."

> Monday night the phone rings. It is my friend Marjorie. I detect a darkness in her voice . . . Then she tells me that John M. is dead. I hear her. My mind, my heart, are shocked, and at some larger, deeper level, I know about this and way deep in a place of light it is said, "Oh, now he will be there to meet me."

Immediately Tessa was aware of at least two levels of her response to death. She felt the shock that would soon turn to grief, but she also touched a knowing that told her she had not lost John. Her communication within Self — through feeling and knowing — was clear. She continued her account:

> Alone, I look at my living room. I hug my dog Wunjo. I see colors very distinctly. I know that I have been deeply struck. And I also begin to be aware that this death is different. I feel an under-chorus of "John is dead." A whole part of me feels it is agreeing with this extraordinary knowledge, and another part absolutely cannot believe or encompass it.

Tessa was awake within her waking dream. She was attentive to the messages from the real Self. There had been a wounding, but it was somehow in harmony with a larger reality. Her thoughts could not yet grasp the message, but she remained open to it:

> I waken early the next morning and am with John. Loving John. Knowing that he is well. Knowing that he is on his true path. His life/death is in order. I reach for really knowing that he is dead, and he is and he is not.

Tessa struggled with the message. John was dead, but he was not. The knowing stretched her ordinary way of viewing things. It was not easy, by thinking, to grasp such a paradoxical truth.

> For the next two days I seem to grieve, to practice the awareness of John's being dead, to get hold of this

world. And all the while I know that something is very different. I am not broken by grief. I am not dark and destroyed and hopeless, as I have always been before with the death of one I loved. Something in me is freed, some thing in me is fluttering wide, expanding.

To stay awake and alert took concentration, but Tessa was able to sustain the effort. She was discovering the purpose of all these waking dreams about death. She was hearing the message from the real Self. She was learning what there was for her to learn:

> I feel how different I am from all past death times. I know that there is no difference between life and death. I feel this in my body. . . . Then it begins - an upsweep of joyous light and energy, like a great wave of sound, pulsing from feet to head and beyond. I am a great chord of sound, wave after wave of life resounds through me. I say aloud, "John is helping me, John is healing me" — and I know it. I know that John is doing his/our work from the other side. We are great companions, friends. We are in this life/death together, doing the work. All through the day I speak to John from time to time. I am filled with laughter and joy and astonishment. I really have changed, can change, am changing. There is no death.

Tessa experienced a remarkable transformation because she stayed awake in her waking dream and communed with herself through the various languages available to her. Tessa realized that her sense of self had empowered her:

> I was the Awakener, struggling to become real, becoming real. I was the perceiver, and the receiver of a gift.

In her sense of self as the awakener, Tessa moved from her theme, "death of beloveds," to rename this waking dream, "The Changing/Changed Meaning of Death in My Life. The Healing of Death in My Life:"

> This event tells me that I have changed, that all the work I have been doing with fear, survival, death and life, has made a difference. Also, that I am apt to hold on to old images of myself as fearful, etc. It also has shown me that I am living life within and from myself, not needing to be sustained by another. It shows me that I have a life. It is telling me that my functioning, not just my head, knows that life and death really are not separate and that nothing is lost and that I am grounded on this earth at this time. I work for that. This dream says I have it. Surely death of a loved one has always been the greatest test of my caring to live and be. And I have passed the test. I did not lose myself in losing John on this plane. I gained myself and a larger relationship with him.

The Ancient Wisdom teaches that we have come into this life to learn and to grow. A life theme is a major learning we have undertaken. If we live it consciously, we call it an overall life objective. Tessa might have framed her life objective as "To know that death does not separate and nothing is lost." By staying awake within this particular waking dream episode, Tessa fulfilled a lifelong objective. No wonder she was filled with laughter, joy, and astonishment!!

After studying her life as a waking dream for about a year, Nancy made a whole list of life themes she had uncovered:

- Playing Victim
- Believing I cannot have what I want
- Believing that freedom excludes committed relationships
- Being "there" instead of "here"
- Rejecting the Mother
- Doing it my way
- Doing things the hard way
- Censoring fun as frivolous and not adult-like
- Giving and not receiving
- Letting others unduly influence my decisions
- Others betray me and are undependable

With such a list, Nancy was preparing for new awareness as she approached the days ahead of her. She was able to watch for these themes and she kept asking herself, "What do I really want here? How can I change the theme?" That helped her to choose objectives.

Objectives are statements of what we want. We formulate them with active verbs so that we can see how they can be accomplished. Nancy's life themes translated into the following life objectives:

Life Themes ☞ *Life Objectives*

Playing victim ☞ *To take charge of my life*

Believing I cannot have what I want ☞ *To enjoy having what I want*

Doing it my way ☞ *To live in the flow*

Doing things the hard way ☞ *To live with ease*

Believing that freedom excludes committed relationships ☞ *To experience my freedom to be in committed relationships*

Being "there" instead of "here" ☞ *To live in the "now"*

Rejecting the Mother ☞ *To learn to love the Mother*

Censoring fun as frivolous and not adult-like ☞ *To have fun*

Giving and not receiving ☞ *To receive what others give with both gratitude and joy*

Letting others unduly influence my decisions ☞ *To make choices based on my own preferences, objectives, and purposes*

By setting out these life objectives and living them consciously, Nancy completely transformed her life-dream over the course of only a few years. She is fulfilling these objectives, and she finds deep gratification in her new life, which is full of joy and love.

Translating unconscious life themes into conscious objectives is very empowering. It enables us to create our own realities, rather than feeling that we have no power, that life merely happens to us. Once we discover the thread of purpose that weaves all the events of our life together, we'll be able to fill every moment of every day with soul-satisfying, spirit-enhancing meaning.

Life As A Myth

Each life event that awakens sharp physical sensations, deep feelings, or strong intuitions contains a mythological statement of some kind about the real Self. It signals something that we are ready to discover, learn, know, develop, and integrate. Waking dreams are communications between the real Self and our sense of self. When we look at what we don't know about an event, we discover how small the sphere of awareness of our sense of self actually is. The not-knowing is always so much larger than the knowing.

By approaching life as a waking dream we awaken gradually to the reality of the Great Unknown. We learn to have deep reverence and respect for all that is unknown to us. Therein lies the next phase of our unfolding. Carl Jung said, "Our present lives are dominated by the goddess Reason, who is our greatest and most tragic illusion."[2] To return to alignment with nature, we must restore the balance of the yin and yang by opening to all we cannot know with yang reason. "Whatever the unconscious may be, it is a natural phenomenon producing symbols that prove to be meaningful."[3] We open to those symbols when we study our life experiences as waking dreams.

This is a yin way of doing spiritual work. It requires an attitude that has been beautifully captured by Rainer Maria Rilke:

> Be patient to all that is unsolved in your heart .
> . . try to love the questions themselves like locked
> rooms and like books that are written in a very
> foreign tongue.

Do not now seek the final answers which cannot be given you because you would not be able to live them.

And the point is to live everything.

Live the questions now. Perhaps you will then gradually, without noticing it, live along some distant day into the answer.

We approach our vivid life experiences with abundant expectancy that they will reveal their messages to us. About our waking dreams we ask:

▶ What is my sense of self?

▶ How are the yin and yang at work in my life?

▶ What qualities and characteristics would help me to fully develop the two polarities?

▶ Am I awake to the information being communicated to me through all the components of Self?

▶ What is the meaning of the symbols that appear in my life?

▶ What is not well-integrated into my sense of self?

▶ What is not well-developed in me?

▶ What life themes am I living out, and how can I adopt them as conscious life objectives?

▶ What is my life purpose?

▶ What is this particular waking dream episode telling me, or asking of me?

As we live, we slowly reveal to ourselves the answers to our questions. We must value our inner work. We must give ourselves the gift of doing it even though the rush and stress of our lives seem to leave little room for introspection and contemplation. Those of us who have worked with our lives as waking dreams have found that the process of examination and reflection feeds and nourishes the spirit and brings greater insight into our lives.

The work we do in our journals is vital, because it is there we record our questions and the insights that follow. Between journal writings, we hold in our consciousness the information we are gathering, and our awareness deepens. From time to time we reread what we have written, noticing how our consciousness is moving and changing. There is nothing more spiritually gratifying than recognizing our own inner growth, and this is one effective way of doing that.

Waking dreams occur while our ego-defenses are still active. As a consequence, "consciousness [yang] naturally resists anything unconscious and unknown [yin]."[4] This is the reason most vivid life experiences are highly repetitive and last over long periods of time. It can be very difficult to discover what a waking dream episode seeks to reveal, and there are often many layers of meaning.

Looking at life as a waking dream is a way of going very yin to our life experiences. Our waking dreams can help us to uncover the next steps to take in specific situations. By viewing our lives this way we foster a deep appreciation for our everyday experiences and how they can teach and guide us.

Our waking dreams can also make us aware of the larger reality in which we are integrated, and to which we are waiting to awaken. To grasp the meaning of waking dreams, therefore, requires conscious surrender: willingness to admit that we don't know, and willingness to trust that we will find deeper meaning in our lives. This is a way to heal our psyches and the gap between body and spirit.

It is this healing that will make it possible for us to mend our relationships with each other and with the planet. We can learn to live in this world with consciousness and presence, and we can remain awake and alive to the purpose for our being.

As we learn to penetrate the meaning of our life experiences, we will find that we are increasingly filled with a deep and abiding sense of presence and the knowledge that we are co-creators of the realities of our lives. This is the promise and the challenge that lies before us. To respond, we must go forward asking "What don't I know?" in relation to every life experience, and "What steps can I take to respond to what I am learning?"

Epilogue:
Suggestions for
Your Ongoing Work with
Life As A Waking Dream

It is important in consciousness work that you never do anything as though it were for another, or in imitation of another, or because another tells you that it is of value. Do not try to fulfill another's expectations, or do the work because you have made a commitment to another person. Rather, come to feel the relationship with Self to be the primary relationship. The commitment to inner work is a commitment to Self, and you keep that commitment because your own fulfillment is important to you.

Consciousness work at its best is self-guided and self-directed. Sometimes you will use the reflection of direction and guidance given to you from the outside. Perhaps that has happened as you read this book. The value lies, however, in developing your ability to guide and direct your own unfolding, in cooperation with the inner impulses you register of the larger Will.

Consciousness work is also self-motivated. You need to have a clear purpose for learning this or any other method of inner work so that you have a strong motivation for sitting down with your journal and taking time with yourself. What is the overall purpose by which you direct the activities of your life? What is your objective? In other words, what do you want to get from looking at your life as a waking dream and how will that help to fulfill your life purpose?

If you write down your purposes and objectives, it will be far easier to stay focused as you follow the suggestions given in this book and use them to guide and direct your own inner work.

MY EARLY LIFE DREAM

QUESTIONS TO GUIDE YOU IN YOUR EXPLORATION

Title of Your Early Life Dream:
Record this only after you have completed your work on the questions that follow.

Step One: Write Your Early Life Dream
Tell the story of your first seven years simply and without embellishment. Write the bare bones of the story, the important and essential elements. **Do not include a lot of detail.** *If a given event stands out for you, you can write it up in a subsequent account of a vivid life experience.* **A paragraph** for each time period should be sufficient. Try to tell the story in one or two (at the most) pages.

Read all the way through these questions before you begin writing. Knowing what you will explore under each of the questions will help you to keep the essential story *simple.* Spend as much time answering the questions as you do writing the story.

Include in your story the people who were important to your emergence, the events that were pivotal, and the places and groups that helped form you.

Start your account with the words "I dreamed," to emphasize that you are looking at this early life story as a waking dream.

Step Two: Revisiting Your Early Life Dream

Aware of yourself as the dreamer who has now awakened within the Life Dream, ask yourself the following questions and write your responses.

Identify with the Power-to-be-Conscious of your dream experience rather than with a sense of self that is immersed in the dream.

1. Describe the self that lived this Early Life Dream.

Stand back far enough to gain a general sense of the principal character in this dream (you). What qualities and characteristics are essential to your way of being in your dream, without which you wouldn't be who you were. Also describe your special talents, gifts, life skills and abilities, if they were apparent in those early years.

2. What was your sense of self *as you lived the dream?*

This is a difficult question, because of course you have had many different senses of self over the years. But was there a predominant sense of self in those early years?

(Here are some examples to get you going: for most of my early childhood, I was in my "mother's helper" sense of self, or my "loner" sense of self, or my "orphan" sense of self.)

3. What predominant feelings do you have about this early life dream as you reread it?

Record what you are aware of as you breathe back into the experience. Do your feelings now represent a change in how you have felt about your life story in the past? If so, what is different now?

4. What was the state of your physical health during this early life dream?

Give a general assessment of your physical response to life, rather than a listing of various conditions or ailments. If, however, there were major ailments that were pivotal, mention those.

5. Were there any strong intuitions that were formative in those early years?

Write only about those knowings that stand out as vital or formative.

6. The formative yin and yang polarities:

a. Describe your mother (symbol of your formative yin force) in both her yin *and yang* characteristics as you experienced her in those early years.

b. Describe your father (symbol of your formative yang force) in both his yang *and yin* characteristics as you experienced him in those early years.

c. As you look back on your predominant way of

functioning, would you describe yourself as primarily yin or yang?

7. Were the Great Yin and Great Yang present in your consciousness in those early years?

a. Were your grandparents close?

b. Did you feel unconditionally loved by them?

c. What special things did you learn from them?

d. What stands out about your experiences with them?

8. What symbols stand out for you in these early years?

a. Answer this question in the light of the whole dream. What persons, key objects, or places stand out for you? Select only a few (four or five), and thus only the most important. Persons who were formative in their influence. Key objects (or animals) that were central somehow. Places that still evoke an emotional connection. Etc. Describe each symbol to convey what it was *to you*. (Do not try to give an *objective* description of the person, place, etc.; stay with its subjective meaning to you.)

b. Then see if you can identify what this person, object, or place symbolizes in you.

c. *Do not include yourself as a symbol.* You talk about yourself under the "sense of self" question (number 2 above).

9. What don't you know about your early life dream?

Usually we fail to pay attention to all that we *do not know* about our lives. It may be precisely in that area that we can discover what we need to learn. Make a note of what you don't know.

10. What remains unresolved for you in this early life dream?

Something is unresolved if you still have a lot of feeling tied into it and you have not found a way to deal with those feelings.

11. What do you feel especially good about when you reread your early life dream?

Mention anything that leaves a warm feeling, brings a smile to your face, or evokes a feeling of satisfaction or pride.

12. Your question(s) and insights:

What questions do you ask yourself as a result of this exploration?

What insights into your life patterns have you gained from this exploration?

WRITING YOUR ENTIRE LIFE DREAM

QUESTIONS TO GUIDE YOU

Title of Your Life Dream:

Record this only after you have completed your work on these questions.

Step One: Write Your Life Dream

Tell the story of your life simply and without embellishment. Write the bare bones of the story, the important and essential elements. **Do not include a lot of detail.** *If a given event stands out for you, you can write it up as a subsequent vivid life experience.* **A paragraph** for each time period should be sufficient. Try to tell the whole story in two or three (at the most) pages.

Read all the way through these questions before you begin writing. Knowing what you will explore under each of the questions will help you to keep the essential story *simple*. Spend as much time answering the questions as you do writing the story.

Include in your story the people who were important to your emergence, the events that were pivotal, and the places and groups that helped form you.

Start your account with the words "I dreamed," to emphasize that you are looking at this life story as a waking dream.

Step Two: Revisiting Your Life Dream

Aware of yourself as the dreamer who has now awakened within the Life Dream, ask yourself the following questions and write your responses.

Identify with the Power-to-be-Conscious of your dream experience rather than with a sense of self that is immersed in the dream.

1. Describe the self that has lived this Life Dream until now.

Stand back far enough to gain a general sense of the principal character in this dream (you). What qualities and characteristics are essential to your way of being in your dream, without which you wouldn't be who you are? Also describe your special talents, gifts, life skills and abilities.

2. What was your sense of self *as you lived the dream?*

This is a difficult question, because of course you have had many different senses of self over the years. But is there a predominant sense of self in each time-period, a way of knowing and experiencing yourself that might be called your "default" sense of self over those years? (Here are some examples to get you going: for most of my childhood, I was in my "mother's helper" sense of self, or my "loner" sense of self; or, in my teen years, I tended to function in my "outsider" sense of self, or my "leader" sense of self; or, in my adult years I have functioned primarily in my "responsible" sense of self, or my "entrepreneur" sense of self.)

3. What predominant feelings do you have about this life dream as you reread it?

Record what you are aware of as you breathe back into the experience. Do your feelings now represent a change in how you have felt about your life story in the past? If so, what is different now?

4. What has been the history of your physical health during this life dream?

Give a general assessment of your physical response to the life dream over the years, rather than a listing of various conditions or ailments. If, however, there were major ailments that were pivotal, mention those.

5. What strong intuitions have been formative in your life?

Write only about those knowings that stand out as vital or formative.

6. How have the yin and yang polarities been active in your life dream?

a. Describe your mother (symbol of your formative yin force) in both her yin *and yang* characteristics as you see her now, from your present vantage point.

b. Describe your father (symbol of your formative yang force) in both his yang *and yin* characteristics as you see him now, from your present vantage point.

c. As you look back on your predominant way of functioning, would you describe yourself as primarily yin or yang? Were there differences in different time-periods? Do you see one of the polarities as under- or over-developed? Have you developed a greater balance of the two forces as you have moved through your life dream?

7. What symbols stand out for you in this life dream?

a. Answer this question in the light of the whole dream. What persons, key objects, or places stand out for you? Select only a few (five to ten), and thus only the most important. Persons who were formative in their influence. Key objects (or animals) that were central somehow. Places that still evoke an emotional connection. Etc. Describe each symbol to convey what it was *to you.* (Do not try to give an *objective* description of the person, place, etc.; stay with its subjective meaning to you.)

b. Then see if you can identify what this person, object, or place symbolizes in you.

c. Do not include yourself as a symbol. You talk about yourself under the "sense of self" question (number 2 above).

8. What don't you know about your life dream?

Usually we fail to pay attention to all that we *do not know* about our lives. It may be precisely in that area that we can discover what we need to learn. Make a note of what you don't know.

9. What remains unresolved for you in this life dream?

Something is unresolved if you still have a lot of feeling tied into it and you have not found a way to deal with those feelings.

10. What do you feel especially good about when you reread your life dream?

Mention anything that leaves a warm feeling, brings a smile to your face, or evokes a feeling of satisfaction or pride.

11. Your question(s):

What questions do you ask yourself as a result of this exploration?

What other observations do you want to make?

12. What does this life dream tell you about your personal and/or spiritual expansion?

What does it reveal about your major challenges in personal or spiritual growth? Are these challenges you have already met, or are they still before you? How can you move forward in your growth?

Appendix

QUOTATIONS FROM PERCEIVERS AND PHILOSOPHERS

Below are selected quotations from perceivers and philosophers related to life as a waking dream. They are organized by their connection with the concepts explored in this book. The intent is to whet your appetite for further reading in order to expand your mental understanding of the nature of reality and your place within it.

Re The Great Unknown:

From P. D. Ouspensky's *The Fourth Way* (New York: Vintage Books, 1971), regarding lying to ourselves:

> When I know that I do not know something, and at the same time say that I know, or act as though I knew it, it is lying. For instance, we know nothing about ourselves, and we really *know* that we know nothing, yet we never recognize or admit the fact; we never confess it even to ourselves; we act and think and speak as though we knew who we are. This is the origin, the beginning of lying. (page 30)

From P. D. Ouspensky's *A New Model of the Universe* (New York, N.Y.: Vintage Books, 1971), on the unknown:

> . . . it is man's misfortune that at those moments

when something new and unknown becomes possible he does not know what he wants, and the opportunity which suddenly appeared as suddenly disappears.

Man is conscious of being surrounded by the wall of the Unknown, and at the same time he believes that he can get through the wall and that others have got through it; but he cannot imagine, or imagines very vaguely, what there may be behind this wall. He does not know what he would like to find there or what it means to possess *knowledge*. It does not even occur to him that a man can be in different relations to the Unknown. (page 15)

. . . what we think we know occupies only a very insignificant place amidst that which we do not know. (page 65)

From P. D. Ouspensky's *Tertium Organum: A Key to the Enigmas of the World* (New York: Vintage Books, 1970), regarding life's mystery:

But if a man *knows* of the existence of the contents of the book — the *noumenon* of life — if he knows that a mysterious meaning is hidden under visible phenomena, there is the possibility that in the long run he will discover the contents. (page 129)

The mystery of life dwells in the fact that the *noumenon*, i.e.., the hidden meaning and the hidden function of a thing, is reflected in its *phenomenon*. A phenomenon is merely the reflection of a noumenon in our sphere. THE PHENOMENON IS THE IMAGE OF THE NOUMENON. It is *possible* to know the noumenon by the phenomenon. . . . (page 145)

Re Life As An Illusion:

From P. D. Ouspensky's *Tertium Organum: A Key to the*

Enigmas of the World (New York: Vintage Books, 1970), regarding the nature of reality:

> *I see it; therefore this exists.*
>
> This affirmation is the principal source of all illusions. To be true, it is necessary to say: *I see it; therefore this does not exist* — or at least, *I see it; therefore this is not so.* (page 89)

> First of all we must get rid of our assurance that we see and sense that which exists in reality, and that the real world is like the world which we see — i.e., we must rid ourselves of the illusion of the material world. We must understand *mentally* all the illusoriness of the world perceived by us in space and time, and know that the *real* world cannot have anything in common with it; to understand that it is impossible to imagine the real world in terms of form; and finally we must perceive the conditionality of the axioms of our mathematics and logic, related as they are to the unreal phenomenal world. (page 238)

From G. I. Gurdjieff's *Views From The Real World* (New York, N.Y.: Penguin Books, 1973) on the Wisdom Tradition:

> The Great Knowledge is handed on in succession from age to age, from people to people, from race to race. The great centers of initiation in India, Assyria, Egypt, Greece, illumine the world with a bright light. The revered names of the great initiates, the living bearers of the truth, are handed on reverently from generation to generation. Truth is fixed by means of symbolical writings and legends and is transmitted to the mass of people for preservation in the form of customs and ceremonies, in oral traditions, in memorials,

in sacred art through the invisible quality in dance, music, sculpture and various rituals. It is communicated openly after a definite trial to those who seek it and is preserved by oral transmission in the chain of those who know. . . .

. . . From time to time separate streams break through to the surface, showing that somewhere deep down in the interior, even in our day, there flows the powerful ancient stream of true knowledge of being.

To break through to this stream, to find it — this is the task and the aim of the search; for, having found it, a man can entrust himself boldly to the way by which he intends to go; then there only remains "to know" in order "to be" and "to do." On this way a man will not be entirely alone; at difficult moments he will receive support and guidance, for all who follow this way are connected by an uninterrupted chain. (pages 56-57)

From P. D. Ouspensky's *A New Model of the Universe* (New York: Vintage Books, 1971, on the Wisdom Tradition:

. . . I see the unbroken line of thought and knowledge which passes from century to century, from age to age, from country to country, from one race to another; a line deeply hidden beneath layers of religions and philosophies which are, in fact, only distortions and perversions of the ideas belonging to the line. I see an extensive literature full of significance which . . . feeds the philosophy we know, although it is scarcely mentioned in the text-books on the history of philosophy. And I am amazed now that I did not know it before, that there are so few who have even heard about it. . . . (page 6)

From Ken Wilber's *Grace and Grit* (Boston & London: Shambhala, 1993), regarding the unity of the Wisdom Traditions:

Exoteric religions vary tremendously from each other; esoteric religions the world over are virtually identical. Mysticism or esotericism is, in the broad sense of the word, scientific, as we have seen, and just as you don't have German chemistry versus American chemistry, you don't have Hindu mystical science versus Muslim mystical science. Rather, they are in fundamental agreement as to the nature of the soul, the nature of Spirit, and the nature of their supreme identity, among many other things. This is what scholars mean by "the transcendental unity of the world's religions" — they mean esoteric religions. Of course, their surface structures vary tremendously, but their deep structures are virtually identical, reflecting the unanimity of the human spirit and its phenomenologically disclosed laws. (page 177)

Re Life As A Waking Dream:

From W. Y. Evans-Wentz' *Tibetan Yoga and Secret Doctrines* (London: Oxford University Press, 1973), regarding life as a dream:

. . . the *Yogin* is taught to realize that matter, or form in its dimensional aspects, large or small, and its numerical aspects, of plurality and unity, is entirely subject to one's will when the mental powers have been efficiently developed by *yoga*. In other words, the *yogin* learns by actual experience, resulting from psychic experimentation, that the character of any dream can be changed or transformed by willing that it shall be. A step further and he learns that form, in the dream-state, and all the multitudinous content of dreams, are merely playthings of mind, and, therefore, as unstable as mirages. A further step leads him to the knowledge that the essential nature of form and of all things perceived by the senses in the waking-state are equally as unreal as their reflexes in the dream-state, both states alike being *sangsaric*. The final step leads to the Great Realization, that nothing within the *Sangsara* is or can be other than unreal like dreams. (pages 221-22)

From P. D. Ouspensky's *The Fourth Way* (New York: Vintage Books, 1971), regarding the need to awaken to consciousness:

. . . All study, all thinking and investigation must have one aim, one purpose in view, and this aim must be attaining consciousness. . . . The first step in acquiring consciousness is the realization that we are not conscious. (page 28-29)

Another illusion is that we are awake. When we realize that we are asleep we will see that all history is made by people who are asleep. Sleeping people fight, make laws; sleeping people obey or disobey them. The worst of our illusions are the wrong ideas among which we live and which govern our lives. If we could change our attitude towards these wrong ideas and understand what they are, this in itself would be a great change and would immediately change other things. (page 29)

From P. D. Ouspensky's *In Search of the Miraculous: Fragments of an Unknown Teaching* (New York: Harcourt Brace Jovanovich, 1949), regarding life as a waking dream:

Both states of consciousness, sleep and the waking state, are equally subjective. Only by beginning to *remember himself* does a man really awaken. And then all surrounding life acquires for him a different aspect and a different meaning. He sees that it is *the life of sleeping people,* a life in sleep. All that men say, all that they do, they say and do in sleep. All this can have no value whatever. Only awakening and what leads to awakening has a value in reality. (page 143)

From A. R. Orage's *Psychological Exercises* (New York: Samuel Wiser, 1930), regarding stages leading to waking up:

It may be feared that . . . an effort to see our waking life as merely a special form of sleep must diminish its importance for us and ours for it. But this attitude towards a possible and probable fact is itself morbidly timid. The truth is that just as in night-dreams the first symptom of waking is to suspect that one is dreaming, the first symptom of waking from the waking state — the second awaking of religion — is the suspicion that our present waking state is dreaming likewise. To be aware that we are only partially awake is the first condition of becoming and making ourselves more fully awake. (page 92)

From Rudolf Steiner's *Theosophy* (Hudson, NY: Anthroposophic Press, 1971), on the possibility of experiencing the "hidden wisdom":

. . . We ought not to doubt for one moment the possibility of opening the eyes of every earnest person to [the hidden wisdom]. On this supposition all those have written and spoken who have felt within themselves that the inner sense-instrument had developed, thereby enabling them to know the true nature and being of man, which is generally hidden from the outer senses. Hence from the most ancient times such a *hidden wisdom* has been spoken of again and again. Those who have grasped some understanding of it feel just as sure of their possession as people with normal eyes feel sure of their ability to visualize color. For them this hidden wisdom requires no proof. They know also that this hidden wisdom requires no proof for anyone else to whom the "higher sense" has unfolded itself. They can speak to such a person as a traveler can speak about America to people who have themselves never seen that country but who can visualize it, for they would see all that he has seen were the opportunity to present itself to them. (page xviii)

Re The Creative Forces:

From Theodore Heline's *The Archetype Unveiled: A Study Of the Sound Patterns Formed By the Creative Word* (La Canada, CA: New Age Press, 1965), regarding the imprinting function of the two-in-one, the Aum, and the nature of the seed of self:

God enters upon manifestation according to plan. That plan is growth. It is a progressive unfoldment of latent potentialities. Step by step, stage by stage, the plan unfolds. This is observable in the four kingdoms of nature. The divine life permeates them all but in differing degrees of expression. In the mineral kingdom that life is asleep, in the plant kingdom it dreams, in the animal kingdom it awakens and in the human kingdom it arrives at a state of individualized self-consciousness. This is the state at which man be comes a rational creature, morally accountable for its acts under the acquired prerogatives of free will.

In all these four kingdoms every entity takes form in accordance with an archetype which had its source in the mind of the Creator. Such was the teaching of Plato, who held that in the Divine Mind there exists the eternal ideas or pure forms according to which all things are formed. Also, in the words of the illumined mystic, Jacob Boehme, "The Ideal Man, the Ideal Animal and the Ideal Plant, precede the natural."

From this original seed Idea there develops the symbolical pattern that contains within it the essence of all it has experienced through the conditions and circumstances it passes in obedience to the cosmic evolutionary forward thrust imparted to it when the Divine Words were first sounded.

All archetypes, from the most embryonic to the most complex and radiant, are really crystallized sound waves. Just as geometrical designs are created by drawing a violin bow over the edge of a glass plate which contains sand, so all forms in the world about us are the result of physical matter being drawn into an archetypal mold by the energies that permeate all space and which were set in motion and given their divine directives by the Creator at the very dawn of manifestation. Thus we come to realize that sound creates patterns in accordance with which all physical forms come into being. As St. John expresses it in the opening verse of the Gospel that bears his name, "In the beginning was the Word, and the Word was with God, and the Word was God." It was in accordance with this Word, John goes on to say, that "by it all things were made, and without it was not anything made that was made."

As previously indicated, it is not only man that carries about with him a kind of super-physical portrait of his inmost being. This is something shared by every created being and object. . . . its position in man and animal is directly above the head; in the plants, at their tap-root, while in the mineral it is contained within itself. The spoken word, too, takes on a definite form.

Studies of the animal kingdom are intensely interesting. They bear out what occultism teaches as to their evolutionary status in relation to their center of intelligence. Animals are governed by a Group Spirit. All members of a species come under the guidance of an overshadowing Intelligence of the archangelic Hierarchy. They are not yet bearers of an indwelling ego. They cannot pronounce "I." That status awaits them in the future when they will enter upon a stage of development comparable to that now achieved by man. (pages 20 & 21)

. . . Heredity, declares occult science, pertains to the physical body only; the higher vehicles, and the archetype, with which we are dealing, is the product of the individual Ego only. It is that which survives the death of the physical body and which develops through repeated incarnations which, as previously stated, is the method by which the soul mounts the ladder of being step by step from life to life, from age to age. (page 23)

From Vitvan's *Self-Mastery Through Meditation* (Baker, NV: School of the Natural Order, 1982), regarding the AUM and the indivisibility of the two fundamental forces:

Aum is called the "sacred word," "the word of Glory," "the Pranava," the sound of conscious life itself, as it is breathed forth into all earth sphere forms. It is designated the word symbolizing the substance of the solar sphere [the Great Mother] united with the cosmic sphere [the Great Father], and is intended to establish the informing powers or controlling energies of these configurations or forms. . . .(page 76)

. . . in understanding the highest form of meditation [we must] reunite in our mental consciousness the Positive Power with the Negative Substance. In order to clearly delineate what we mean by those terms we artificially separate them into two sections for discussion. But on the functional level they are never separate. We cannot differentiate the Father from the Mother. Our mental processes focus first on the Power and then on the Substance, but eventually we will need to comprehend both aspects of the creating process in one act of consciousness. (page 97)

. . . [That] separation is invalid on the grounds that when we work our consciousness into the Higher Self (which is identification with the Power with which we are conscious), then we will experience the very act of being conscious as the activity of the Mother and the Power which motivates that activity as the Father. The unmoving but all-powerful Positive Power will be experienced in one act of consciousness with the activation of the Substance. (page 98)

From P. D. Ouspensky's *Tertium Organum: A Key to the Enigmas of the World* (New York: Vintage Books, 1970), regarding the process of Creation:

The Tao which can be expressed in words is not the eternal Tao; the name which can be uttered is not its eternal name. (page 262)

Tao produced Unity; Unity produced Duality; Duality produced Trinity; and Trinity produced all existing objects. (page 263)

From Rudolf Steiner's *Theosophy* (Hudson, NY: Anthroposophic Press, 1971), regarding human unfoldment:

. . . If we want to understand a human spirit we must, therefore, know two different things about it. Firstly, how much of the eternal has been revealed to it, and secondly, how much treasure from the past lies stored up within it.

These treasures by no means remain in the spirit in an unchanged shape. The impressions that man acquires from his experiences fade gradually from memory. Not so, however, their fruits. We do not remember all the experiences lived through during childhood while acquiring the arts of reading and writing. Yet we could not read or write had we not had such experiences, and had not their fruits been preserved in the form of abilities. Such is the transmutation that the spirit effects in the treasures of memory. The spirit consigns to its fate whatever can lead to pictures of the separate experiences, and extracts therefrom only the force necessary for enhancing its abilities. Thus not a single experience passes by unutilized. The soul preserves each one as memory, and from each the spirit draws forth all that can enrich its abilities and the whole content of its life. The human spirit grows through assimilated experiences, and although one cannot find past experiences in the spirit as if in a storeroom, one nevertheless finds their effects in the abilities that man has acquired. (pages 46-47)

The fruits of learning are acquired capacities. . . . (page 58)

. . . The human spirit is its own species. Just as man as a physical being belonging to a species bequeaths his qualities within the species, so does the spirit bequeath its qualities within its species, that is, within itself. *In each life the human spirit appears as a repetition of itself with the fruits of its former experiences in previous lives.* This life is consequently the repetition of others and brings with it what the spirit self has, by work, acquired for itself in the previous life. When the spirit self absorbs something that can develop into fruit, it permeates itself with the life spirit. Just as the life body reproduces the form from species to species, so does the life spirit reproduce the soul from personal existence to personal existence. (page 59)

Re **A Sense of Self:**

From Sogyal Rinpoche's *The Tibetan Book of Living and Dying* (San Francisco, California: HarperSanFrancisco, 1992), regarding the Hindu philosophy of Creation:

Imagine a person who suddenly wakes up in hospital after a road accident to find she is suffering from total amnesia. Outwardly, everything is intact: she has the same face and form, her senses and her mind are there, but she doesn't have any idea or any trace of a memory of who she really is. In exactly the same way, we cannot remember our true identity, our original nature. Frantically, and in real dread, we cast around and improvise another identity, one we clutch onto with all the desperation of someone falling continuously into an abyss. This false and ignorantly assumed identity is "ego".

So ego, then, is the absence of true knowledge of who we really are, together with its result: a doomed clutching on, at all costs, to a cobbled together and makeshift image of ourselves, an inevitably chameleon charlatan self that keeps changing and has to, to keep alive the fiction of its existence. (page 116)

From Kabir Edmund Helminski's *Living Presence: A Sufi Way to Mindfulness & the Essential Self* (New York: Jeremy P. Tarcher/Perigee, 1992), regarding identification with a sense of self:

What characterizes the human being is a gift of conscious awareness that offers us the possibility of real will and creativity, as well as the opportunity to know the source of this conscious awareness, the

Spirit from which it emanates. Usually, however, this conscious awareness is absorbed in experience and embedded in the structures of perception. This is life as most people know it: the complete identification of one's awareness with all the events and subjective experiences that life on earth offers. This consciousness is also identified with a self-construct, an ego that is ruled by contradictory desires and conditionings. (page 43)

From P. D. Ouspensky's *The Fourth Way* (New York: Vintage Books, 1971), regarding the many different "I's":

. . . Man . . ., before he begins to study himself in connection with some system which gives him the possibility of self-study, passes all his life in sleep. He only looks as though he is awake; he is really never awake, or occasionally he awakes for a moment, looks round and falls asleep again. . . . though he has many different 'I's, some of these 'I's do not even know one another. Man can have quite definite attitudes, definite convictions or definite views, and on the other hand he can have quite different convictions, quite different views, quite different likes and different dislikes, and one of them does not know the other. . . . Men are very divided and they do not know and cannot know it, because each of these 'I's knows only certain 'I's that it meets by association; other 'I's remain quite unknown. 'I's are divided according to functions; there are intellectual, emotional, instinctive and moving 'I's. Round themselves they know something, but beyond that they know nothing, so until man begins to study himself with knowledge of this division, he can never come to a right understanding of his functions or reactions.

This sleep of man, and absence of unity in him,

create another very important characteristic, and this is, the complete mechanicalness of man. Man in this state . . . is a machine controlled by external influences; he has no possibility to resist these external influences, and no possibility to distinguish them from one another, no possibility to study himself apart from these things. He sees himself always on the move, and has a long-established and very strong illusion that he is free to go where he wills, that he can move according to his wish, and that he can go to the right or to the left. He cannot do this; if he moves to the right, that means that he could not move to the left. . . . Will can exist only in man who has one controlling 'I', but as long as he has many different 'I's which do not know one another he has just as many different wills; each 'I' has its own will, there can be no other 'I' or other will. But man can come to a state when he acquires a controlling 'I' and when he acquires will. He can reach this state only by developing consciousness. . . . (pages 15 & 16)

From P. D. Ouspensky's *Tertium Organum: A Key to the Enigmas of the World* (New York: Vintage Books, 1970), regarding the impermanent sense of self and the structure of the human being:

Our "I" is also that *battlefield* on which this or that emotion, this or that habit or inclination gains an advantage, subjecting to itself all of the rest at every given moment, and identifying itself with the I. Our I is *a being*, having *its own* life, imperfectly conscious of that of which it itself consists, and identifying itself with this or another portion of itself. . . . (page 173)

If we abandon analogies and return to facts, so far as these are accessible to our observation, it then becomes necessary to begin with several somewhat artificial divisions of the human being. The old division into body, soul and spirit, has in itself a certain authenticity, where the soul ends and the spirit begins, and so forth. There are no strict limits at all, nor can there be. In addition to this, confusion enters in by reason of the *opposition* of body, soul and spirit, which are recognized in this case as *inimical* principles. This is entirely erroneous also, because the body is the expression of the soul, and the soul of the spirit.

The very terms, body, soul and spirit need explanation. The "body" is the physical body with its (to us) little understood mind; the soul — the *psyche* as studied by scientific psychology — is the reflected activity which is guided by impressions received from the external world and from the body. The "spirit" comprises those higher principles which guide, or under certain conditions may guide, the soul-life.

Thus a human being contains in itself the following three categories.

First: *the body* — the region of instincts, and the inner "instinctive" consciousness of the different organs, parts of the body, and the entire organism.

Second: *the soul* — consisting of sensations, perceptions, conceptions, thoughts, emotions and desires.

Third: *the region of the unknown* — consciousness, will, and the one I, i.e., those things which in ordinary man are in potentiality only. (pages 182-183)

From Kabir Edmund Helminski's *Living Presence: A Sufi Way to Mindfulness & the Essential Self* (New York: Jeremy P. Tarcher/Perigee, 1992), regarding the nature of the human being:

The personality can either serve as the reflecting lamp of our Essence — magnifying or focusing the light of the soul — or be the bushel that hides that light. Every human being carries a seed of the Essence that is meant to be actualized. This Essence has no limits. Limits are imposed only by the condition of the vehicle that carries it. (page 84)

From Ouspensky's *Conscience: The Search for Truth* (New York: Arkana, 1988), regarding identification:

'Identifying' or 'identification' is a curious state in which man passes about half of his life, the other half being passed in complete sleep. He identifies with everything: with what he says, what he feels, what he believes, what he does not believe, what he wishes, what he does not wish, what attracts him, what repels him. Everything becomes *him*, or it is better to say *he* becomes *it*. He becomes all that he likes and all that he dislikes. This means that in the state of identification man is incapable of separating himself from the object of his identification. It is difficult to find the smallest thing with which man is unable to identify. At the same time, in a state of identification man has even less control over his mechanical reactions than at any other time. (page 119, footnote 1)

Re Communicating with Self:

From Vitvan's *Self-Mastery Through Meditation* (Baker, NV: School of the Natural Order, 1982), regarding the facets of the One Self:

When for the sake of study we segregate . . . humanity, from the Oneness of the Whole and mentally isolate one man or person for investigative purposes, we find that he microcosmically exhibits a three-in-one-person. In the old Aristotelian cycle these three were called: spirit, soul and body. . . . The term, *spirit-'in'-man*, or the word *spirit* when reference is made to a given person, stands for a differentiated sphere or field of conscious Light-energy. We often use the term *autonomous field* as the source which controls the other two departments — soul and body — of the objective self-conscious state, or man. The word *soul*, or *psyche*, symbolizes the seat of feelings and thinkings, 'psychological' processes of a person. . . . The word *body* signifies the configuration of energy-living-matter substances which, while it can only act (i.e., cannot feel or think), enables the spirit through soul to exert an influence on the lowest level of Cosmos. . . . (pages 20-21)

From Sogyal Rinpoche's *The Tibetan Book of Living and Dying* (San Francisco, California: HarperSanFrancisco, 1992), regarding the nature of the mind:

Because in our culture we overvalue the intellect, we would imagine that to become enlightened demands extraordinary intelligence. In fact many kinds of cleverness are just further obscurations. There is a Tibetan saying that goes, "If you are too clever, you could miss the point entirely." Patrul Rinpoche said: "The logical mind seems interesting, but it is the seed of delusion." People can become obsessed with their own theories and miss the point of everything. In Tibet we say: "Theories are like patches on a coat, one day they just wear off." . . . (page 54)

From Arnold Mindell's *Working with the Dreaming Body* (London: Arkana, 1985), regarding communication with self, which he calls "process work":

. . . Processes can switch suddenly from hearing to feeling, from feeling to visualization, or from seeing to moving, like lightning. If you can follow processes as they move in and out of the body, you are then able to move with the flow of life, and sometimes witness surprising things. . . . (page 37)

From Rudolf Steiner's *Theosophy* (Hudson, NY: Anthroposophic Press, 1971), regarding the importance of feelings:

Feeling is the life and activity of the soul within itself. What is called the *comfort* of the soul depends on the way the feelings of liking and disliking, attraction and repulsion, interact within the soul. (page 84)

From Kabir Edmund Helminski's *Living Presence: A Sufi Way to Mindfulness & the Essential Self* (New York: Jeremy P. Tarcher/Perigee, 1992), regarding identification with the real Self:

Spiritual attainment is a fundamental transformation of the "I" from a separate, limited, and contracted identity into a rich and infinite one. It is a movement from separation to union.

One of the first steps in this process is to observe and understand the chaotic and fragmented nature of the ordinary self and to understand that a very practical integration and harmony can be achieved. This integrated self is the drop that contains the ocean. At the dimensionless center of our identity is the creative potential of Cosmic Mind. (pages 85-86)

When we can listen to and express the Self, we will find what is needed to meet life's demands. Having brought the conscious mind into resonance with a dimensionless point within, which contains all qualities in potential, each of us comes spontaneously to the Truth. We will be able to embrace life and those we need to love. This dimensionless point within is our point of contact with the qualities of Spirit. If we can regularly silence the mind and be aware at this core of our being, we will receive help from the Source of life. Presence is the empty center that attracts and manifests the qualities of Spirit. (page 129)

Through this deeper refinement of attention and an ever more subtle focusing, the false identity collapses. The supports on which it once depended have been removed, and the self begins to feel like a unique point of view of the Whole, a reflector of cosmic awareness. (page 45)

Re Symbols and Meaning:

From P. D. Ouspensky's *In Search of the Miraculous: Fragments of an Unknown Teaching* (New York: Harcourt Brace Jovanovich, 1949), regarding myths and symbols:

The aim of 'myths' and 'symbols' was to reach man's higher centers, to transmit to him ideas inaccessible to the intellect and to transmit them in such forms as would exclude the possibility of false interpretations. 'Myths' were destined for the higher emotional center; 'symbols' for the higher thinking center. (page 279)

From Vitvan's *Functional Activities* (Baker, NV: School of the Natural Order), regarding seeing *through* images:

What constitutes growth and development into the consciousness of Reality? To surmount the images and see the Reality. It is right here all the time; you are in it. You are not going to get a thing that you do not already have. Open your eyes and see what you have and what you are here-now. See yourself in life-facts, in livingness. Not the way you create images and then try to chase them. (page 77)

Re The Question "Why Wake Up?":

From Sogyal Rinpoche's *The Tibetan Book of Living and Dying* (San Francisco, California: HarperSanFrancisco, 1992), regarding the question "Why wake up?"

Two people have been living in you all your life. One is the ego, garrulous, demanding, hysterical, calculating; the other is the hidden spiritual being, whose still voice of wisdom you have only rarely heard or attended to. As you listen more and more to the teachings, contemplate them, and integrate them into your life, your inner voice, your innate wisdom of discernment, what we call in Buddhism "discriminating awareness," is awakened and strengthened, and you start to begin to distinguish between its guidance and the various clamorous and enthralling voices of ego. The memory of your real nature, with all its splendor and confidence, begins to return to you. (page 120)

More and more, then, instead of the harsh and fragmented gossip that ego has been talking to you all your life, you will find yourself hearing in your mind the clear directions of the teachings, which inspire, admonish, guide, and direct you at every turn. The more you listen, the more guidance you will receive. If you follow the voice of your wise guide, the voice of your discriminating awareness, and let ego fall silent, you come to experience that presence of wisdom and joy and bliss that you really are. A new life, utterly different from that when you were masquerading as your ego, begins in you. (page 121)

All the spiritual teachers of humanity have told us the same thing, that the purpose of life on earth is to achieve union with our fundamental, enlightened nature. The "task" for which the "king" has sent us into this strange, dark country is to realize and embody our true being. There is only one way to do this, and that is to undertake the spiritual journey, with all the ardor and intelligence, courage and resolve for transformation that we can muster. . . . (page 127)

From P. D. Ouspensky's *In Search of the Miraculous* (New York: Harcourt Brace Jovanovich, 1976), on "self-remembering:"

I was once walking along the Liteiny towards the Nevsky, and in spite of all my efforts I was unable to keep my attention on self-remembering. The noise, movement, everything distracted me. Every minute I lost the thread of attention, found it again, and then lost it again. At last I felt a kind of ridiculous irritation with myself and I turned into the street on the left having firmly decided to keep my attention on the fact that I *would remember myself* at least for some time, at any rate until I reached the following street. I reached the Nadejdinskaya without losing the thread of attention except, perhaps, for short moments. Then I again turned towards the Nevsky realizing that, in quiet streets, it was easier for me not to lose the line of thought and wishing therefore to test myself in more noisy streets. I reached the Nevsky still remembering myself, and was already beginning to experience the strange emotional state of inner peace and confidence which comes after great efforts of this kind. Just around the corner on the Nevsky was a tobacconist's shop where they made my cigarettes. Still remembering myself I thought I would call there and order some cigarettes.

Two hours later I *woke up* in the Tavricheskaya, that is, far away. I was going by *izvostchik* to the printers. The sensation of awakening was extraordinarily vivid. I can almost say that I *came to.* I remembered everything at once. How I had been walking along the

Nadejdinskaya, how I had been remembering myself, how I had thought about cigarettes, and how at this thought I seemed all at once to fall and disappear into a deep sleep.

At the same time, while immersed in this sleep, I had continued to perform consistent and expedient actions. I left the tobacconist, called at my flat in the Liteiny, telephoned to the printers. I wrote two letters. Then again I went out of the house. I walked on the left side of Nevsky up to the Gostinoy Dvor intending to go to the Offitzerskaya. Then I had changed my mind as it was getting late. I had taken an *izvostchik* and was driving to the Kavalergardskaya to my printers. And on the way while driving along the Tavricheskaya I began to feel a strange uneasiness, as though I had forgotten something — *And suddenly I remembered that I had forgotten to remember myself.*

I spoke of my observations and deductions to the people in our group as well as to my various literary friends and others.

I told them that this was the center of gravity . . . of all work on oneself, that now work on oneself was not only empty words but a real fact full of significance thanks to which psychology becomes an exact and at the same time a practical science.

I said that European and Western psychology in general had overlooked a fact of tremendous importance, namely, that *we do not remember ourselves*; that we live and act and reason in deep sleep, not metaphorically but in absolute reality. And also that, at the same time, we *can* remember ourselves if we make sufficient efforts, that we *can awaken*. (pages 120-121)

From P. D. Ouspensky's *The Fourth Way* (New York: Vintage Books, 1971), regarding "work:"

'Work' in the sense we use this word . . . means work for acquiring knowledge and for the study of change of being. You have to have some clear objective and work for it, so 'work' includes acquiring knowledge and self-control in order to reach your objective. (page 46)

From Kabir Edmund Helminski's *Living Presence: A Sufi Way to Mindfulness & the Essential Self* (New York: Jeremy P. Tarcher/Perigee, 1992), regarding the nature of the human being:

The essential Self is an objective reality, but it cannot be known in a state of sleep, any more than the ordinary facts of reality can be known in a dream. In the Sufi tradition it is written that the absolute Spirit said, "And I breathed My Spirit into humanity." We are each enlivened by this inbreath. The essential Self, the soul, can be understood as this individualization of Spirit. The soul, however, is such a fine subtle energy that it can be obscured by coarser energies of our existence, the energies of thought, desire, instinct, and sensation. These are the veils over the essential Self, the substances of intoxication that numb us to our essential Self.

If the essential Self, the soul, is engaged, it has the powers of Being, Doing, Living, Knowing, Speaking, Hearing, and Loving. From essential attributes like these proceed all the qualities that we need to live an abundant life. Within this nondimensional point of the essential Self (nondimensional because it has its existence in the realm of true Being, which appears to us as nonexistence) is the treasury of all qualities. We may receive what we need to be of service from this treasury through a process of conscious or unconscious activation, but it is our right as human beings to receive consciously. The human being is a channel for the creative power of the universe. Through the use of will — conscious choice — we can activate the qualities and powers of the essential Self. (page 59)

Re Using the Life As A Waking Dream Method to Wake Up Gradually:

From P. D. Ouspensky's *A Record of Meetings* (New York: Arkana, 1951), regarding the need to see through images:

. . . When one grows up among sleeping people one can become awake only by effort. (page 53)

From P. D. Ouspensky's *The Fourth Way* (New York: Vintage Books, 1971), regarding efforts to wake up:

Then, when one awakes for a moment, one realizes that generally one is asleep, that one is not conscious, and how dangerous it is. The more you put into it, the more you understand it, the better the result will be. If you realize what you lose by not remembering yourself and what you gain by remembering yourself, you will have a greater incentive for making efforts to self-remember. You will see that not remembering yourself is like finding yourself in an aeroplane, high above the earth, and fast asleep. This is in fact our situation, but we do not wish to realize it. If a man does realize it, then naturally he will make efforts to awake. But if he thinks he is just sitting in an easy chair and nothing particular is happening, he will think that there is no harm in sleeping. (page 112)

But if you find yourself in a moment of very strong emotional stress and try to remember yourself then, it will remain after the stress is over, and then you will be able to remember yourself. So only with very intense emotion is it possible to create this foundation for self- remembering. But it cannot be done if you do not prepare yourself beforehand. Moments may come, but you will get nothing from them. These emotional moments come from time to time, but we do not use them, because we do not know *how* to use them. If you try sufficiently hard to remember yourself during a moment of intense emotion, and if the emotional stress is strong enough, it will leave a certain trace, and this will help you to remember your self in the future. (page 118)

[To conquer inertia, one must make an] effort to self-remember, to observe, not to identify. Consciousness is a force, and force can only be developed by overcoming obstacles. Two things can be developed in man — consciousness and will. Both are forces. If man overcomes unconsciousness, he will possess consciousness; if he overcomes mechanicalness he will possess will. If he understands the nature of the powers he can attain, it will be clear to him that they cannot be given; these powers must be developed by effort. . . . It is in the very nature of things that consciousness and will cannot be given. If someone could give them to you, it would not be an advantage. This is the reason why one must buy everything, nothing is free. The most difficult thing is to learn how to pay. But if it could be explained in a few words, there would be no need to go to school. One has to pay not only for consciousness but for everything. Not the smallest idea can become one's own until one has paid for it. (pages 119-120)

From Arnold Mindell's *Working with the Dreaming Body* (London: Arkana, 1985), regarding going deeper into a process through the body in order to learn more:

Mindell says that the dreambody uses many channels for communication:

> dreams are *a visual channel*, and he calls the signals "symbols" (visualization);
>
> bodies are *a proprioceptive channel*, and he calls the signals "symptoms" (proprioception, or body feelings);
>
> *audition* uses signals he calls "voices;"
>
> *kinesthesis* uses signals he calls "movements," body postures, or gestures;
>
> and *events on the street*, which he calls "synchronicities."
>
> . . . I think that it's the absolute real personality, what I call the "dreambody," that creates the bodily symptoms. . . The dreambody is a term for the total, multi-channeled personality. It expresses itself in any one or all of the possible channels I mentioned. It can also use the telepathic channel and can manifest itself in dreams. If you amplify a dream symbol, the process that results is the real you, the one you were before you were born and the one that you'll be after you die. The same result occurs when you amplify a body symptom. The eternal and total personality is exposed. The dreambody is the empirical name for a mystery which appears in practice as dreams and body life. With the discovery of the dreambody, dreamwork and bodywork have be come interchangeable. . . . The dreambody is the part of you that is trying to grow and develop in this life. The dreambody is your wise signaler, giving you messages in many different dimensions. When it signals to you in the body, we call it a symptom. When it signals to you through a dream, we call it a symbol. (page 39)
>
> . . . the dreambody is symmetrical; it is like a many-faceted jewel, a diamond, since all its sides,

i.e. each of its channels, the world, dream and body, reflect the same information in different ways. The dreambody is a diamond body and each of us is potentially a symmetrical jewel. Becoming yourself can be understood as knowing your dreambody, becoming whole or round, developing your full experience through awareness of each of your different channels. (page 45)

. . . Your dreambody is yours, yet it's not yours. It's a collective phenomenon, belonging to nature and the world around you. Your dreambody is you, but it's also the entire universe. . . . (page 71)

Notes

Chapter One: The Great Unknown

1. This is perhaps close to what Mary M. Watkins means by the term "waking dream." She says, "By waking dream we mean not just an experience of dreamlike character received while awake, but an experience of the imagination undertaken with a certain quality or attitude of awareness. This conscious awareness differentiates the experience of imagination (whether conveyed through auditory and visual imagery, or activities such as automatic writing or dancing, or less translatable experiences of imagination) from daydreams and hallucinations." *Waking Dreams,* New York: Harper Colophon Books, 1976, page 31. The meaning she gives the term "waking dream" differs from the way I use it.

2. By "waking dream" I refer to those experiences we ordinarily call "real life." When we look at our life experiences *as if they were dreams*, we can penetrate their meaning in a much more expansive way. Ray Grasse, in his book *The Waking Dream,* Wheaton, IL: Quest Books, 1996, uses the term in the same sense I do.

3. "The inner shrine by which God's name is hallowed can be developed only through letting go, releasing some of the clutter inside that keeps us too busy to be silent and receptive to the 'still, small voice.' The prayer also leads us to consider our 'feeling heart,' the place that mystics of all paths have called the inner temple. Jesus recommended going to this 'heart-shrine' (one of the meanings of 'enter into thy closet' — Matt. 6:6) whenever we pray. In another setting, Virginia Woolf called this 'a room of one's own.'" Neil Douglas-Klotz, *Prayers of the Cosmos,* HarperSanFran-cisco, 1990, page 17.

Chapter Two: Life As A Waking Dream

1. Ouspensky, *Tertium Organum: A key to the Enigmas of the World,* New

York: Vintage Books, 1970, page 155.

2. All waking dreams recounted in this book were lived and then explored by students in Waking Dream classes conducted by the author. The authors have given permission for their Waking Dreams to be published in this book, but I have changed their names to protect their privacy.

3. Jung, in his Introduction to *The Tibetan Book of the Dead*, by W. Y. Evans-Wentz, New York: Oxford University Press, 1960, page xlvii.

4. Prigogine, *From Being to Becoming,* New York: W. H. Freeman and Co., 1980, pages 241-248, as quoted by Danah Zohar in *The Quantum Self,* New York: William Morrow and Co., 1990, page 47.

5. Ouspensky, *In Search of the Miraculous: Fragments of an Unknown Teaching,* New York: Harcourt Brace Jovanovich, 1949, page 143.

6. Orage, *Psychological Exercises,* New York: Samuel Wiser, 1930, page 92.

7. LaBerge uses this term in his book *Lucid Dreaming: The Power of Being Awake & Aware in Your Dreams,* New York: Ballantine Books, 1985. He speaks of lucid dreaming as an important tool for approaching the philosophical question as to whether we are only partially awake in our ordinary state of consciousness. In *Flow: The Psychology of Optimal Experience,* New York: Harper Perennial, 1990, page 26, Mihaly Csikszentmihalyi contrasts dreams and consciousness by pointing out that when awake we have the power to choose: "In dreams we are locked into a single scenario we cannot change at will [whereas the] events that constitute consciousness - the things we see, feel, think, and desire - are information that we can manipulate and use." This suggests that when we are lucid or conscious within our life experiences, we gather data that serves us in the choice-making process.

8. Ouspensky, *In Search of the Miraculous,* page 143.

9. A holy man from India believed by his followers to be an incarnation of God, an Avatar.

10. To expand your understanding of the value of journaling, read Ira Progoff's *At a Journal Workshop*, New York: Dialogue House Library, 1975, and Christina Baldwin's *Life's Companion: Journal Writing as a Spiritual Quest,* New York: Bantam Books, 1990.

Chapter Three: The Sense of Self

1. Jung, *Memories, Dreams, and Reflections,* New York: Vintage Books

Edition, 1965, page 323.
2. Ouspensky, *Tertium Organum*, page 155.
3. Zohar, *The Quantum Self,* New York: William Morrow & Co., 1990, pages 141-142.

Chapter Four: The Creative Forces: Yin and Yang

1. A reference to the principles and philosophy attributed to Hermes Trismegistus (which means "the thrice greatest", the greatest of all philosophers, the greatest of all priests, and the greatest of all kings), "regarded by the ancient Egyptians as the embodiment of the Universal Mind. While in all probability there actually existed a great sage and educator by the name of Hermes, it is impossible to extricate the historical man from the mass of legendary accounts which attempt to identify him with the Cosmic Principle of Thought." (Manly P. Hall, *The Secret Teachings of All Ages,* Los Angeles: The Philosophical Research Society, 1977, p. XXXVII) Hermes was the Greek name for the Egyptian Thoth, who was the god of wisdom, learning, and magic. "It is doubtful that the deity called *Thoth* by the Egyptians was originally Hermes, but the two personalities were blended together and it is now impossible to separate them." (*Ibid.,* page XXXVIII.)
Some of the principles attributed to Hermes are: the law of balance (also stated: counterbalancing opposition builds strength); the law of orderly trend (or, the cosmos is orderly); the law of polarity (meaning that everything has its opposite); the law of vibration; the law of periodicity (also called reincarnation); the law of rhythm; the law of analogy or correspondence (also known in the form "as above, so below; as below, so above; as without, so within; as within, so without"); the law of sequence or the principle of absolute justice (which affirms that nothing happens alone or by chance, and that there is cause and effect); the law of gender (everything has its masculine and feminine polarities); all is mind; and, attunement brings liberation. Generally these laws are variously stated as seven. Cf. Manly P. Hall, *Questions and Answers,* pages 28-32, and Jonathan Goldman, *Healing Sounds: The Power of Harmonics*, Rockport: Element, Inc., 1992, page 12.
2. Manly P. Hall, *Questions and Answers: Fundamentals of the Occult Sciences*, Los Angeles: Philosophical Research Society, 1965, page 31.
3. Freeman, in his introduction to *Man and His Symbols,* page 14.

Chapter Five: Communicating with Self

1. Wisdom is knowledge brought into form. Through the body, humans have access to a massive bundle of data accumulated over millions of years through the process of evolution. The body's wisdom, therefore, is vast.

2. There are always exceptions, even to the "rule" of instinct. Some infants do not seem to know how to suck and must be taught. Others do not respond to loud noises by contracting, jumping, etc. Nevertheless, the rule holds often enough to serve our purpose here.

3. Kinesthesia is, according to *Webster's Unabridged Dictionary,* Second Edition, "the sensation of position, movement, tension, etc. of parts of the body perceived through nerve end organs in muscles, tendons and joints."

4. Dr. Moshe Feldenkrais, an Israeli scientist, developed a revolutionary method of working with the body to restore its natural capacities of strength and flexibility. Feldenkrais classes help people reeducate their bodies to enhance their functionality.

5. Mindell, *Working with the Dreaming Body,* London: Arkana, 1985, page 37. Mindell speaks of the dreambody as "the total, multi-channeled personality . . . your wise signaller, giving you messages in many different dimensions." I use the term *real Self* with much the same meaning.

6. *Psyche* is the Greek word translated in English as "soul." The spirit is different from the soul. Spirit is the animating life principle; it is both life and Will.

7. These memories are held in what Carl Jung called the "collective unconscious." *Cf.* pages 67-82 in *Man and His Symbols,* New York: Doubleday & Co., 1964. "Like the instincts, the collective thought patterns of the human mind are innate and inherited." *(*page 75).

8. The formation of the personality is a vast subject on which countless books have been written. My intent here is to provide only the broadest outlines of the structure of the Self according to the Wisdom Tradition, not to explore all possible psychological theories and their ramifications.

9. Understanding how the thought processes work is the subject matter of the science of General Semantics.

10. Compare *Learn To See: An Approach To Your Inner Voice Through*

Symbols, by Mary Jo McCabe, Blue Dolphin Publishing, 1994.

11. See also *Awakening to Wisdom,* by Diane Kennedy Pike writing as Mariamne Paulus, Teleos Imprint, 2003.

12. Zohar, *The Quantum Self,* pages 100-101.

13. Purce, *The Mystic Spiral: Journey of the Soul,* London: Thames and Hudson, 1994, page 10.

Chapter Six: The Meaning of Our Waking Dreams

1. Jung, *Man and His Symbols,* New York: Doubleday & Co., 1964, page 21.

2. Jung, *Op. cit.,* page 89.

3. Ouspensky, *The Fourth Way,* New York: Vintage Books, 1971, page 16.

4. See the Bibliography, page 315, for suggested resources on dream interpretation. Remember that the meanings given in dictionaries of dream symbolism are not magic formulas which you can automatically apply to your waking dreams. Use them to evoke your own intuition.

5. Jung, *op. cit.,* page 53.

6. Jung, *op. cit.,* pages 20-21.

7. John Freeman, in his introduction to *Man and His Symbols,* page 13.

8. Ouspensky, *In Search of the Miraculous,* page 279.

Chapter Seven: Realizing Our Potential

1. Steiner, *Theosophy,* Hudson, NY: Anthroposophic Press, 1971, page 84.

2. Kabir Edmund Helminski, *Living Presence: A Sufi Way to Mindfulness & the Essential Self,* New York: Jeremy P. Tarcher/Perigee, 1992, pages 85-86.

Chapter Eight: Life Themes

1. Cf. Karpman's Drama Triangle, "Fairy Tales and Script Drama Analysis," by S. Karpman. In *Transactional Analysis Bulletin,* 1968, pages 7, 39-43.

2. Jung, *Man and His Symbols,* page 101.

3. Jung, *op. cit.,* page 102.

4. Jung, *op. cit.,* page 31.

Glossary

ANCIENT WISDOM: Traditional teachings about the nature of reality and the place human beings have in that reality, compiled by great seers and found at the heart of all major world religions and philosophies. A comparison of the wisdom tradition from diverse cultures reveals that the teachings are strikingly similar. Based on direct perception rather than belief, the wisdom tradition also teaches methods for developing the capacity to experience directly the reality described. The teachings predate recorded history and have a continuity that is uninterrupted through to the present day. Also known as the perennial wisdom or philosophy.

AWAKENED: Identified with the real Self.

DREAMER: The power-to-be-conscious which empowers our sense of self but with which we are not identified. The real Self.

ENERGY EVENT: What occurs in reality, and is therefore available to all people to experience. An occurrence before it is interpreted or explained by anyone. A happening without any meaning ascribed to it.

ENERGY POLARITIES: Two forces fundamental to all reality, tending to have opposing characteristics, yet dependent on one another for the release of their potential to create. See "Yin" and "Yang."

ENERGY WORLD: The real world of waves and particles, as described by seers and modern physicists. The energy world is contrasted with the seemingly objective world of waking dreams. See "Objective World."

ENFOLDING PROCESS: The first movement in the cosmic process of bringing the pattern of the original One into manifestation. This first movement is, in the Eastern tradition, called the "out-breath" of Brahma. In the Hebrew tradition it was thought of as "the rolling up of the scroll." The "writing" on the scroll is the pattern of the One, referred to in the Hebrew tradition as "the Law" or "the Lord." In the Judeo-Christian tradition this phase of the cosmic process is called "the creation." In science, it is called "evolution." It is the bringing of the unmanifest into physical manifestation. It is the work of the Mother-God, the Yin.

The enfolding process is characterized by growing specialization and diversification as organisms become more and more complex. Finally an organism develops which is capable of being a microcosmic expression of the original One. That organism is the human being. The emergence of the human being marks the beginning of the second movement in the cosmic process. See "Unfolding Process."

FORMATIVE FORCES: The forces that brought us into being. See "Energy Polarities."

HERMETIC: The principles and philosophy developed by Hermes Trismegistus (which means "the thrice greatest"), or attributed to him. Hermes is the Greek name for the Egyptian Thoth, who was the god of wisdom, learning, and magic.

IDENTIFY WITH: To know something *as* Self: "I am that."

INDIVIDUALIZING: The process by which we human beings differentiate from the groups to which we belong, developing our uniqueness until we become representations of the original "One," whole in ourselves and one with the universal Whole, that is, indivisible and therefore true individuals.

INDIVIDUALIZED SELF/BEING: A true individual: one who is indivisible in her/his internal experience of self and in her/his sense of relationship with others and the whole.

LIFE AS A WAKING DREAM: A method for fostering our own awakening by studying the books of our own lives to discover their hidden meaning. This method synthesizes concepts from wisdom teachings, General Semantics, and Quantum Physics with approaches to dream interpretation from both spiritual and psychological traditions.

LIFE-DREAM: A lifetime, when viewed as a whole and seen as a waking dream.

OBJECTIVE CONSCIOUSNESS: Consciousness in duality. The perceiver experiences self as separate from the perceived, so that everything perceived appears to be an object, having an existence independent of the perceiver.

OBJECTIVE MIND: The human mind when functioning in the objective state of consciousness.

OBJECTIVE REALITY: The world as it is perceived in the human state of consciousness, as if it were composed of discrete objects, each occupying its own space, separate from every other. Even the internal parts of things (such as internal organs) are viewed as separate from the whole (in this case, the body) and thus interchangeable and replaceable.

(THE) ONE: That which was before anything came into existence: the unknown and the unknowable. In various traditions it is given the name God, Brahma, Allah, T'ai Chi, etc.

PERCEIVERS: Individuals in whom the faculty of direct perception has opened and who have clear vision into the nature of reality. See "Seers."

POWER-TO-BE-CONSCIOUS: The force released by the dynamic interplay between the fundamental energy polarities, the yin and yang, enabling human beings to be both aware and self-aware; the one power which can never be called into doubt because to doubt it we use that very power. See "Real Self."

PRIVATE WORLD: The mental or abstracted inner world in which most people believe they live, although the functional energy reality is far different, more vast and universal. Each person's private world is unique, and can never be completely understood or shared by anyone else, since it is made up of memories filled with feeling (both personal and group), interpretations, beliefs, values, rationalizations, justifications, etc. In effect, the private world is a selectively edited videotape of an individual's life.

PSYCHE: See "Soul."

REAL SELF: The power-to-be-conscious which empowers the sense of self; the individualizing energy field (yin polarity) and the invisible pattern held within it (yang polarity) with which one identifies after awakening from the life-dream.

RECALL (OF A PAST LIFE): An experience in which one seems to remember being a different person at a different time in history. Often such recalls include vivid detail which can be verified through other sources of historical documentation previously unknown to the one who had the recall.

SEERS: Individualized beings who perceive the energy world itself, without the overlay of objectified images of that reality, and who, therefore, describe reality with such universal validity that their depictions are nearly identical across cultures. See "Perceivers."

SELF: The energy field with which the "I" identifies.

SENSE OF SELF: A name or an image that expresses our internal experience of ourselves during an event. The noun or phrase may express the relationship we felt, a self-image, or what we did or said, not according to external definitions, roles, or expectations, but only according to how we felt about ourselves.

SOUL: The faculties of feeling and thinking, including the memory, and the patterns which develop as a result of exercising those faculties. Often called the personality or the psyche.

SPIRIT: The individualizing field of energy that forms when the faculties of intuition and knowing are developed.

STATE OF CONSCIOUSNESS: A particular way of viewing, knowing, and/or experiencing the world and self. See, for example, "Objective Consciousness."

SYMBOL: A person, an object, a name, a term, or a place in a waking dream which represents a facet of Self but with which our sense of self is not identified.

UNFOLDING PROCESS: The second movement in the cosmic process of bringing the original One into manifestation. This second movement is, in the Eastern tradition, called the "in-breath" of Brahma. In the Christian tradition it has been called the return to the Father's house. In the Hebrew tradition it was thought of as "the unrolling and reading of the scroll," the scroll being a symbol for consciousness of the manifested universe.

This phase of the cosmic process is not addressed by modern science. In most Wisdom Traditions it is called the process of awakening or the pathway to enlightenment. It is the manifest reality being brought into full consciousness by individual human beings. This is what is referred to as "the individualizing process."

The unfolding process is characterized by synthesis and union. The sense of self of each individual human expands until his/her consciousness of Self encompasses the Whole of what exists. The unfolding process takes place entirely in consciousness. This is the process by which the One comes to know Itself one being by one being until its knowing of Self is complete. See also "Enfolding Process."

VIVID LIFE EXPERIENCE: Any event that stands out in our consciousness when we look back over a period of time: feelings are still alive in us about the event, we keep replaying the event in our minds, we wish we could relive it differently, etc.

WAKING DREAM: A life experience which we believe to be real but which is actually an out-picturing of our inner state of consciousness. The experience is not recognized as a waking dream because we are asleep, unconscious of our real Self.

THE WHOLE: Cosmos; the Universe; all that is.

THE WILL: The original pattern imprinted within that guides the unfolding process and is experienced by humans as inner guidance or direction when brought into consciousness; the power of self-direction or self-control, residing in our real Self.

WISDOM TEACHINGS: See "Ancient Wisdom."

WISDOM TRADITION: The teachings of the ancient wisdom as passed down from teacher to student within any given cultural tradition.

WORK: Effort to acquire knowledge about the nature of reality and about Self; effort to gain self-control in order to change ourselves and align our Self-expression with our life purpose.

YANG: One of two polarities of energy fundamental to the nature of reality, characterized by the tendency to initiate, to set the pattern, to organize, and to direct; often called the father force, masculine force, or positive (meaning electric) polarity of the One.

YIN: One of two polarities of energy fundamental to the nature of reality, characterized by the tendency to receive, to give form to, to manifest, and to respond; often called the mother force, feminine force, or negative (meaning magnetic) polarity of the One.

Bibliography

References for Dream Interpretation

Conscious Dreaming, by Robert Moss. New York: Crown Trade Paperbacks, 1996.

The Dream Book: Symbols for Self- Understanding, by Betty Bethards. Rockport, MA: Element, 1995.

Dream Dictionary: A Guide to Dreams and Sleep Experiences, by Tony Crisp. New York: Dell Publishing, 1991.

Dream Symbolism, by Manly P. Hall. Los Angeles, California: The Philosophical Research Society, 1965.

Dictionary of all Scriptures and Myths, by G. A. Gaskell. New York: The Julian Press, Inc., 1969.

A Dictionary of Symbols, by J. E. Cirlot, translated from the Spanish by Jack Sage. New York: Philosophical Library. 1971.

Dreams: Your Magic Mirror, by Elsie Sechrist. New York: Dell Publishing Co., 1968.

The Herder Dictionary of Symbols, English Translation by Boris Matthews. Ph.D. Wilmette: Chiron Publications, 1986.

The Hidden Power of Dreams, by Denise Linn. New York: Ballantine Books, 1988.

Jungian Dream Interpretation: A Hand book of Theory and Practice, by James A. Hall, M.D. Toronto, Canada: Inner City Books, 1983.

The Jungian-Senoi Dreamwork Manual, by Strephon Kaplan Williams. Berkeley, California: Journey Press, 1980.

The Lost Language of Symbolism, by Harold Bayley. New York: Carol Publishing, 1993.

The Lost Language of Symbolism, Vol.II, by Harold Bayley. New York: Carol Publishing, 1990.

Metaphysical Bible Dictionary. Unity Village, MO: Unity School of Christianity, 1931.

The Mystical, Magical, Marvelous World of Dreams, by Wilda B. Tanner. Tahlequah, Oklahoma: SparrowHawk Press, 1988.

Our Dream Language: A Guide to the Symbols of Dreams, by John Schmidt. Santa Barbara: Fithian Press, 1989.

The Secret Language of Waking Dreams, by Mike Avery. Golden Valley, MN: Illuminated Way Publishing, Inc., 1992.

Wisdom of the Heart: Working with Women's Dreams, by Karen A Signell, Ph.D. New York: Bantam Books, 1990.

The Woman's Encyclopedia of Myths and Secrets, by Barbara G. Walker. San Francisco: HarperSanFrancisco, 1983.

The Woman's Dictionary of Symbols and Sacred Objects, by Barbara G. Walker. San Francisco: HarperSanFrancisco, 1983.

General

Baldwin, Christina. *Life's Companion: Journal Writing as a Spiritual Quest.* New York: Bantam Books, 1990.

Campbell, Joseph. *The Inner Reaches of Outer Space: Metaphor as Myth and as Religion.* New York: Alfred Van Der Marck Editions, 1985.

Csikszentmihalyi, Mihaly. *Flow: The Psychology of Optimal Experience.* New York: Harper Perennial, 1990.

Chopra, Deepak M.D. *Ageless Body, Timeless Mind.* New York: Harmony Books, 1993.
——— *Quantum Healing: Exploring the Frontiers of Mind/Body Medicine.* New York: Bantam Books, 1990.

Choyin, Detong. *Waking from the Dream.* Boston: Charles E Tuttle Co., Inc. 1996.

The Dalai Lama. *Sleeping, Dreaming, and Dying.* Edited and narrated by Francisco J. Varela, Ph.D. Boston: Wisdom Publications, 1997.

Douglas-Klotz, Neil. *Prayers of the Cosmos: Meditations on the Aramaic Words of Jesus.* San Francisco: HarperSanFrancisco, 1990.

Evans-Wentz, W. Y. *Tibetan Yoga and Secret Doctrines.* London: Oxford University Press, 1935.

————— , ed. *The Tibetan Book of the Dead.* New York: Oxford University Press, 1960.

————— , ed. *The Yoga of the Dream State.* New York: Julian Press, 1964.

Gendlin, Eugene T., Ph.D. *Focusing.* New York: A Bantam New Age Book, 1978.

————— *Let Your Body Interpret Your Dreams.* Wilmette, IL: Chiron Publications, 1986.

Godwin, Malcolm. *The Lucid Dreamer: A Waking Guide for the Traveler Between Worlds.* New York: Simon & Schuster, 1994.

Goldman, Jonathan. *Healing Sounds: The Power of Harmonics.* Rockport: Element, Inc., 1992.

Grasse, Ray. *The Waking Dream: Unlocking the Symbolic Language of Our Lives,* Wheaton, IL: Quest Books, 1996.

Gurdjieff, G. I. *Views from the Real World.* New York: Arkana, 1984.

Haddon, Genia Pauli. *Body Metaphors: Releasing God-Feminine in Us All.* New York: Crossroad, 1988.

Hall, Manly P. *Questions and Answers: Fundamentals of the Occult Sciences.* Los Angeles: Philosophical Research Society, 1965.

————— *The Secret Teachings of All Ages.* Los Angeles: The Philosophical Research Society, 1977.

Hannah, Barbara. *Encounters with the Soul: Active Imagination As Developed by C. G. Jung.* Sigo Press, 1981.

Heline, Theodore. *The Archetype Unveiled: A Study Of the*

Sound Patterns Formed By the Creative Word. La Canada, California: New Age Press, Inc., 4636 Vineta Avenue, 91011, 1965.

Helminski, Kabir Edmund. *Living Presence: A Sufi Way to Mindfulness and* the Essential Self. New York: Jeremy P. Tarcher/Perigee, 1992.

Heyneman, Nicholas E. *DreamScape: The Personal Interactive Dream Analysis System.* New York: Fireside, Simon & Schuster, 1996.

I Ching (The Book of Changes). Richard Wilhelm, Trans. New York: Princeton University Press, 1950.

Jung, Carl G. *Man and His Symbols,* New York: Doubleday & Co., 1964.
——— *Memories, Dreams, Reflections.* New York: Vintage Books, 1965.

Kushi, Michio. *The Book of Macrobiotics.* Tokyo: Japan Publications, 1977.

LaBerge, Stephen, Ph.D. *Lucid Dreaming.* New York: Ballantine Books, 1985.

Lockhart, Russell Arthur. *Psyche Speaks: A Jungian Approach to Self and World.* Wilmette, Illinois: Chiron Publications, 1982.

McCabe, Mary Jo. *Learn to See: An Approach To Your Inner Voice Through Symbols.* Grass Valley, CA: Blue Dolphin Publishing, 1994.

Mindell, Arnold. *River's Way: The Process Science of the Dreambody.* London and New York: Routledge & Kegan Paul, 1985.

———— *Working with the Dreaming Body.* London: Arkana, 1985.

———— *Working on Yourself Alone: Inner Dreambody Work.* London: Arkana, 1990.

Norbu, Namkhai. *Dream Yoga and The Practice of Natural Light.* Ithaca, New York: Snow Lion Publications, 1992.

Orage, A. R. *Psychological Exercises.* New York: Samuel Wiser, 1930.

Ouspensky, P. D. *Conscience: The Search for Truth.* New York: Arkana, 1988.

———— *The Fourth Way.* New York: Vintage Books, 1971.

———— *A New Model of the Universe.* New York: Vintage Books, 1971.

———— *The Psychology of Man's Possible Evolution.* New York: Vintage Books, 1974.

———— *A Record of Meetings.* New York: Arkana, 1951.

———— *In Search of the Miraculous: Fragments of an Unknown Teaching.* New York: Harcourt Brace Jovanovich, 1949.

———— *Tertium Organum: A Key to the Enigmas of the World.* New York: Vintage Books, 1970.

Pike, Diane Kennedy writing as Mariamne Paulus. *Awakening to Wisdom.* Scottsdale, AZ: Teleos Imprint, 2003.

Progoff, Ira. *At A Journal Workshop.* New York: Dialogue House Library, 1975.

———— *The Symbolic & the Real.* New York: McGraw-Hill Book Company, 1973.

Purce, Jill. *The Mystic Spiral: Journey of the Soul.* London: Thames and Hudson, 1994.

Secter, Mondo. *I Ching Clarified: A Practical Guide.* Rutland, VT: Charles E. Tuttle Company, 1993.

Sogyal Rinpoche. *The Tibetan Book of Living and Dying.* San Francisco, California: HarperSanFrancisco, 1992.

Steiner, Rudolph. *Theosophy.* Hudson, NY: Anthroposophic Press, 1971.

Van de Castle, Robert L. *Our Dreaming Mind.* New York: Ballantine Books, 1994.

Vitvan. *The Christos.* Baker, NV: School of the Natural Order, 1982.
—— *Clear Thinking.* Baker, NV: School of the Natural Order.
—— *Self-Mastery Through Meditation.* Baker, NV: School of the Natural Order, 1951.
—— *The Veil of Maya.* Baker, NV: School of the Natural Order, 1946.
—— Lesson Series (available from School of the Natural Order, P.O. Box 578, Baker, NV 89311):
   Cosmology (1950)
   A Description of the Psychic World (1954)
   Expanding States of Self- Awareness (1956)
   Four Somatic Divisions of Man (1949)
   Functional Activities (1956)
   The Natural Order Process: Basic Teachings of the School of the Natural Order (volumes 1, 2, & 3)
   The Tree of Life (1949)
   Understanding the Psychic Nature (1960)

Watkins, Mary M. *Waking Dreams.* San Francisco: Harper Colophon Books, Harper & Row, 1976.

Wilber, Ken. *A Brief History of Everything*. Boston & London: Shambhala, 1996.

———— *No Boundary*. Boulder, CO: New Science Library, 1981.

———— *Sex, Ecology, Spirituality: The Spirit of Evolution*. Boston & London: Shambhala, 1995.

———— *The Spectrum of Consciousness*. Wheaton, IL: The Theosophical Publishing House, 1977.

Zohar, Danah. *The Quantum Self.* New York: William Morrow and Co., 1990.

▬▬▬▬▬▬▬▬▬▬▬▬▬▬▬▬▬▬▬▬▬▬▬▬▬

About the creator of the Cover Art:

Reverend Rebecca Hanna Ph.D. is  a visionary assemblage artist and ordained Metaphysical Interfaith Minister. She earned her B.F.A. from the Maryland Institute College of Art and has been working as a professional artist since 1981. Rebecca has her Masters degree in Metaphysical Science and her Ph.D. in Transpersonal Psychology from the University of Sedona. Rebecca is also a certified teacher of **Life as Waking Dream**. For more information on go to www.wakingdreamwisdom.com.